American Lazarus

AMERICAN LAZARUS

Religion and the Rise
of African-American
and Native American
Literatures

Joanna Brooks

OXFORD
UNIVERSITY PRESS

2003

OXFORD
UNIVERSITY PRESS

Oxford   New York

Auckland   Bangkok   Buenos Aires   Cape Town   Chennai
Dar es Salaam   Delhi   Hong Kong   Istanbul   Karachi   Kolkata
Kuala Lumpur   Madrid   Melbourne   Mexico City   Mumbai   Nairobi
São Paulo   Shanghai   Taipei   Tokyo   Toronto

Copyright © 2003 by Oxford University Press, Inc.

Published by Oxford University Press, Inc.
198 Madison Avenue, New York, New York 10016

www.oup.com

Oxford is a registered trademark of Oxford University Press

Library of Congress Cataloging-in Publication Data
Brooks, Joanna, 1971–
American Lazarus : religion and the rise of African-American and
native American literatures / Joanna Brooks.
p. cm.
Includes bibliographical references and index.
ISBN 978-0-19-533291-9
1. American literature—African American authors—
History and criticism. 2. Christianity and literature—United States—
History—18th century. 3. American literature—Revolutionary period, 1775–1783—
History and criticism. 4. American literature—Colonial period, ca. 1600–1775—
History and criticism. 5. American literature—Indian authors—History and criticism.
6. Indians of North America—Intellectual life—18th century. 7. American literature—
1783–1850—History and criticism. 8. Hymns, English—United States—History
and criticism. 9. Christian literature, American—History and criticism.
10. African Americans—Intellectual life—18th century. 11. African
Americans in literature. 12. Occom, Samson, 1723–1792.
13. Indians in literature. I. Title.
PS153.N5 B668   2003
810.9′96073—dc21   2002013708

Printed in the United States of America
on acid-free paper

Acknowledgments

I am indebted to Michael Colacurcio, Richard Yarborough, and Karen
Rowe at the University of California, Los Angeles, who nurtured this project through its formative stages and continue as generous and inspiring
mentors. I also thank Paula Gunn Allen, Vincent Pecora, Kenneth Rein-
hard, Samuel Weber, Muriel McClendon, and Greg Sarris for their influence and Meredith Neuman, Mark Quigley, Kris Fresonke, Bill Handley,
Maurice Lee, Jim Lee, Colette Brown, Karen Wallace, and my SAGE/
UAW brothers and sisters for their camaraderie at UCLA. At the University of Texas at Austin, I have been sustained by a collegial community including Bill Scheick, Evan Carton, Shelley Fisher Fishkin, Ann Cvetko-
vich, Phil Barrish, Sabrina Barton, Lisa Moore, Helena Woodard, Martin
Kevorkian, Shirley Thompson, and Maria Franklin, all of whom I thank
for their advice, encouragement, and feedback. Additional thanks to fellow early Americanists Kristina Bross, Lisa Gordis, Jacquelyn Miller, Laura
Rigal, John Saillant, David Shields, and Hilary Wyss. I am certainly thankful to Elissa Morris, Jeremy Lewis, and many others at Oxford University
Press who believed in this book and brought it to life.

My gratitude goes to the women of Feminist Home Evening at
Brigham Young University (1991–93) and the broader community of Mor-
mon feminist scholars for being good examples. I am also thankful for the
city of Gallup, New Mexico, and for broader *Dinetah*, which fed me on fry-
bread, turquoise, thunderstorms, and red rocks as I finished this book.
Asale Angel-Ajani is my number-one junior faculty homegirl; Bryan Wa-
terman is my number-one junior faculty homeboy. Love and gratitude to
my parents James and Michele Brooks, my grandmother America Pearl
Leonis, my late grandfather Frank J. Leonis, Jr., and my late grandmother
Dorothy Brooks; this book belongs to you as much as it does to me. Love
also to brothers and sisters Melissa, MaryBeth, John, Chris, Laurie, and

Steve, and to Michael and Carole Kamper. Finally, deep love and devotion to my husband and best friend David Kamper, for loving Zion and loathing Babylon, and for being the kind of man who would gladly pull a handcart across the desert.

This book was written with fellowship and grant support from the University of California, Los Angeles, the Charlotte W. Newcombe–Woodrow Wilson Foundation, and the University of Texas at Austin. I also thank staff members from the Rauner Special Collections Library at Dartmouth College, the Connecticut Historical Society, the State Library of Pennsylvania, the Boston Public Library, and the Inter-Library Loan department of the University of Texas at Austin. Earlier versions of chapters 3 and 4 appeared as "The Journal of John Marrant: Providence and Prophecy in the Eighteenth-Century Black Atlantic," *The North Star: A Journal of African American Religious History* 3.1 (fall 1999): http://northstar.vassar.edu/, and "Prince Hall, Freemasonry, and Genealogy," *African-American Review* 34.2 (summer 2000): 197–216.

Contents

American Lazarus

Introduction

> Oh Mary don't you weep,
> Tell Martha not to moan,
> Pharaoh's Army
> Drowned in the Red Sea,
> Oh Mary don't you weep,
> Tell Martha not to moan.

American Lazarus tells a story of redemption and regeneration. It reconstructs the founding moments of African-American and Native American literatures. These American literary traditions emerged during the era of the American Revolution, when blacks and Indians faced not only the crushing legacies of slavery and colonization but also the chaos of war, epidemic, resettlement, exile, and the political uncertainties of the new nation. In this portentous and dangerous time, pioneering black and Indian writers used literature to create a new future for their peoples. They redirected the democratizing, charismatic, and separatist energies of American evangelicalism and its powerful doctrine of rebirth into the formation of new religious communities, new theologies, and new literatures for people of color. By adapting, politicizing, and indigenizing mainline religious discourses, African-Americans and Native Americans also established a platform for their critical interventions into early national formulations of race. This book tells the story of how the earliest black and Indian authors established themselves as visionary interlocutors of secular nationalism and the American Enlightenment.

The most famous proponents of that Enlightenment did not regard their black and Indian contemporaries so highly. This is what Thomas Jefferson had to say about one of America's first black authors: "Religion indeed has produced a Phyllis Whately; but it could not produce a poet. The compositions published under her name are beneath the dignity of criticism." Jefferson issued this blunt and bruising judgment of Wheatley's *Poems on Various Subjects, Religious and Moral* (1773) in his *Notes on the State of Virginia* (1787), a work itself designed to defend American nature and culture against charges of inferiority. The French philosophe Georges-Louis Leclerc, comte du Buffon, had argued that environment and climate determine human development; the North American environment, he judged, was so poor as to be degenerative. Jefferson countered Buffon by compiling his own observations on Virginia's rich natural resources; the quality and variety of its flora and fauna; and the laws, customs, and cultures invented by its "native" inhabitants, aboriginal and modern. Among those distinctly American social inventions were certain laws sustaining a system of race slavery. This system, too, Jefferson attempted to naturalize as the necessary consequence of the inherent inferiority of the enslaved, who were by his estimation incapable of improvement. Phillis Wheatley was no natural genius, he insisted, but rather an unnatural and artificial production. Critics of Jefferson joined the argument with their own interpretations of Wheatley's career. Thomas Clarkson, an advocate of African colonization and author of *An Essay on the Slavery and Commerce of the Human Species, Particularly the African* (1786), presented Wheatley as "proof" that blacks might attain equality if their "impediments" under slavery were "removed." In *The Capacity of Negroes for Religious and Moral Improvement Considered* (1789), Richard Nisbet repented of his previously published opinions against black intelligence by offering the "moral natural and ingenious productions of Phillis Wheatley" as evidence of her race's capacity for "rational moral" agency. Finally, Gilbert Imlay, a would-be rival in the field of natural science, argued in his *Topographical Description of the Western Territory of North America* (1797) that no "white person upon this continent has written more beautiful lines" than she had.[1]

Wheatley did not live to see her role in this political and scientific controversy: she died impoverished in Boston in December 1784. However, her letters and poems reveal her to have been an acute critic of the limitations of rationalist philosophy and empirical science. In a February 1774 letter to her friend, the Mohegan minister Samson Occom, Wheatley criticized the inconsistencies of American slaveholders, "our modern Egyptians": "How well the cry for Liberty, and the reverse Disposition for the exercise of oppressive Powers over others agree,—I humbly think it does not require the penetration of a Philosopher to determine." Her poem "To the University of Cambridge, in New-England" chastises the privileged "sons of science" who "scan the heights" and "mark the systems of revolving worlds," yet cannot appreciate the implications of their studies. The worlds *do* revolve; the heavenly systems are *not* fixed; rather, a sovereign God who will redeem the just and damn the unregenerate orders their motions. "Improve your privileges while they stay," Wheatley warns the young scientists. Speaking as an "Ethiop" with the voice of anciency and prophecy, she exhorts them to remember that the powerful and chaotic forces of sin will quickly sink their ethereal aspirations into an "immense perdition," reducing the "transient sweetness" of privilege and human presumption to "endless pain."

This is what Phillis Wheatley knew that the "sons of science" were unwilling to acknowledge: that neither rational causes nor natural forces governed the events of this world. Having been seized by a slaver from her African home; having survived the horrors of the middle passage; having arrived in Boston wearing a scrap of dirty carpet at the age of six or seven, or so they guessed by her missing front teeth; having been purchased by a white family and named for the schooner which conveyed her—Phillis knew that there was nothing inevitable or natural about her arrival in America. Indeed, there was nothing inevitable or natural about the expropriation of 12 million Africans to the Americas and their perpetual enslavement. Reason did not appoint the death of at least 4 million North American Indians consequent to colonization, nor did nature direct the European appropriation of their aboriginal homelands.[2] Indeed, there was nothing inevitable or natural about the state of Virginia, the state of Massachusetts, nor the newly incorporated United States of America, notwithstanding the rhetoric of "natural rights" espoused by those who organized its national formation. Those "sons of science" would never acknowledge it, but Phillis Wheatley knew it, and Thomas Jefferson knew it too.

Jefferson knew that the "natural" nation was no inevitability but rather an argument to be won through careful scientific and political reasoning. Moreover, he knew that this construct was particularly vulnerable to the African-American population within its borders, then numbering more than 750,000 and comprising almost 20 percent of the United States total. According to Jefferson, this unnatural presence, this dark "blot" on the national body, threatened the stability of the whole:

> Indeed I tremble for my country when I reflect that God is just: that his justice cannot sleep for ever: that considering numbers, nature and natural means only, a revolution of the wheel of fortune, an exchange of situation is among possible events: that it may become probable by supernatural interference! The Almighty has no attribute which can take side with us in such a contest. . . . I think a change already perceptible, since the origin of the present revolution. The spirit of the master is abating, that of the slave rising from the dust, his condition mollifying,

the way I hope preparing, under the auspices of heaven, for a total emancipation, and that this is disposed, in the order of events, to be with the consent of the masters, rather than by their extirpation.[3]

Jefferson did not think himself a supernaturalist. His was "Nature's God"—a deistic set of regulating principles, expurgated of miracles and mysteries—a force as straight and solid as the law of gravity. But this rare and fearful moment in the natural-scientific *Notes*, this vision of a "supernatural interference" in the course of human events, establishes a competing pattern and a haunting presence. Who was this other God reaching for the "wheel of fortune"? Was this the darker God dwelling in the shadows of the system, working unnamed and silent alongside the slaves to maintain its timely order? Did they plot together, God and the slaves, in the holy darkness of their Monticello quarters, behind an inscrutable veil of blackness, to overturn that very system? Was it not this same God who also "produced" through "religion" a slave poet named Phillis Wheatley? Jefferson's mind grouped slave poets and religion, slave emancipation and divine intervention, into the same occultish and threatening space. Indeed, it appears that for Thomas Jefferson, God was black.[4]

Jefferson correctly sensed that the birth of the American nation was closely shadowed by a parallel rebirth, a resurrection, a "rising from the dust" in its communities of color. Like an American Lazarus, African-Americans and Native Americans were creating from the chaos of colonization and slavery new identities, new communities, and new American literary traditions. The 1760s and 1770s saw the first published works by black and Indian authors: *A Narrative of the Uncommon Sufferings and Surprizing Deliverance of Briton Hammon, A Negro Man* (1760); enslaved poet Jupiter Hammon's "An Evening Thought. Salvation by Christ, with Penitential Cries" (1760); Mohegan minister Samson Occom's *Sermon at the Execution of Moses Paul* (1772); and Wheatley's *Poems* (1773). These pioneering works were soon followed by Occom's *A Collection of Hymns and Spiritual Songs* (1774); John Marrant's *A Narrative of the Lord's Wonderful Dealings with John Marrant, A Black (Now Going to Preach the Gospel in Nova Scotia)* (1785), *Sermon to the African Lodge of Freemasons* (1789), and published missionary *Journal* (1790); Prince Hall's two *Charges* to the African Lodge (1792, 1797); and the *Narrative of the Black People* (1794), penned by Absalom Jones and Richard Allen during the 1793 Philadelphia yellow fever epidemic.[5]

Now, more than two centuries after their initial imprints, the foundational works of African-American and Native American literature have been resurrected from the archives and restored to literary publication, study, and instruction.[6] Consequently, there is a significant need for more information about pioneering black and Indian authors, the extent of their careers, and the diversity of their literary products. This book will introduce new and little-known works by eighteenth-century authors of color and establish the contexts for their creation. It strives to answer the questions raised by these lately remembered, twice-born texts: how did literature take shape out of the imposed chaos of slavery and colonialism? What were the necessary conditions for this genesis? How did slaves, ex-slaves, and indigenous peoples assume and exercise literary authority in the new United States of America?

In 1955, R. W. B. Lewis produced an abidingly influential account of American cultural and literary formation in *The American Adam: Innocence, Tragedy, and Tradition in the Nineteenth Century*. Lewis distilled from classic American literature a powerful and pervasive myth, which held that history began anew in the American experiment and which personified America as a prelapsarian Adam. He described this mythic persona as follows:

> An individual emancipated from history, happily bereft of ancestry, untouched and undefiled by the usual inheritances of family and race; an individual standing alone, self-reliant and self-propelling, ready to confront whatever awaited him with the aid of his own unique and inherent resources. . . . His moral position was prior to experience, and in his very newness he was fundamentally innocent. The world and history lay all before him. And he was the type of creator, the poet par excellence, creating language itself by naming the elements of the scene about him. All this and more were contained in the image of the American as Adam.[7]

This ingenious summary characterization of early nationalist ideology has shaped the way we think about our literature and its history. After Lewis, it seems, the American Adam appears everywhere in early national literature, striding with protagonistic boldness through novels, narratives, histories, and poems. Indeed, it sometimes appears that the American Adamic myth has taken on a life of its own as a master narrative for the "birth" of American literature. Adam's footprints appear wherever scholars propose an innocent and ahistorical account of American literary beginnings, whenever we neglect the messier aspects of our history so as to preserve an exceptionalist or ethnocentric concept of national culture.

The earliest African-American and Native American authors did not share in this mythology. To them, the history of cultural and national origination was no fable of foreordained progress but rather a chronicle of cataclysmic change and determined survival. Their American story begins not in the natural inheritance of the garden, but rather in the unnatural horrors of enslavement and colonization, in the Middle Passage, in forced displacement, in near extermination. From the residue of this shared suffering, from the detritus of scientific and political racism, they conscientiously constructed new identities as black and Indian people. The first black and Indian authors wrote from this space of instability and transformation. If their first forays into literature seem accidental, if their earliest works seem simple, this image masks the deeper paradox of their circumstances: the imperative to express inexpressible losses, to create community out of mutual alienation, to assert authority despite being denied basic humanity. It makes sense, then, that when they turned to their Bibles, early African-American and Native American authors sought out stories that honored their haunted and paradoxical circumstances and offered some key into the mystery of personal and community redemption. Their primary concern was not genesis but regeneration: not the static economies of prelapsarian innocence, but the tumultuous and emancipatory traversing of the Red Sea, the forty years' wandering in the wilderness, the deliverance from the tomb. The collective character of their stories resembles not the prototypical American Adam but instead an American Lazarus.

In this book, I will use the term *American Lazarus* to characterize a complex of concerns textualized in early African-American and Native American literatures. The biblical character Lazarus appears in two New Testament stories. The first, related in John 11, features Lazarus the ailing brother of Mary and Martha. Four days after his death, this Lazarus is summoned forth from the tomb by Jesus in a demonstration of the overruling power of God. His resurrection transforms Lazarus into a living example of this godly power, or even into a spectacle. But his witness is mute: if he did speak of his own experience, his words were not recorded in scripture. Thus the story of Lazarus invites unsettling questions: how does the world look to one who has faced and survived death? Is it possible to convey in human terms such a profound break in consciousness and existence? How is catastrophic change processed in body, mind, and spirit? What effects does it have on the body, experience, memory, relationship, and language? Similar questions arise in relationship to early African-American and Native American cultures. How does the world look to those who have faced and survived death, be it the involuntary deaths of kinspeople in the dark holds of slave ships, the suicides who threw themselves into the Atlantic rather than surrender their lives to slavery, or the carnage of colonial contagion—epidemic diseases, smallpox blankets, famine, and alcohol? Slavery and colonization entailed not only physical but also social death, as the distinguished sociologist Orlando Patterson has explained, in alienation from homeland, family, culture, language, and humanity. How does the world look to those who have faced and survived this social death, to those who have been appropriated as chattel, displaced from ancestral lands, disabused of their native languages, rent from their kinspeople, hated, and hunted? Is it possible to convey in language— indeed, in the language of the enslaver and colonizer—such a profound break in consciousness and existence? How does such catastrophic change affect experience, culture, and language, not only in the first generation but in perpetuity? Unlike the resurrected Lazarus, African-American and Native American peoples did not remain entirely mute on these subjects. Their early writings reflect the imposed discontinuities, cruelties, and mortalities of life under slavery and colonialism, and they demonstrate the drive to claim life from death and meaning from chaos.

Just as the story of Lazarus encompasses both death and resurrection, this book will show how communities of color reclaimed and revived themselves in eighteenth-century America. Religious revivalism played a critical role in their creation of new black and Indian identities, new communities, and new literatures. Without exception, the first African-American and Native American authors were deeply implicated in the evangelical movements inspired by the first Great Awakening. Phillis Wheatley first won wide literary recognition for her "Elegiac Poem on the Death of That Celebrated Divine, and Eminent Servant of Jesus Christ, the late Reverend, and Pious George Whitefield" (1770), wherein she ventriloquizes and thus resurrects the voice of this celebrity preacher and friend to the Wheatley family. Whitefield's sponsor, Selina Hastings, the countess of Huntingdon, endorsed the publication of Wheatley's *Poems* in 1773. Jupiter Hammon also chose religious themes for his first publication, and his literary career benefited from his associations with the New Light preacher Ebenezer Pemberton and with the Society of Friends. Samson Occom was educated by the New Light preacher Eleazar Wheelock at Moor's Indian Charity School and later ordained by the Long Island Presbytery. His *Sermon at the Execution of Moses Paul* drew a large audience on the day it was preached at the gallows and later became a best-selling publication. John Marrant, Richard Allen, and Absalom Jones were also ordained ministers, empowered by the separatist impulses of evangelicalism and by the pressing needs of their own peoples to create their own churches, theologies, and modes of worship. Their pioneering contributions to American literature came about in connection with this broader regeneration, and they reveal how religious formulas such as conversion, revival, and resurrection answered the alienating and mortifying effects of slavery, colonialism, and racial oppression.

Tropes of revival and resurrection in general and the story of Lazarus in particular have long been important features of black religious and popular culture. Lazarus has figured in black visual arts, religious music, and popular music; this chapter opened with lines from "Mary Don't You Weep," a spiritual that compares the resurrection of Lazarus to the deliverance of slaves from Egypt, thus paralleling resurrection with freedom. This book shows that the Lazarus tradition reaches back into early black and Indian literatures, where we find the story of Lazarus explicitly referenced and implicitly incorporated in cycles of backsliding and renewal, in the life-and-death exigencies of survival on the colonial margins, and, importantly, as a performed feature of religious and spiritual ritual. The physical performances of death and rebirth I will describe in this book—baptisms by immersion, "falling out" at revivals, and Masonic ritual performances of resurrection—signified not only the transformation of the individual, but also his or her entrée into new communities which themselves sought collective regeneration. In choosing the story of Lazarus as a metanarrative for early black and Indian literatures, I do not seek to overimpose a Christian narrative against pre-Christian African and Indian cultural histories. Rather, Lazarus is also a surrogate for the multiple, unnamed, unspecified indigenous African and indigenous American belief systems that survived in and through Christian practices. The Lazarus trope recycles and binds together the multiple influences that constituted early African-American and Native American understandings of regeneration.

The figure of Lazarus also binds my work to recent studies of death and resurrection in culture and performance. In *Cities of the Dead: Circum-Atlantic Performance* (1996), Joseph Roach writes that black and Native-informed performance traditions remember the role of "officially forgotten" "diasporic and genocidal histories of Africa and the Americas, North and South, in the creation of the culture of modernity."[8] Similarly, Sharon Holland's provocative study, *Raising the Dead: Readings of Death and (Black) Subjectivity* (2000), asserts that literature and performance by black and Indian subjects can be understood as "speaking from the dead," or, the rehabilitation of dispossessed and silenced spaces. In these "liminal" or "inverted" spaces—spaces outside the coercion of law, the state, the rational, the visible—"the living and the dead converge, mingle, and discourse," remembering together unspeakable modern histories of violence and dispossession.[9] Both Roach and Holland situate literary and cultural criticism as a conversation with the dead, whose memories survive in text and performance, transgressing the boundaries modernity has constructed between this life and the next.

Finally, Lazarus represents questions of method and theory facing the reader or scholar of early African-American and Native American literatures. These textual considerations are captured in a second New Testament Lazarus story. In Luke 16, a beggar named Lazarus dies and is taken up into the proverbial "bosom of Abraham"; meanwhile, the rich man who despised him is cast down into hell. The rich man begs Abraham to send Lazarus as a messenger to his living relatives, to warn them of their imminent damnation. Replies Abraham, "If they hear not Moses and the prophets, neither will they be persuaded, though one rose from the dead" (Luke 16: 31). Like the story of Lazarus the resurrected, the story of Lazarus the beggar also indicates the overruling power of God in the overturning of human expectations and social hierarchies. It too assigns value to the lives of the afflicted and oppressed, suggesting that God chooses such lives as a medium for the revelation of the divine. However, Abraham raises an important question about the power of these Lazarus stories and the circumstances of their reception. He asks, Will those who ignore "Moses and the prophets" be convinced by a messenger arisen "from the dead"? Will those who ignored Lazarus the beggar in life hear him better in his death? Or, Will those skeptical of resurrection find any convincement in the testimony of Lazarus the resurrected? Abraham suggests that the significance of these Lazarus stories is contingent on the faith of the hearer or reader. Only those willing to see meaning in these lives, only those prepared for the strange and unsettling stories they tell will be able to fully appreciate them. The same may be said of early African-American and Native American literatures. It is not enough to recover these texts from the archival tomb. We must also be willing to believe in and search out their meaningfulness, even if that search entails a reformulation of our assumptions about literature, history, race, and religion.

Abdul JanMohamed and David Lloyd emphasize this important positivistic component of literary research in their introduction to *The Nature and Context of Minority Discourse* (1990). They argue that "archival work"— especially as it unearths forgotten or neglected works by minority authors—can be a potent "form of counter-memory."[10] This potential can be realized, however, only if readers and researchers are willing to value textual features specific to historically marginalized literatures, features that may indicate the legacies of historical oppressions. JanMohamed and Lloyd explain:

> The positive theoretical work involves a critical-discursive articulation of
> alternative practices and values that are embedded in the often-damaged,
> -fragmentary, -hampered, or -occluded works of minorities. This is not to
> reassert the exclusive claim of the dominant culture that objective

grounds for marginalization can be read in the inadequacy or underdevelopment of 'minority' work. On the contrary, it is to assert that even the very differences that have always been read as symptoms of inadequacy can be reread transformatively as indications and figurations of values radically opposed to those of the dominant culture.[11]

Our challenge in the field of early American minority literatures is to recognize that differences in content, shape, and texture, which have been read as markers of "inadequacy," are in fact elements of signification. Even apparently simple texts can present a radical challenge to conventional understandings of American literature and, further, to the way we conceptualize literature, authorship, genre, tradition, nation, and history. In order to appreciate these radical possibilities, we must not underestimate the resourcefulness of early black and Indian authors. We must be willing to read in every textual feature the potential for intelligence and strategy. Understanding this literature requires a rigorous attention to details of publication, including place, printer, edition, and date; it requires careful examination of title pages, attestations, subscription lists, prefaces, and appendices; it enjoins us to consider carefully the mediating roles of amanuenses, editors, sponsors, and publishers, without summarily declaring a text compromised by association. Perhaps we must rethink our narrow notion of authorship as the exercise of an independent genius, for by that definition there were few authors in early America as a whole, let alone in its black and Indian communities. We must also use our full register of skills in literary analysis, to be alert to structure and repetition; to coded language use, unannotated scripture references, the shadows of earlier texts; to adaptations of or diversions from conventions of genre. We must consider the history of literary canonization: what happened to these texts after their initial imprints? Were they reissued? If so, when, where, how, and by whom? Did these texts remain important to specific social or religious communities? Who were the first literary critics or historians to remember them? We must review critically the various critical templates that have been recently applied to these literatures. Contemporary critical studies of early African-American and Native American literatures have been inclined to new historicism and especially to its concern with subjectivity. Is the lens of subjectivity the most germane and valuable way of viewing these texts? Does an occupation with subject-formation not lead us to concentrate only on a narrow set of eighteenth-century life writings by authors of color, some of these narratives conscripted or confessional, and to ignore more interesting and complex works by the same authors? Take, for example, the literary career of Mohegan tribal leader and Presbyterian minister Samson Occom. Occom scholarship has sometimes privileged an unpublished autoethnographic confession he delivered in 1768 to a prejudiced and skeptical faction of Boston ministers; almost no consideration has been given to the major literary project of his career, *A Collection of Hymns and Spiritual Songs* (1774), a work groundbreaking in its interdenominational inclusiveness, rich with insight into the cohesive strategies of Christian Indian communities, and republished consistently into the nineteenth century. This book examines Occom's hymnal as well as underacknowledged works of early African-American literature. It seeks to locate meaning in the tropes, discursive devices, and tensions that emerge from these texts. I have sought to answer as many questions as I have raised, but I do not pretend to have mastered the often-occluded histories of early African-American and Native American authors and their writings.

Indeed, historical occlusion is a condition endemic to this field. This is because slavery, colonialism, and racism impacted not only the writing of literature but also the writing of histories and the keeping of records. Race, class, and gender determined the differential documentation of early American lives in government, church, business, and private records. Not all had equal access to literacy, political representation, church membership, or property ownership. Poverty, warfare, exile, illness, family separation, and forced displacement made poor conditions for the preservation of letters, manuscripts, and libraries. All of these factors make it impossible to reconstruct with confidence and perfect clarity the lives or careers of pioneering authors of color. More fundamentally, the way we conventionally think about history—as a continuous and developmental narrative, or as an epic driven by the decisions of individual heroes—denies the legitimacy of black and Indian experience in early America. Existing scholarship in African-American and Native American histories do provide information and insight essential to our interpretation of this literature. However, we must also be alert to the inevitable limitations of these scholarly histories, and we must consider the potential value of oral and tribal traditions as alternate means to decoding and understanding early literatures of color. Finally, no work of early African-American or Native American literature should be disqualified solely because we cannot verify against historical records the identity of its author or the authenticity of its contents. I do not mean to suggest that historical research is not important, or that vigilance is not required. Rather, I am arguing that the historical record is incomplete and that literature may in fact map out new facets of African-American and Native American experience. I would also argue that historical fidelity is not the first responsibility of literature. We are mistaken to think that early black and Indian authors did not exercise creative agency, even in texts presented as autobiographical.

What Abdul JanMohamed and David Lloyd argued for relationship of minority literature to conventional literary expectations may also be argued for its relationship to conventional history: "damaged," "fragmentary," "hampered," or "occluded" historical documentation is not a "symptom of inadequacy" but rather a positive indictment of the difficult conditions under which early American writers of color worked and thus a consideration integral to the interpretation of their writings.

In summary, the story of Lazarus indicates the regenerative power of early American literatures of color as well as the methodological and textual challenges that attend their reading and interpretation. To honor those challenges, to appreciate now the value of eighteenth-century black and Indian writings is to participate in the regeneration of memory and thus the raising of the dead.

This book advances our understanding of how race was lived and how racial identities were formed in eighteenth-century America. I will show how the earliest African-American and Native American authors used religion and literature as instruments for transforming the meaning of race.[12] In their writings, race no longer designates some individuals for appropriation, expropriation, or annihilation; rather, it assumes new value as a site of common identification, shared histories and experiences, mutual allegiances and affiliations, and new communities—physical, social, cultural, theological, and ideological. This reclamation, recontextualization, and resignification is the same process Anthony Marx calls "race making from below" and which Howard Winant and Michael Omi term a "rearticulation" of racial identities.[13] Failing to recognize these processes of racial formation, too many contemporary literary critics have measured pioneering black and Indian authors against contemporary notions of racial authenticity. For example, some read Samson Occom's profession of Christianity as compromising his Indian identity; others search in vain for a familiar black consciousness in the writings of Phillis Wheatley. While such readings imply that race is a transhistorical and natural essence, this book is premised on my understanding of race as a historically contingent and ideologically invested construction.

More recently, studies of early African-American and Native American literatures have focused on the ways authors strategically adopted dominant literary and cultural conventions to win and persuade white audiences. In *We Wear the Mask: African-Americans Write American Literature, 1760–1870*, Rafia Zafar describes this phenomenon as a wearing of literary "whiteface." The calculated appeal to white readers both empowered and limited early authors of color, who sometimes masked their own profound revulsion, despair, anger, and frustration.[14] It is important to recognize that interracial mediation or negotiation with Euro-American forms and audiences is not the only story encoded in early black and Indian writings—not the only, and perhaps not even the most compelling. *American Lazarus* engages another side of the story, revealing how early black and Indian writings mattered to black and Indian communities, documenting and instrumentalizing movements toward common identification and community regeneration. This book, then, redresses the misconception that early black and Indian authors wrote only for white audiences, that a significant filial community of readers and auditors did not exist until the nineteenth century. It resituates early literatures of color in relation to communities of color in early America.

In so doing, I honor calls by scholars of color to respect the intellectual integrity and longevity of their respective traditions. Native scholars like Jace Weaver (Cherokee), Robert Warrior (Osage), Craig Womack (Creek), and others have challenged readers to recognize the intellectual sovereignty of Native American literary culture. Weaver argues that the defining quality of Native literature is not its mediation of white expectations but rather its commitment to Indian communities, which he defines as a "we-hermeneutics" or "communitism."[15] He explains:

Writing prepares the ground for recovery, and even recreation, of Indian identity and culture. Native writers speak to that part of us the colonial power and the dominant culture cannot reach, cannot touch. They help Indians imagine themselves as Indians. Just as there is no practice of Native religions for personal empowerment, they write that the People might live.[16]

Accordingly, I read early Indian texts as generative of new modes of community, new social histories, new theories and practices for Indian peoples.[17] I also read early black texts as both representative and constitutive of new social, cultural, religious, and political formations among African-Americans.[18] Together, then, this book takes early black and Indian literatures as builders of distinctive African-American and Native American intellectual histories.

As a study of early American racial formation, this book also responds to an emergent trend in early American studies to assert the ultimate "fluidity" or "hybridity" of race in early America, or to summarize early African-American and Native American literatures as products of "hybridization." This trend often results from a misreading of postcolonial theory as simple anti-essentialism. The introduction of postcolonial theory to early American studies has furnished scholars with new models for understanding the circum-Atlantic movement of persons, cultures, and ideas. However, some critics have mistaken concepts such as Paul Gilroy's black Atlantic to discount the power of race as a shaper of modern identities and cultures. For example, the editors of a recent collection of essays on early black Atlantic literature conflate Gilroy's formulation of the black Atlantic as a new geographical "unit of analysis" with the "decentering of ethnic identity" propounded by Homi Bhabha; consequently, they claim that the very idea of a "black literary 'tradition'" is a "teleological distortion."[19] I find this claim objectionable for several reasons.

First, reducing the "black Atlantic" to a celebration of "fluid" identities overlooks the profound philosophical and political underpinnings of Gilroy's theory. For Gilroy, the black Atlantic is not only a supranational conceptualization of culture; the black Atlantic theorizes blackness as a "counter-culture of modernity" distinguished by its "politics of transfiguration." His formula demonstrates how black people have creatively, conscientiously, and electively reorganized the circuits of the slave trade into conduits for the expression of resistance to the violence of modernity. Locating the philosophical roots of blackness in the Hegelian master-slave dialectic, Gilroy suggests that blackness poses a fundamental challenge to modern conceptions of the nation, nature, reason, and freedom. Neither of these political or philosophical aspects of the black Atlantic is sufficiently articulated in the notion of "hybrid" or "fluid" identity.[20]

Second, declaring "hybridity" or "fluidity" of eighteenth-century racial identities wrongly suggests the ephemerality, immateriality, or evanescence of race in the eighteenth-century Atlantic world. It is right to recognize that among eighteenth-century Europeans and Euro-Americans there was no consensual philosophical theorization, scientific formulation, or literary imagination of race. However, it does not follow that race was not a major determinant of lived experience. The inconsistency of learned discourses about race in eighteenth-century Europe does not correlate with the instrumental power of race in eighteenth-century America. Indeed, American legal theorists and historians of race have demonstrated that race—independent of scientific and philosophical theorization—consolidated as a legal concept in the British North American colonies from the 1660s onward. The determination of race in America was driven by political and economic conditions specific to the colonies and the new nation: the persistence of large-scale race slavery and the campaign to expropriate indigenous landholders. Gilroy's formulation accounts for these economic and historical forces driving the construction of race, as well as for the agency of people of color in reconstructing their own identities. The notion of "hybridity" evacuates these considerations of power.[21]

A third hazard that attends the classification of black and Indian cultures as "hybrid" inheres in the historical usage of the term *hybridity* itself. As Robert Young demonstrates in *Colonial Desire: Hybridity in Theory, Culture, and Race* (1995), the very notion of hybridity—especially as it is used in relation to people of color—originated in nineteenth-century racist theories of polygenism. Originally, it was developed to classify the offspring of interracial sexual unions; now, cultural critics use it to describe cultural production by non-European peoples under colonial and postcolonial conditions. The sexual overtones of the term *hybridity* suggests that these cultural products better reflect the successful penetration and replication of the colonizers' culture than the original creative agency of the colonized.[22] Consequently, notions of "purity" and "hybridity" are often used to denigrate the legitimacy of modern Native American and African-American cultures.[23]

Finally, using hybridity as a rationale for rejecting the notion of "black literary 'tradition'" devalues the continuing institutional and intellectual value of African-American studies. Early Americanists benefit tremendously from the labors of our predecessors and colleagues in African-American studies and American Indian studies. By their pioneering efforts in scholarship, teaching, and activism, by their determined defense of the intellectual value of these cultures, and by their struggles to obtain institutional support for work in these fields, they have made it possible to research, write about, and teach early American literatures of color. If we teach, write about, or profit from early American literatures of color without a conscientious reckoning of our relationship to the broader legacies and commitments of African-American and American Indian studies, then our labors can amount only to opportunistic antiquarianism.

Early African-American and Native American literatures demand that we grapple not only with race but also with the value of religion to early communities of color. Engaging the vital religious aspects of these writings is an enterprise fraught with its own complications. The scripture references—annotated and unannotated—that ripple through these texts privilege readers who know the Bible. Such references helped authors of color encode meaning and create insider discourse communities in the eighteenth century; in the contemporary college classroom, these same references can make outsiders of non-Bible literate students. Greater responsibility, then, falls to teachers of early African-American and Native American literatures to explicate the particular strategic and significant value of religion. This, of course, means that we must understand these values better ourselves. Our subject authors were trained, ordained, and sophisticated interpreters of major currents in American religious thought, as well as visionary innovators of new strands of religious belief and practice. They were not merely dupes, apologists, or victims of missionary colonialism, as they are sometimes made out to be. Such views typically hinge on a rigid and outmoded Marxist rejection of religion as ideological delusion; they do not reflect a more contemporary cultural studies understanding of religion as a venue for creative and political agency.

Recent studies in early American literatures of color have called for this better understanding. For example, Katherine Clay Bassard in *Spiritual Interrogations: Culture, Gender, and Community in Early African American Women's Writing* (1999) urges us to develop "greater sophistication in the theorizing of connections between literature and religion in general, given that it is becoming increasingly difficult to 'bracket' religion and religious experience as somehow extraliterary or not germane to issues of textuality."[24] Scholars in the fields of postcolonialism and subaltern studies have also called for greater attention to the role of religion in histories of empire and anti-imperialism. Gauri Visnawathan has presented an especially compelling analysis of conversion among the religious minorities and colonial subjects of the British Empire in *Outside the Fold: Conversion, Modernity, and Belief* (1998). Conversion, she argues, should not be interpreted merely as missionary mastery over the convert but rather as a convert act of resistance against traditional hierarchy, imperial control, and nascent secular nationalism. Following Visnawathan, we may read the religious aspects of early African-American and Native American writings as potential expressions of resistance against the ascendant secularization and rationalization of the late eighteenth century. Tropes of conversion figure the processes—death and resurrection, loss and reclamation, scattering and gathering, forgetting and remembering, abjection and testimony—through which blacks and Indians became "peoples." Religious discourse thus mattered not only to individual African and Native Americans but collectively as a language for their common condition. Acts of conversion were acts of self-determination.

Given their religiously expressed commitments to community regeneration, these literatures invite us to consider the regenerative possibilities of our own work as literary scholars and teachers. Who are we but revivalists, breathing life into old texts as we read them? If, as Derrida notes, the word *religion* can be traced to dual Latinate roots in *relegere*—"bringing together in order to return and begin again"— and *religare*—"linking religion to the link, precisely, to obligation, ligament"—is not our effort to rehabilitate these forgotten literatures in some measure a religious undertaking?[25] Walter Benjamin, in his "Theses on the Philosophy of History," characterized historical research as a work of redemption and revelation:

The past carries with it a temporal index by which it is referred to re-demption. There is a secret agreement between past generations and the present one. Our coming was expected on earth. Like every generation that preceded us, we have been endowed with a *weak* Messianic power, a power to which the past has a claim. That claim cannot be settled cheaply.[26]

Understanding early African-American and Native American literatures may require of us unusual faith in their potential meaningfulness. It may also require us to abandon comfortable notions of literary value, histori-cal verification, and racial authenticity. Intelligent receptivity is the price of literary redemption, and revelation, or a new understanding of the past, is its reward.

American Lazarus will chart an itinerant path through several eighteenth-century American communities and cultures, traveling from theological controversies at the colonies' learned centers to gospels preached at the crossroads and margins. These scattered sites belong to a transatlantic web of connection established in the collective movements of colonizers, slaves, and exiles, reconstructed by traveling evangelists and religious communities, and individually negotiated by the authors featured in this book. Chapter 1, "Race, Religion, and Regeneration," reviews the domi-nant theologies, religious movements, and racial ideologies of the late eighteenth-century. Chapter 2, "Samson Occom and the Poetics of Native Revival," focuses on Mohegan minister and tribal leader Samson Occom's *A Choice Collection of Hymns and Spiritual Songs* (1774). The composition and contents of the hymnal—which includes hymn texts written by Occom himself and perhaps as well by his Native colleague Joseph Johnson—reflect the strategic adaptation of Christian theologies to In-dian separatist movements and particularly to the Occom-led founding of an intertribal Christian community at Brotherton, New York. Occom and Johnson were the only Native American authors who wrote and pub-lished their literary works in the eighteenth century; consequently, they are the only Indian authors who fit the historical contours of my study. Their historical isolation underscores the value of a comparative ap-proach to early literatures of color, as do Occom's friendships with black authors like Phillis Wheatley and the frequent intermingling of black and Indian religious communities in early America.

Chapter 3, "John Marrant and the Lazarus Theology of the Black At-lantic," follows African-American evangelist John Marrant (1755–90) dur-ing his three-year mission to Birchtown, Nova Scotia, where thousands of exiled black Loyalists had formed North America's largest all-black settlement. Marrant's published missionary *Journal* (1790) establishes a covenant theology specific to this black Atlantic community and promulgates a collective narrative of gathering, exodus, and Zionistic fulfillment. Many Birchtowners made an exodus to Sierra Leone in 1791. Marrant, however, continued his ministry as chaplain to the first African Lodge of Freemasons in Boston, Massachusetts. Chapter 4, "Prince Hall Freemasonry: Secrecy, Authority, and Culture," examines three speeches delivered by Marrant and lodge founder Prince Hall (1735?–1807), which construct from scripture, Masonic lore, and mystical earlier texts a new and ennobling concept of black history and black identity. Absalom Jones and Richard Allen, members of Philadelphia's Prince Hall Masonic Lodge and founders of the African Methodist Episcopal church, are the subjects of chapter 5, "Black Identity and Yellow Fever in Philadelphia." Philadelphia's civic leaders impressed African-Americans, who were erroneously thought immune to yellow fever, into hazardous service as nurses and gravediggers during the epidemic. Jones and Allen narrate their community's travails and disprove allegations of criminality against them in *A Narrative of the Proceedings of the Black People, During the Late Awful Calamity in Philadelphia* (1794). The *Narrative* counters the lethal falsehoods of racialist science with a spiritual conception of the black community and their survival of the epidemic.

Three considerations have governed my choice of subject texts. First, I have focused primarily on published texts by early American authors of color; unpublished documents play only a supporting role in this study. I have also selected texts that until now have received little or no literary-critical examination. Their neglect cannot be attributed to their archival inaccessibility; their eighteenth-century publication has secured almost all of these works a place in the widely available *Early American Imprints* microform series. Consequently, I hope my work serves as a reminder that the archives do not own the past. We who live at some geographical distance from archives of early American materials, or who cannot travel extensively due to funding constraints, teaching responsibilities, or family obligations, nonetheless can explore rich and uncharted regions of American literary history. Finally, I have focused on writings closely connected to religious and spiritual communities of color in early America that document and contribute to the lives of their respective constituencies. These texts best illustrate the central themes of *American Lazarus*: that early African-American and Native American literatures were endeavors of community regeneration, and that these literatures can also incur in contemporary readers a regenerate understanding of American religion, race, resistance, and culture, past and present.

I

Ho

Race, Religion, and Regeneration

The advent of African-American and Native American literatures is inextricably connected to the rise of American evangelicalism in the eighteenth century. From the first Great Awakening (1737–45) through the New Light Stir (1778–82) to the dawn of the Second Great Awakening at century's end, revivals rumbled through American religion, from north to south, from seaboard to frontier, across denominations, ethnicities, races, and classes. Critics warned that the revivals would unleash on the American strand an old and troublesome spirit of enthusiasm. In Benjamin Franklin's *General Magazine and Historical Chronicle* of February 1741, "Theophilus Misodemon" reported the American advent of "a wonderful WANDERING SPIRIT," lately arrived from European and Near Eastern exploits among the "Bachanals," "Mahomet," "Jacob Behmen," and the "Enthusiasts of Munster." Misodemon described the effects of its American manifestation:

> When it possesses the Mob, which it delights to torture, they swell and shake like *Virgil's* enthusiastick Sybil, or those possess'd with the Devil in the Gospel. . . . It also loves to be esteemed among us a gifted Brother, or a Lay-holder-forth. . . . It acts the Busy-Body, is here and there, and everywhere, and above all Things, hates Rules and good Order, or Bounds and Limits. It is unwearied in issuing Warrants and Commissions under the broad Seal of an inward Call to all that have Conceit and Self-sufficiency enough to run its Errands. . . . [It] carefully excuses all from the Number of the Faithful who will not tell every impertinent hypocritical Canter he meets, his Sins and Experiences. . . . All that it bewitches generally bid farewell to Reason, and are carried by it to the Land of Clouds and Darkness, under the Pretence of divine Light. . . . It hates *Greek* and *Hebrew*, because Holy Languages, and tells its Admirers, that it

can make a sanctified Cobler at once an abler Divine than either *Luther* or *Calvin*.[1]

Other antirevivalists asserted that the same "Spirit" which activated the revivals had in the last century emboldened Ann Hutchinson, Mary Dyer, and other so-called "antinomians" and "familists." The Old Light leader and Congregationalist minister Charles Chauncy sternly charged, "It has made strong attempts to destroy all property, to make all things common, wives as well as goods."[2] Its itinerant operations, its disorderly "wandering," its transgression of established priestly domains, its disregard for standing ministers, its discounting of conventional clerical training, and most fearsomely, its agitation of common persons to prophetic speech: these characteristics of the "Spirit" and the American evangelical movement were perceived not only as a threat to established churches but also to the established social orders they sustained.[3]

Especially provocative was visible and vocal participation in the revivals by African- and Native Americans. Anecdotes of Indian conversions and black exhortations circulated like currency among both New Lights and Old Lights. During the first Great Awakening, such stories were transmitted by letter from American ministers to their English evangelical colleagues and faithfully reprinted in both British and American print organs of the evangelical movement. Prominent among these was the *Christian History* (1743–44), a weekly magazine dedicated entirely to the revivals, published in Boston by Thomas Prince, Jr. In addition to featuring missives from John Sargeant and other missionaries among the Indians, the *Christian History* adopted a peculiarly American strategy of using indigenous peoples to naturalize and legitimate controversial features of New Light evangelicalism. In September 1743, the magazine published a defense of "Outcries and bodily Distresses attending a Work of the divine Spirit," compiled from English and American religious writings. To show that such expressions were "no new Things," Prince first and foremost cited the example of American Indians: "We find there were some Appearances of these among the Natives of this Country, upon our Forefathers coming over and preaching among them."[4] Another species of anecdote emphasized emotive affinities between George Whitefield and the African-Americans who attended his preachings. For example, in October 1741, the English prorevival *Weekly History* reported that certain Boston "gentlemen" disdainful of the revival had gathered to enjoy the spectacle of a black slave impersonating Whitefield but were instantaneously and effectively converted by the performance. "Such is the work of God by the Hands of poor Negroes," the *Weekly History* concluded, "We have such Instances every Week from some Part of the Country or other."[5] Such accounts appealed to popular racial stereotypes—Indian primitivism, black mimicry—but they also demonstrate a positive valuation of racial difference as a significant element within the spectacular lexicon of the revivals.

Conversely, Old Lights seized on black and Indian participation in the revivals as a symptom of New Light errancy and excess. Their public and private writings rehearse with striking consistency a catalog of undesirable characters roused by the New Lights. Opponents protested in the Boston *Weekly Post-Boy* for July 12, 1742, that the New Light "Shepherd's Tent" ministerial school in New Haven, Connecticut, appealed to "Teachers, Exhorters, and Armour-Bearers, Whites and Blacks, Young and Old, from the Shopkeeper, the Deacon, the Barber, to the Cobler, and . . . particularly the good Women." Similarly, in his *Seasonable Thoughts on the State of Religion in New England* (1743), Charles Chauncy observed that the exhorters of the Awakening were "chiefly indeed young Persons, sometimes Lads or rather Boys: Nay, Women and Girls; yea, Negroes, have taken upon them to do the Business of Preachers."[6] Chauncy's concerns were echoed by a minor Massachusetts antirevivalist named Nathan Bowen, who privately observed that individuals "of the meanest Capacity ie women & even Common negros" began to "take upon them to Exhort their Betters even in the pulpit, before large assemblys."[7] This imputation of subversive and even revolutionary tendencies to popular religion survived beyond the first Great Awakening and into the early national era.[8]

Indeed, contemporary scholars continue to view the Great Awakening as a watershed in American intellectual and social history, which forever reformulated notions of experience, learning, authority, textuality, and religion. It has become customary to think about the Great Awakening and its evangelical sequels in the oppositional terms set forth by the distinguished intellectual historians Perry Miller and Alan Heimert: "Old Lights" against "New Lights," elite against popular, churched against unchurched, Arminianism versus Calvinism, pietism against empiricism, emotion against reason, head against heart.[9] More recently, Nancy Ruttenburg has keyed to the Awakening the emergence of a "democratic personality," a popular, vernacular, and sometimes unruly mode of subjective performance that both prepared the way for and marked the limits of the Habermasian public sphere.[10] What was the racial character of this "democratic personality"? How did race figure into the polarized "Old Light" versus "New Light" controversies of the eighteenth century? Why did African-Americans and American Indians figure so consistently in the folklore and history of the eighteenth-century revivals, and what did their spectacular presence signify? Why were so many black and Indian writers deeply implicated in American and British evangelical movements?

This chapter will provide essential background on the evangelical movements most attractive to pioneering black and Indian authors and examine their respective racial policies and theologies. I will argue that most eighteenth-century American evangelists, beginning with the eminent and influential Jonathan Edwards, marked the spectacular value of black and Indian conversions but failed to develop a clear theological outlook on race or to enlarge on the potentially progressive energies of revivalism. This cognitive lapse was especially egregious given the rapid advancement of racialist thinking in natural science and the legal institution of racial identities in the new nation. It fell, then, to a powerful group of black and Indian evangelist-authors to marshal religion against the degradations of racialist science and racist politics, producing in their efforts toward community regeneration new identities, religious traditions, and literatures. This chapter will show how eighteenth-century American evangelicalism, national politics, and natural science constructed race as a significant category of human experience. It will also show how people of color rose up to answer these constructions, telling their own stories and thus transforming the course of American literary history.

Many historians of American religion have summarized black and Indian participation in the eighteenth-century revivals as a function of revivalistic enthusiasm and its particular attractiveness to people of color. However, this sweeping claim obscures the complex and often-uncertain dynamics at work within American evangelicalism at large and within communities of color. Eighteenth-century revivals were not merely a venting of religious enthusiasm but rather a profound retooling of established religion in the American colonies, with lasting impacts on theology, ecclesiastical polity, and denominational organization and with specific consequences for communities of color. These communities were especially influenced by the era's increasing religious pluralism, which introduced them to multiple modes of Christianity: not only the dominant strains of colonial Anglicanism, Congregationalism, and Catholicism but also the Moravian Brethren, the Dutch Reformed Church, Baptists, Quakers, Shakers, and other indigenous Protestant sects. Thus, American Indian and African-American responses to evangelicalism must be understood not as simple, affectionate attraction but rather as conscientious choices determined by compound historical, political, economic, cultural, regional, and denominational factors. Correspondingly, because they were engaged and influential participants in the revivals, America's first writers of color must be understood in relation to the religious movements that most impacted their careers: the Whitefield-Huntingdon Connexion, American New Light evangelicalism, Wesleyan Methodism, and the New Divinity School.

Celebrity English evangelist George Whitefield made six highly successful and widely publicized preaching tours of the American colonies from October 1739 until his death in Newburyport, Massachusetts, in September 1770. The Oxford-educated and Anglican-ordained Whitefield developed a trademark evangelical style that included theatrical oratory, use of outdoor venues, open disregard for sectarian differences and established church authorities, unremitting emphasis on the necessity of the new birth, unrelenting criticism of ministers perceived to be "unconverted," and as Frank Lambert has shown, a highly coordinated "preach and print" publicity campaign. During the first Great Awakening, he was unrivalled not only as an orator but as a print celebrity: 30 percent of all works published in America during 1740 were either by or about George Whitefield, and no other author matched his sales record in the years from 1739 to 1745.[11] In 1741, Whitefield split from the Methodist movement led by his former Oxford classmates John and Charles Wesley over key theological and ecclesiastical differences. Whitefield was a committed Calvinist and predestinarian, whereas the Wesleys endorsed a more Arminian conception of regeneration as human perfection; Whitefield in his itinerancy paid little heed to local authorities or established church precincts, while the Wesleys emphasized local society building. In 1748, Whitefield found a powerful sponsor in Selina Hastings, the countess of Huntingdon, who had abandoned Wesleyan Methodism and appointed him her personal chaplain. Together, they developed a cohort of Anglican ministers committed to constant itinerancy and Calvinist doctrine. Under the direction of the countess, the Huntingdon Connexion issued distinctive gowns and scarves to its member ministers; opened chapels, the most famous being at Bath and then at Spa-Fields; established Trevecca College for the training of ministers, in 1768; issued a fifteen-article Calvinist "Confession of Faith," in 1783; and finally, separated from the Church of England.[12]

On issues of race and slavery, George Whitefield and the Huntingdon Connexion compiled a very uneven record. The countess of Huntingdon was known to fancy or even fetishize foreign missions and converts; similarly, Whitefield was noted in his sentimental regard for black people, and especially for those who attended his revivals. An exemplary entry from Whitefield's journal records that during his tour of Philadelphia in 1740, he had "been much drawn out in prayer for" the African-Americans in his audience and had "seen them exceedingly wrought upon under the Word preached."[13] His *Letter to the Inhabitants of Maryland, Virginia, North and South-Carolina, Concerning Their Negroes*, published in Philadelphia in 1740, challenged the religious bases of white supremacy: "Think you, your children are in any way better by nature than the poor negroes? No! In no wise! Blacks are just as much, and no more, conceived and born in sin, as white men are; and both, if born and bred up here, I am persuaded, are naturally capable of the same improvement."[14] Some whites suspected Whitefield and his preaching of inciting rebellion amongst free blacks and slaves, especially during the New York Slave Revolt of 1741, and his black audiences occasionally expressed disappointment when Whitefield failed to enlarge on this theme. At least one member of the Huntingdon Connexion *did* preach slave rebellion: David Margate, a black Briton educated at Trevecca College and ordained in 1774, was recalled from the American South after he declared himself a "Moses" "called to deliver his people from slavery." In its official politics and practice, however, the Connexion was unmistakably proslavery. George Whitefield himself lobbied Parliament and the Trustees of Georgia to permit slavery in the colony, and after the legalization of slavery in 1750, he quickly obtained dozens of slaves for his orphanage and for the countess.[15]

His proslavery politics notwithstanding, George Whitefield was remembered fondly by a majority of the eighteenth-century's black Atlantic authors, including Phillis Wheatley, James Albert Ukawsaw Gronniosaw, Olaudah Equiano, John Jea, and John Marrant. Most memorable is Equiano's description of his own encounter with Whitefield:

> I saw this pious man exhorting the people with the greatest fervour and earnestness, and sweating as much as I ever did while in slavery on Montserrat beach. I was very much struck and impressed with this; I thought it strange I had never seen divines exert themselves in this manner before, and was no longer at a loss to account for the thin congregations they preached to.[16]

Whitefield's American and English associates in the Huntingdon Connexion formed a transatlantic network of influence that proved critical to the careers of several authors in this study. Whitefield regularly corresponded with Eleazar Wheelock, founder of Moor's Indian Charity School and mentor to Samson Occom; when Occom made fund-raising tour of England in 1768, Whitefield was a generous host and an affectionate friend. Through Whitefield, Occom was introduced to Susannah and Phillis Wheatley. Susannah corresponded with Occom and generated financial support for his ministries, while Phillis ingratiated herself into the powerful transatlantic networks of the Connexion. George Whitefield's untimely death afforded the occasion for Phillis Wheatley's breakthrough work "An Elegiac Poem, on the Death of that Celebrated Divine, and Eminent Servant of Jesus Christ, the Late Reverend and Pious George

Whitefield, Chaplain to the Right Honourable the Countess of Hunting-don" (1770), and the countess herself endorsed and advised the publication of Wheatley's *Poems on Subjects, Religious and Moral* (1773). Finally, Whitefield was instrumental in the conversion of John Marrant, who later joined the Huntingdon Connexion and traveled to Nova Scotia as its emissary. In Nova Scotia, Marrant gathered a fiercely loyal black Huntingdonian congregation, which maintained its distinctive sectarian identity even through their emigration to Sierra Leone, in 1792.[17]

While the Huntingdon Connexion maintained its English base and character, George Whitefield's itinerancy inspired similar networks and alliances among sympathetic American religionists. Whitefield's colonial "New Light" allies came from different sectarian backgrounds and different regions, but they agreed that the revivals of the first Great Awakening were divinely inspired. They also shared a Calvinist insistence on salvation by justification alone, and they emphasized the necessity of an experiential "new birth" rather than a merely intellectual or sacramental conversion. Some New Lights openly criticized Arminian tendencies within the established and urbane churches, and a few extended their criticisms to the conservative, elite, and highly educated "Old Light" clerics who, they judged, preached "head" religion without heartfelt conviction. Most infamous in this regard was James Davenport, a Yale-educated, ordained Congregationalist, who left his Long Island congregation in 1740 to undertake a radical itinerant career: Davenport publicly humiliated Old Lights whom he perceived to be "unconverted," shocked small towns by leading singing throngs of revivalists through their streets, and in New London, Connecticut, in 1743, instigated a public book burning of antirevival writings. More moderate forces within the New Light movement included the esteemed Jonathan Edwards. Edwards had led a pioneering revival at Northampton, Massachusetts, in 1734–35; his published account of that event—*A Faithful Narrative of the Suprising Work of God* (1737)—attracted the attention of English evangelists like Isaac Watts and George White-field, and effectively set American evangelicalism into motion. Even after the initial revival controversies of the 1740s had cooled, the New Light movement continued to incur change and division within New England Congregationalism. By 1770, almost one hundred New England churches had declared themselves "Separate" or "Strict" Congregationalists; the "New Light Stir" during the War of Independence furthered the erosion of established state religion by fostering a patchwork of autonomous, charismatic, and uniquely local sectarian experiments. As Stephen Marini has observed, the New Light movement culminated in "nothing less than the creation of alternative cultures, complete models for human life structured by religious priorities and fabricated by a native constituency intent on finding ultimate meaning amid rapid and violent change."[18]

New Light itinerants made significant inroads into rural and isolated communities of color. David Brainerd, who was expelled from Yale in 1742 for accusing his tutor of "having no more grace than this chair," was subsequently licensed by the Scottish Society for Propagating Christian Knowledge (SPCK) and expended his life preaching to tribal communities in southern New England, Long Island, Delaware, New York, Pennsylvania, and New Jersey. James Davenport effected the conversion of Samson Occom and several other Mohegan. According to Occom, the Mohegan and other tribes in southern New England did not adopt Christianity until the first Great Awakening. "We heard a Strange Rumor among the English, that there were Extraordinary Ministers Preaching from Place to Place and a Strange Concern among the White People," he recalled. "These Preachers did not only come to us, but we frequently went to their meetings and Churches."[19] The first Great Awakening also initiated new experiments in American Indian education, sponsored by patrons of the revival in England and America. Inspired by the example of the Shepherd's Tent ministerial college, a New Light itinerant named Eleazar Wheelock—a Yale classmate and brother-in-law to James Davenport—established a similar school for the training of Indian missionaries. His Moor's Indian Charity School (now Dartmouth College) produced a notable cohort of pioneering Native ministers and authors, including Samson Occom, David and Jacob Fowler, and Joseph Johnson. Several lay and ordained Native ministers followed separatist tendencies within the New Light movement to establish their own independent Christian Indian congregations and settlements, the most notable of which was the Brotherton community founded by Occom, Johnson, and the Fowlers in upstate New York.[20]

Traveling on orders to proselytize Indians neighboring the Anglican pastorate at Savannah, Georgia, John Wesley introduced his Methodist brand of Anglicanism to America in 1736. His greatest impact in the American South would not be on tribal communities but rather on enslaved and free African-Americans. His first significant interaction with black slaves came during a 1737 visit to the South Carolina plantation (slave-holding was not then permitted in Georgia), where he conversed with a young black Barbadian slave named Nanny, who had been denied by her master, an Anglican minister, even a rudimentary religious education. This interaction incited Wesley to a serious consideration of slavery and the religious instruction of African-Americans. Inspired in part by this cause, he established an infrastructure of classes, circuits, and conferences, which was extended throughout the American colonies after 1770.

This Methodist Society was designed to supplement rather than supplant established Anglicanism by fostering piety according to the Wesleyan doctrine of perfectionism. Its close ties with the Church of England caused some crisis for the society during the American War of Independence. At the onset of the war, John Wesley withdrew his preachers from America; after the war, American Methodism separated from its British parent.

One consequence of this separation was a softening of antislavery sentiment within American Methodism. John Wesley had condemned the slave trade and slave-holding in his "Thoughts Upon Slavery," published in 1774. Such sentiments were then not uncommon among British and American circuit riders and society leaders, including Freeborn Garrettson, Francis Asbury, and Thomas Rankin; in fact, Rankin had preached in 1775 that the coming war was divine retribution for slavery. Despite strong opinions held by individuals and individual conferences, the society never adopted an official antislavery policy and, by the end of the eighteenth-century, retreated from formal engagement with the cause. Still, American Methodism attracted phenomenal numbers of African-Americans, who helped increase society membership from 1,000 members in 1770 to 250,000 in 1820. Methodism also opened to black men like Richard Allen, Harry Hosier, Moses Wilkinson, and Boston King and black women like Jarena Lee and Zilpha Elaw unprecedented (albeit institutionally limited) opportunities for leadership as class leaders, circuit riders, and lay preachers. The institutional church's refusal to ordain these black preachers and local congregations' insistence on segregated seating provoked black walkouts in a number of cities, including Baltimore (1787); Philadelphia (1792); Wilmington, Delaware (1805); and Charleston (1817). These in turn led to the establishment of the African Methodist Episcopal (A.M.E.) and African Methodist Episcopal Zion (A.M.E. Zion) churches in the late eighteenth and early nineteenth centuries.[21]

Another influential development in American evangelicalism involved the theological problems of race and slavery. Coalescing in the early republican era, the New Divinity school of Congregationalist clergy included Samuel Hopkins, Levi Hart, Jonathan Edwards, Jr., and Timothy Dwight. They inherited from the elder Edwards their concept of God as a just sovereign and their dispensationalist understanding of history. By this view, all human events and conditions—even sin—belonged to a grand historical design appointed to achieve the redemption of the regenerate, the damnation of the unregenerate, and the glorification of God. New Divinity men condemned slavery as a practice inherently contrary to the "benevolence" characteristic of God and required of a godly society. However, they also sought to reconcile the historical fact of the slave trade to the grand historical design. This effort produced a highly influential view of slavery as the means appointed by God to the Christianization of Africa, a view articulated most convincingly by Samuel Hopkins in his popular *Dialogue Concerning the Slavery of the Africans* (1776). As the pastor of the First Congregational Church in Newport, Rhode Island, Hopkins witnessed firsthand the cruelties of the slave trade as it was carried out on the docks of his city. He pressured congregants to free their slaves, founded the charitable African Union Society, and aspired to train African-Americans for missionary service in Africa. Hopkins's followers Susannah Anthony and Sarah Osborn educated two prospective candidates—Bristol Yamma and John Quamine; home schools organized by these women drew dozens of regular black attendants, including Phillis Wheatley's friend and correspondent Obour Tanner. (Phillis Wheatley herself had declined Hopkins's invitation to undertake an African mission.) The War of Independence and the war-related death of John Quamine derailed Hopkins's African missionary project, and he subsequently endorsed a new scheme involving the expatriation of black Christians to Africa. Hopkins developed a scriptural rationale for African colonization in his *Treatise on the Millennium* (1793) and appended supporting arguments to a revised edition of his *Dialogue Concerning the Slavery of the Africans* (1793). This turn toward colonization initiated a divide between white and black followers of the movement. Lemuel Haynes, an accomplished New Divinity thinker in his own right, and Prince Hall, founder of Boston's African Lodge of Freemasons, which established a satellite lodge in Providence, Rhode Island, in 1797, both retained the New Divinity's dispensationalist view of slavery but rejected its colonizationist agenda.[22]

The story of these evangelical movements reveals deep ambivalence concerning race and communities of color. By moving religion outside the exclusive domain of the established churches, through itinerant preaching, interdenominational revivals, and educational experiments such as Moor's Indian Charity School, the first Great Awakening did create new opportunities for Native and African-Americans in religious instruction, experience, and expression. However, the revivals did not necessarily change racial politics within organized religious bodies. The Huntingdon Connexion, the Methodist Society, and the New Lights generally maintained the policies and practices worked out by established churches in the seventeenth-century: they supported (with varying degrees of commitment) the conversion and religious instruction of blacks and Indians, while they accommodated themselves to powerful slave-holding and colonialist interests. Just like their Anglican and Congregationalist predecessors, eighteenth-century American evangelists with ties to communities of color—including Eleazar Wheelock, Jonathan Edwards, and Samuel Hopkins—advised colonial, state, and federal governments on American Indian and African-American affairs. They also inherited their predecessors' nominally egalitarian theology, rejecting race as a sign of Calvinist election or inelection. Cotton Mather set forth this position in *The Negro Christianized* (1706): "Their *Complexion* sometimes is made an Argument why nothing should be done for them. A *Gay* sort of argument! As if the great God went by the Complexion of Men, in His Favours to them! As if none but *Whites* might hope to be Favoured and Accepted with God! . . . The God who *looks on the Heart*, is not moved by the colour of the *Skin*."[23] George Whitefield reiterated Mather's sentiments in 1740: "Think you, your children are in any way better by nature than the poor negroes? No! In no wise! Blacks are just as much, and no more, conceived and born in sin, as white men are; and both, if born and bred up here, I am persuaded, are naturally capable of the same improvement."[24] Both Mather and Whitefield agreed that God was no respecter of races; both men also owned slaves. Indeed, none of the churches or societies connected with American evangelicalism officially forbade slaveholding until 1776, when the Philadelphia Yearly Meeting of the Society of Friends recommended that local meetings "disown" members who refused to free their slaves. Similarly, most churches still refused to ordain men of color, and segregationist seating customs persisted in local congregations. The theological ideal of a color-blind God in heaven did nothing to dislodge the myriad daily practices through which race was instituted as an instrument of power and domination.

This profound disjunction between belief and practice symptomized the deeper failure of eighteenth-century American evangelicalism to consider race as a theological problem. More concerned with ecclesiastical expansion than theological introspection, Huntingdonians, New Lights, and Methodists alike happily inherited and reiterated a negative valuation of race: it did *not* signify salvation or damnation; it did *not* matter to God. However, their consistent notation and publication of black and Indian involvement in the revivals suggests that race *did* matter to the evangelists. It mattered to the evangelists just as massive crowds, dramatic conversions, and theatrical oratory mattered: as a sensible indication that the revivals were the work of God, that unprecedented events were unfolding. Racial difference was appreciated chiefly as it enhanced the remarkability and spectacularity of the revivals. White evangelists had yet to recognize or reckon with its growing independent significance as a shaping force of American religion and culture. They viewed racial difference as a spectacle, perhaps as an uncertain portent, but not yet as a sign.

Eighteenth-century American evangelicals demonstrated a growing ecclesiastical interest in communities of color and increasing attentiveness to racial difference. Meanwhile, within American political, legal, and scientific discourses, race was accumulating value as a human classification and as an instrument of governance. Excepting the New Divinity school, which developed its own view of race as an instrumental element of dispensationalist history, mainline white evangelists generally failed to respond to these provocative developments. They insisted on an egalitarian God, and they rejected theories of racial origination that clashed with biblical teachings, but most failed to consider race from a theological perspective. How might theologians answer racialist philosophy and natural science? What, if anything, did race mean to God? Was it a physical, spiritual, or cultural condition? If physical, were the races—white, black, and red—to be understood as consequences of Adam's fall, as conditions of mortality? Would race persist in the afterlife, or in the resurrection? How did the "new birth"—often defined as a regeneration of the "natural man"—affect the racial identity of the convert? If spiritual, was race an inherent property, quality, or faculty of the soul? If not inherent, then did the lived experience of race and racial oppression generate specific spiritual qualities or faculties? How did race inflect, modify, or determine the conversion process? Might racial oppression and race-related suffering be instrumental in preparation for the new birth? Might it not somehow prepare people of color to more readily admit the depravity of humankind, by disabusing them of the notion of the self-sufficiency of human action toward salvation, or by encouraging their "weaned affections" from the things of this world? Was race merely a cultural, or—in language more common to the times—a "national" construct? If so, how did it determine or mediate the lexicon of signs associated with the new birth? How did it mediate the social venues of regeneration, such as the church? These important questions were generally not considered by white American evangelists, most of whom were dedicated more to itinerant preaching than to scholasticism.

The writings of Jonathan Edwards, the most eminent scholarly affiliate of the New Light movement, provide us some insight into how questions of race were theologically manifested and managed. I do not mean to suggest that Edwards represents the common element of his time, place, or profession, which he certainly did not. Rather, by virtue of his dedication to the success of the evangelical movement, his strong influence on subsequent generations of theologians, his exceptional attentiveness to matters of signification and design, and his prodigious literary output, Edwards provides us an exemplary opportunity for understanding the implication of race in New Light theology. Of course, neither Edwards nor his contemporaries used the term *race* in its modern sense, to denote a group identity based in shared physical or cultural characteristics. Instead, they preferred "nation"—a term with strong biblical precedent—to describe different human groupings. To Edwards, the most significant distinguishing characteristic of a nation was its status as Jewish or Gentile, "heathen" or Christian. He also believed that with the accomplishment of the divinely appointed plan for the redemption of humankind, these national distinctions would ultimately dissolve and individuals would be grouped into two general categories: the saved and the damned. This vector from difference to union recurs as a pattern throughout Edwards's writings to indicate the fundamental workings of the divine. Although he prized the concept of divine union and harmony, Edwards also believed that God worked in strange, revolutionary, and sometimes inexplicable ways. Consequently, he prized strangeness or inscrutability in spiritual phenomena as a manifestation of the sovereignty of God and as a weapon against human conceit. Racial and national differences thus assumed a heightened but unspecific significance for Edwards. To him they were emblems of inscrutability.

His private notebooks, now known as the *Miscellanies*, reveal Edwards's early thoughts on national difference. He looked favorably on increasing interaction among the nations as preparatory to the millennial reign of Jesus Christ. His vision of the millennium, as recorded in the early 1720s, drew all continents and peoples into a union of mind:

> How happy will that state be, when neither divine nor human learning shall be confined and imprisoned within only two or three nations of Europe, but shall be diffused all over the world, and this lower world shall be all over covered with light, the various parts of it mutually enlightening each other; . . . sometimes new and wondrous discoveries from Terra Australis Incognita, admirable books of devotion, the most divine and angelic strains from among the Hottentots, and the press shall groan in wild Tartary—when we shall have the great advantages of the sentiments of men of the most distant nations, different circumstances, customs and tempers; [when] learning shall not be restrained [by] the particular humor of a nation or their singular way of treating of things; when the distant extremes of the world shall shake hands together and all nations shall be acquainted, and they shall all join the forces of their minds in exploring the glories of the Creator, their hearts in loving and adoring him, their hands in serving him, and their voices in making the world to ring with his praise. What infinite advantages will they have for discovering the truth of every kind, to what they have now![25]

Although this entry appears to proceed from narrow Eurocentric premises, with the implication that "learning" was then "confined" to Europe alone, its scope quickly broadens to embrace distant nations in a relationship of "mutual enlightenment." This millennial union of "hands," "hearts," "voices," and "minds" reflects Edwards's understanding of the divine as a state of union. The passage also discloses Edwards's understanding of national characters as composed of "singular" "sentiments," "circumstances," "customs," "tempers," and "humors." Inevitably, these characteristics imprinted, then "imprisoned" and "restrained" subjective thinking; interaction with other peoples and other ways of thinking would produce "infinite advantages" in the "discovery" of "truth." To this glorious end, Edwards celebrated technological advances in travel and communication: "so that there need not be such a tedious voyage in order to hear from the other hemisphere, and so the countries about the poles need no longer to lie hid to us, but the whole earth may be as one community, one body in Christ."[26] The church, he testified in another entry, "is not any particular enclosure but is dispersed through the whole world . . . without any walls or dividing bounds."[27]

Edwards systematized this view of the millennium in his *History of the Work of Redemption* (1739; pb. 1774), a series of sermons outlining the historical phases, or dispensations, designed by a sovereign God to achieve the salvation of the righteous, the damnation of the unrighteous, and divine glorification. By this account, the internal differentiation of the human race and its division into separate nations first took place not in relation to the transgressions of Cain or Ham—events which, in fact, assume no special value in the *History*—but rather to the ruin of the Tower of Babel. Edwards explained that the consequential "dispersing [of] the nations and dividing the earth among its inhabitants" served a "great design" encompassing "the future propagation of the gospel among the nations."[28] In connection with this proposition, Edwards invokes two biblical texts. The first, Deuteronomy 32:8–9—"When the most High divided to the nations their inheritance, when he separated the sons of Adam, he set the bounds of the people according to the number of the children of Israel. For the LORD's portion is his people; Jacob is the lot of his inheritance"—suggests that through national differentiation God established the basis for covenant relationships, specifically, with Israel. The second, Acts 17:26–27, insisted that the covenant with Israel did not disqualify other nations from seeking a relationship with God: God "hath made of one blood all nations of men for to dwell on all the face of the earth, and hath determined the times before appointed, and the bounds of their habitation; That they should seek the Lord, if haply they might feel after him, and find him, though he be not far from every one of us." As the debate over race and race slavery escalated in the later decades of the eighteenth century, these lines from Acts would be summoned repeatedly to defend the common humanity of whites and blacks. Edwards used these scriptures to emphasize not similarity but difference, to soften the Old Testament view of the covenant, and to promote a pluralistic understanding of God's relationships with humankind. God would interact individually with different nations and would instrumentalize these national differences toward the achievement of the "great design."

Both the covenant with Israel and the abandoning of other nations to "heathenism" had their unique purposes, Edwards continued. The Old Testament covenant was designed to preserve the gospel through the first phase of the historical design, until the beginning of a second dispensation at the birth of Jesus Christ. The noncovenanted nations—those "wholly rejected and given over to heathenism"—also played an important role: "to prepare the way for the more glorious and signal victory and triumph, and Christ's power and grace over the wicked and miserable world, and that Christ's salvation of the world of mankind might become the more sensible."[29] Non-Israelite nations established the most urgent case for the necessity of the work of redemption. Similarly, as emblems of inscrutability, these heathen nations assumed a literary value within the divine narrative of the work of redemption. The revolutionary conversion of "heathens" heightened the dramatic "visibility" and "sensibility" of the redemption epic. Moreover, if we read the *History of the Work of Redemption* as an analogy for conversion, as William J. Scheick has recommended, then it appears that the "heathenish" nations emblematize the ultimate dependence of *all* humankind on Christ: "They were concluded so long a time in unbelief that there might be a thorough proof of the necessity of a savior, that it might appear by so long a trial past all contradiction that mankind were utterly insufficient to deliver themselves from that gross darkness and misery and subjection to the devil that they had fallen into."[30] By assigning "heathenish" nations historical and emblematic significance within the work of redemption, Edwards complicates the Manichean racial dichotomies so prevalent within contemporary thought.[31]

This is not to say that Edwards escaped or even opposed Manichean thinking in his *History of the Work of Redemption*. As the *History* enters its third dispensation—from the resurrection of Jesus Christ until the end of the world—the narrative unfolds in more oppositional and agonistic terms. Non-Christian nations in this dispensation are described as "Satan's heathenish kingdom"; assuming a more specific racial character, they include "the many nations of Africa, the nations of Negroes and others," "that now seem to be in a state but little above the beasts in many respects and as much below them in many others," as well as the indigenous peoples of "this vast continent of America."[32] Edwards attributes not only the persistence but sometimes the very existence of these non-Christian "nations" to Satan. Especially curious is his explanation of the origins of the American Indian population, which, in a moment of surprising informality, he claimed to have derived from popular anecdote:

'Tis a thing which if I remember right I have somewhere [heard] tell of, as probably supposed from some remaining accounts of things, that the occasion of the first peopling America was this: that the devil being alarmed and surprised by the wonderful success of the gospel that was the first three hundred years after Christ, and [by] the downfall of the heathen empire in Constantine's time, and seeing the gospel spread so fast, and fearing that his heathenish kingdom would be wholly overthrown through the world, led away a people from the other continent into America, that they might be quite out of the reach of the gospel that here he might quietly possess them and reign over them as their god.[33]

Both in his antagonistic view of the Indians and in his description of African peoples as brutish, Edwards inflects this phase of his dispensationalist history with contemporary ethnocentrism. Although he predicted that there would soon arise a "wonderful spirit of pity towards them," his correlation of conversion with civilization confirms that Edwards was limited by the prevailing ideologies of his milieu and era.

Remarkably, though, Edwards managed to account for his own subjective and authorial limitations in the concluding pages of the *History*. There, utilizing an image with some precedent in New England Puritan literary tradition, he describes the overarching pattern of the "great design" as "a large and long river, having innumerable branches beginning in different regions, and at a great distance one from another, and all conspiring to one common issue . . . and all at length discharging themselves at one mouth into the same ocean."[34] The river is an emblem of the unifying tendencies of the divine in the temporal world; it is also a representation of the millennial gathering of once-dispersed peoples. Finally, as Edwards explains, the image of the river bears implications for the nature of human understanding:

The different streams of this river are ready to look like mere jumble and confusion to us because of the limitedness of our sight, whereby we can't see from one branch to another and can't see the whole at once, so as to see how all are united in one. A man that sees but one or two streams at a time can't tell what their course tends to. Their course seems very crooked, and the different streams seem to run for a while different and contrary ways. And if we view things at a distance, there seem to be innumerable obstacles and impediments in the way to hinder their ever uniting and coming to the ocean, as rocks and mountains and the like. But yet if we trace them they all unite at last and all come to the same issue, disgorging themselves in one into the same great ocean. Not one of all the streams fail of coming hither at last.[35]

Here, as in the *Miscellanies*, Edwards acknowledges the limits of the human mind. But whereas he had earlier attributed those limits to the mediation of national "temper" and "custom," in this instance he argues that they stem from the character of the grand design. To advance the work of redemption and heighten its sensibility, God designs to disperse the nations as branches of a tree or a river. The differential situation of the nations—in relation to covenant, history, and geography—determines the experience and understanding of the individual saints. Situated in space and time on "one branch," it is nearly impossible for an individual to appreciate its diversity or to anticipate its ultimate resolution. The Bible affords greater perspective and fuller insight, Edwards argued. But it does not liberate the author of the *History of the Work of Redemption* from this abiding Archimedean paradox. For all his scripture knowledge, scrupulous scholarship, and careful formulation, his *History* still bore the imprint of Edwards's protonationalistic particularities.[36]

His investigations of dispensationalist history did prepare Edwards to recognize the participation of people of color in the first Great Awakening. Although he dismissed so many other socially and physically spectacular phenomena as irrelevant to the effectiveness or authenticity of the revivals, he did note in his own accounts the conversion of African- and Native Americans. In his *Faithful Narrative of the Surprising Work of God* (1737), a report on the "remarkable conversions" taking place during 1734–35 among the members of his Northampton, Massachusetts, congregation, Edwards specifically observed: "There are several Negroes, that from what was seen in them then, and what is discernable in them since, appear to have been truly born again in the late remarkable season."[37] A few years later, in his more extensive *Some Thoughts Concerning the Present Revival of Religion* (1742), he remarked that along with African-Americans, "the poor Indians'" "minds have now been strangely opened to receive instruction, and have been deeply affected with the concerns of their precious souls, and have reformed their lives."[38] These lasting effects on communities of color did not of themselves prove the revival, but they did enhance its "glory" by making more "visible" and "conspicuous" in unexpected ways the power of God.[39] The first Great Awakening served as a proving ground for the emblems of inscrutability. Controversies concerning the trustworthy signs of the New Birth and the validity of the revivals themselves amounted to nothing less than a crisis in signification. As Edwards wrote in *The Distinguishing Marks* (1741), an address designed to settle some of the controversy:

> I know by experience that there is a great aptness in men, that think they have had some experience of the power of religion, to think themselves sufficient to discern and determine the state of others' souls by a little conversation with them; and experience has taught me that 'tis an error. I once did not imagine that the heart of man had been so unsearchable as I find it is. I am less charitable, and less uncharitable than once I was. I find more things in wicked men that may counterfeit, and make a fair shew of piety, and more ways that the remaining corruption of the godly may make them appear like carnal men, formalists and dead hypocrites, than once I knew of.[40]

The revivals had discovered once-familiar signs of piety to be "counterfeits" and once-familiar signs of "carnality" to be but a human residue abiding within otherwise converted men and women. If such discoveries affirmed the sovereign and mysterious character of God, they also encouraged an inclination toward the strange and inscrutable as more reliable indicators of Godly operation. In *Some Thoughts*, Edwards invoked 1 Corinthians 1:27 to support his observation that "God in this work has begun at the lower end, and he has made use of the weak and foolish things of the world to carry on his work."[41] This dynamic of overturning, this aesthetic of inscrutability, comported perfectly with the revolutionary work of conversion.

Edwards viewed the conversion of blacks and Indians as an attestation to the inscrutable, unpredictable, and fundamentally revolutionary nature of the work of God. How, then, did the revolutionary nature of conversion affect the racial identity of the convert? How did the rejection of the natural man and the new birth impact race? This is the thorny problem alluded to by Phillis Wheatley in her poem "On Being Brought from Africa to America": "Remember, Christians, Negroes, black as Cain, / May be refin'd, and join th'angelic train." Even now, these cryptic and controversial lines cause readers to wonder whether Wheatley really believed that redemption negated blackness. Jonathan Edwards correlated the Christianization of heathen nations with their civilization in the *Miscellanies* and the *History of the Work of Redemption*, but for further insights into the way conversion affected the identity of the individual convert, we must consult *A Treatise on Religious Affections* (1746). In this thorough study of soteriology—the theory of the conversion process—Edwards describes how grace endows the convert with "a new spiritual sense" and related "new dispositions." This induction is accomplished through the Holy Spirit, which inhabits and operates within the convert as a "new principle of nature." Edwards carefully explains that this new spiritual "principle" does not confer on the convert new "faculties"—that is, new spiritual, emotional, or intellectual characteristics or capacities—but rather supplies a new motive and new orientation for a "new kind of exercise of the same faculty of understanding."[42] He returns to this point by enlarging on the seventh of twelve attributes distinctive to the saving operation of the spirit, namely, that grace effects "a change of nature."[43] Edwards acknowledges the numerous scriptural configurations of this change, "such as being born again; becoming new creatures; rising from the dead; being renewed in the spirit of the mind; dying to sin, and living to righteousness; putting off the old man, and putting on the new man; a being ingrafted into a new stock; a having a divine seed implanted in the heart; a being made partakers of the divine nature, etc."[44] Whereas these figures give an indefinite idea of the nature and extent of that change, Edwards specifies that it does not involve the eradication of natural human attributes. "Conversion don't entirely root out the natural temper," he explains; "nature is an abiding thing."[45] Rather, the indwelling of the Holy Spirit as a new motivating "principle of nature" works through, renovates, and reorients the constitutional faculties of the individual convert to accord with the nature of the divine.[46] Imagine, then, how this gracious change might operate within a black or Native convert. Would not the Holy Spirit inhabit and renew those constitutional faculties that tended toward righteousness and glory? If one conceived of human differences in terms of "sentiments," "circumstances," "customs," "tempers," and "humors," was it not also conceivable that grace might turn customary and circumstantial national characteristics toward the fulfillment of the grand design? To give a concrete example from the *Faithful Narrative*, Edwards observed that during the revival at Northampton the influence of the Spirit was manifest in congregational psalmody, which was then sung with "unusual elevation of heart and voice."[47] Edwards did not report that the Spirit improved the technical abilities of his congregants, nor did it immediately introduce new songs or new customs of psalmody; rather, it imbued and renewed customary modes of musical worship. Might not the same principle apply to communities of color?

Indeed, it might—unless one believed, as Edwards did, that African and American Indian nations were the dominion of the devil, that their customs of worship were governed by Satan, and that their cultures were simply too barbaric to accord harmoniously with the divine. However promising the implications of his soteriology, he demonstrated no unusual degree of insight or sympathy in his relationship to communities of color. Edwards did not oppose slavery, and like many prominent New England clergymen he owned a small number of slaves. His thoughts on the issue are documented in a private letter drafted between 1738 and 1742 in defense of an unnamed slaveholding minister criticized by his congregation. This slaveholding was no crime, Edwards reasoned, as long as humane treatment and Christian education prevailed. The slave trade, however, was an indefensible inducement to war among nations and to the "disfranchizing" of free Africans. The "Contradict[ory]" and "Circumstan[tial]" quality of this proslavery, antislave trade stance did not escape Edwards, but neither did he seek to address these contradictions in his later writings. At the time of his death, in 1758, Edwards left an estate that included a young male slave named Titus.[48]

Similarly unexceptional was Edwards's disposition toward Indians. Certainly he had imbibed the regional culture of Indian-hating, more acutely, perhaps, as the nephew of a famous captive. His uncle the Reverend John Williams, his aunt, and six cousins were either killed or taken captive during an infamous Kahnawake Indian raid on Deerfield, Massachusetts, in 1704. His grandfather and mentor, the Reverend Solomon Stoddard, also harbored no fondness for Indians, but he preached that God expected the New English colonists to convert indigenous peoples. Edwards himself advocated efforts to evangelize American Indian communities, as did most of his New Light colleagues; his own career concluded at the Indian mission town of Stockbridge, Massachusetts. During his seven-year pastorate there, Edwards administered colonial Indian policy and directed the local Indian mission school. He never learned local indigenous languages but instead prioritized English-language instruction for his young Mahican, Mohawk, Tuscarora, and Oneida pupils, for reasons both political and pastoral: "Their own barbarous languages," Edwards judged, were "exceeding barren and very unfit to express moral and divine things. And their being brought to the English language would open their minds, and bring 'em to acquaintance and conversation with the English, and would tend above all things to bring that civility which is to be found among the English."[49] Edwards did perform acts of kindness and charity toward Indian individuals and some tribal communities, for example, in one noteworthy instance, by helping his missionary-friend David Brainerd to find new lands for displaced Indians in New Jersey. However, this most careful and accomplished American thinker did not interrogate the relationship between civilization and Christianization, nor in Indian affairs did he seek to distinguish the church from the colony. In this, his opinions and practices scarcely diverged from prevailing custom.[50]

During the thirty-five-year ministry of Jonathan Edwards, race took on new significance within American evangelicalism, as ever greater numbers of African- and Native Americans demonstrated interest in Christianity and comprised a visible presence at revivals. This presence drew comment but not explicit or extensive consideration from Edwards, the most dedicated and accomplished theologian of the evangelical movement. His writings in dispensationalist history did provide an alternate view of the origins of national or racial difference, which he described not as the consequence of sins by Cain or Ham but as designated elements within the work of redemption. His treatment of soteriology raised the possibility that conversion might not require an eradication of these differences, but rather initiate their graceful renewal. These possibilities, however, were neither elaborated by Edwards nor implemented in his pastoral practice; it would take a powerful and charismatic late-eighteenth-century cohort of black and Indian ministers to initiate their realization. Edwards did acknowledge that national differences limited subjective understanding, and he anticipated the day when distances would be abridged and understanding improved. Until that millennial day, however, he would continue to view the black faces at his services and the Indian faces in his school as emblems of the mystery, strangeness, and inscrutability of God. He would not yet think to ask the people behind the faces to describe the grand design as it appeared from their vantage point on another branch of its mighty river.

If Edwards and other eighteenth-century evangelists were reticent to theorize race, their contemporaries in science and politics were not. Inheriting an archive of medieval and early modern exploration narratives describing physical, cultural, and linguistic characteristics of encountered "nations," eighteenth-century philosophers and scientists set aside attempts by earlier commentators to reconcile the nations to biblical genealogies.[51] Instead, they organized explorers' observations to accord with philosophical and scientific systems. In 1735, the Swedish biologist Carl von Linné published the first edition of his encyclopedic *System Natura*, which divided the human species into five classifications: the "Wild Man," the "American," the "European," the "Asiatic," and the "African." To each of these, Linné assigned unique constitutional characteristics. The "European," for example, was "fair, sanguine, [and] brawny," while the "African" was "Black, phlegmatic, [and] relaxed." Others in the burgeoning field of natural science attempted to theorize the origins of these variations within the human species. Monogeneticists, subscribing to the biblical account of the creation, proposed that environmental factors such as geography, climate, and diet were responsible for differences within the human species, while polygeneticists espoused the controversial position that the races derived from different genetic origins. Philosophers such as David Hume and Immanuel Kant also joined the debate, assigning the different races, or "nations," specific cultural, aesthetic, and intellectual values. To be sure, eighteenth-century theorists of human difference established no common and consistent terminology.[52] Regardless of its status in European and Euro-American thought, it would be a mistake to imagine that race did not shape lived experience in America.

Questions of natural and national character mattered powerfully to political minds in the American colonies, who were striving to formulate a rational basis for their secession from Britain and their incorporation as a unified political entity. Critical to this project was the construction of white European colonists as American citizens, with "natural" rights to liberty and self-rule. The ideological naturalization of these European immigrants depended on the denaturalization—the extermination or permanent alienation—of indigenous peoples as well as on the dehumanization of black slaves. As Carroll Smith-Rosenberg argues, the white, male, and propertied "national subject" was defined in relation to these racial others. Indeed, whiteness was stipulated as a requirement for citizenship in the Naturalization Law of 1790. Nationalization also determined the construction of blackness and Indianness, vesting invented biological categories with specific political values.[53]

The consolidation of colonial North America under British rule and the establishment of the United States effected the incorporation of the American Indian as a distinct racial category with specific legal properties. During the early centuries of European colonization, Indian affairs had been a variegated business: the British, Spanish, and French vied to establish individual relations with hundreds of indigenous societies, while individual colonists took possession of indigenous lands by myriad strategies of violence, coercion, occupation, deception, marriage, legal stratagem, or purchase. However, at the end of the Seven Years' War in 1763, the British assumed colonial control over all lands east of the Mississippi. Eager to maintain good relations with their war-time allies the Iroquois Confederacy, the crown quickly moved to establish a central office of Indian affairs, forbade colonial officers from interfering in Indian policy, and attempted to protect Iroquois lands east of the Allegheny Mountains from settler incursion. The United States, on declaring its independence from Great Britain, assumed a similar stance in the management of Indian affairs. The *Articles of Confederation* (1783) reserved to the federal government exclusive powers in negotiating treaties, alliances, and land deals with Indian tribes; legally, individual states and private parties were not empowered to negotiate with sovereign foreign nations, as Indians tribes were then considered to be. Three important early nineteenth-century decisions by the U.S. Supreme Court—*Johnson v. McIntosh* (1823), *Cherokee Na-*

tion v. Georgia (1831), and *Worcester v. Georgia* (1832)—downgraded the legal status of tribes to "domestic dependent nations," stripping them of full title to their ancestral lands but still recognizing limited powers of self-determination. (Universal suffrage for American Indians was not granted until 1924.) This denial of land title and citizenship enforced the legal alienation of American Indians, while religious, social, and political programs reinforced their "dependent" status.

Indian boarding schools exemplified this dual strategy of enforced alienation and dependency. First established in the eighteenth century by New Light evangelists and supported by contributions from the British colonial and American federal governments, the boarding schools disrupted tribal integrity and continuity by removing young children from their home communities, forbidding the speaking of native languages or the practice of indigenous religions, insisting on "civilization" through English language instruction and Christianization, and training young boys to serve as missionaries and young girls to serve as domestics. These schools, ironically, became important organs for the formulation of resistant pan-Indian politics, as young people of differing tribes developed common bases for identification and solidarity. The dual dynamics of alienation and dependency were also manifest, as Philip Deloria has brilliantly observed, in the early national custom of "playing Indian," a practice whereby Anglo-Americans performed their independence from Britain by adopting the guise of the "savage" natives they had displaced or exterminated during colonization. For Euro-Americans, American Indianness thus assumed a political significance intricately related to the identity of the United States but essentially opposed to its dominion. American Indians as a race were to be both pitied and feared, embraced and extinguished.[54]

The move from colonial to national governance also hastened the construction of an African-American racial identity with specific legal attributes. Momentum in this direction had been building since the 1640s, when Virginia established legal differentiation between white and black servitude. In the 1660s, some southern colonies formulated legal support for the institution of slavery in deciding that slave status and blackness were both conferred matrilineally. Also during the last decades of the seventeenth century, six colonies passed acts ruling that Christian conversion did not confer freedom on black slaves, thereby negating an older justification for slavery—that Christian nations were entitled to enslave heathens or infidels—and newly affirming the explicitly racial basis for slavery in British North America. With the shift toward large-scale plantation slavery in the South at the turn of the eighteenth century, blacks were substituted into the economic position formally occupied by the English peasantry; meanwhile, an emergent white solidarity cemented a racial compact between nonslaveholding and slaveholding whites, despite social, ethnic, and economic breaches. Even regional differences were abridged by shared white desires and fears. Indeed, from the seventeenth-century onward, printed accounts of black slave revolts against white masters circulated throughout the colonies, stoking the fears of white colonists from Massachusetts to the Carolinas that the black underclass like the Indians at their borders might rise up to "cut them off" from what they believed to be their rightful or covenanted colonial possessions. Colonies north and south enacted restrictive legal codes that tightened control over black populations and reinforced the association between black and unfree by imposing restrictions on travel, suffrage, public assembly, property ownership, and education for all African-Americans.[55]

Similar sentiments did not prevail in England. In the first edition of his *Commentaries on the Laws of England* (1765), the distinguished jurist William Blackstone asserted that the "spirit of liberty is so deeply implanted in our constitution, and rooted even in our very soil, that a slave or a negro, the moment he lands in England, falls under the protection of the laws, and so far becomes a freeman."[56] In 1772, Chief Justice Lord Mansfield ruled that a slave-owner named Charles Stewart could not forcibly transport his escaped slave James Somerset to the West Indies; this decision was broadly interpreted in harmony with Blackstone's *Commentaries* to mean that black slaves were free on arrival in England. Further, it codified the difference between the policies of England and the policies of its slave-dependent economic colonies. Unfree in America, free in Britain—Phillis Wheatley herself tested the power of the Massachusetts colony against the crown when she traveled to England in 1773 and returned quite probably having secured from the Wheatleys their promise of her manumission.[57]

This strange and contradictory state of affairs was further exacerbated when colonists appropriated the rhetoric of freedom and slavery in their campaign for independence from Britain. Following the War of Independence, some states moved to correct the blatant hypocrisy of slavery with revolutionary ideals and, through judicial decisions and legislative acts, provided for the gradual emancipation of slaves. These provisions for emancipation were often so gradual as to be cruel. For example, in the state of Pennsylvania, the first state to enact emancipation legislation, children born to slave parents after March 1, 1780, were not immediately free but rather legally obliged to twenty-eight years of indentured servitude. Similar *post nati* statues passed by Connecticut and Rhode Island in 1784 prescribed between eighteen and twenty-four years of indenture for the children of slaves. These limited measures modified but did not redefine the legal attributes of blackness. In fact, as Joanne Pope Melish shows, these so-called emancipation statutes incurred tremendous anxiety among whites, who feared the loss of economic and social dominance and who responded to these fears by inventing and enforcing racial distinctions. "The characteristics of availability, dependency, and instrumentality associated with slave status," Melish explains, "were redefined as uniquely innate and permanent biological traits in persons of color, irrespective of their status."[58] Similarly, in his study of black identity formation in the northern United States, Patrick Rael finds that free blacks in the North were not so free as in other societies of the African diaspora: "Throughout the North, policy and informal practice often subjected blacks in toto to degradations shared by elite and popular alike. . . . The relative uniformity of their social experience led them, too, towards a more highly integrated notion of black identity."[59] Segregation, denial of education, disenfranchisement, white-on-black mob violence, criminalization, colonization, and racist images in literature, popular culture, and political discourse enacted and sustained the legal subjugation of African-Americans.[60]

Thus, in those crucial years of national formation, when whiteness assumed a positive legal value in the United States, blackness and Indianness were constructed in negative and oppositional terms. The naturalization of whiteness took shape in relationship to the denaturalization or alienation of black and Indian people. Slavery, as Orlando Patterson has argued, was a state of "social death" or "natal alienation"; postemancipation racist practices perpetuated the alienation of African-Americans from the full benefits of American citizenship. Similarly, colonialism and early national Indian policy sought to extinguish the relationship between indigenous societies and their homelands—a relationship critical to tribal identities and cultures—thereby making American Indians aliens in their own land. The physical and spiritual deficiencies attributed to these races by natural scientists further compounded the negative definition of blackness and Indianness.

It is no coincidence that this era of intensive racialization also saw the first articulation of conscious and oppositional African-American and Native American identities and the birth of African-American and Native American literatures. By processes as historically determined, ideologically informed, and imaginatively inventive as those that produced the concept of race itself, blacks and Indians gradually reclaimed and reinvested racial identity with positive values. Africans violently alienated from their homelands, societies, and cultures brought meaning out of chaos as they began to develop from their shared experiences of alienation new and common "black" identities.[61] Indigenous peoples also developed new bases for continuance and identification in their shared experience of colonialism as "Indians." By this positive and creative rearticulation, they opposed their own negation in legal and scientific discourse. As Abdul Jan Mohammed writes, "The hegemonic formation of minorities is itself based on an attempt to negate them—to prevent them from realizing their full and equal participation in civil and political society"; all minority discourse, he argues, emerges from "the will to negate the hegemony."[62] In early African- and Native American literatures, this will to negate the negative formation of blackness and Indianness is expressed in religious terms. For if empiricist philosophy, natural science, and nationalist politics all aimed for the negation of these racialized subjects, then it would take a supernatural and spiritual force to revive, renew, and resurrect them. Even a man as disinclined to religious thinking or immediate racial emancipation as Thomas Jefferson sensed that divine intervention might overturn American racial hierarchies: "Indeed I tremble for my country when I reflect that God is just: that his justice cannot sleep for ever: that considering numbers, nature and natural means only, a revolution of the wheel of fortune, an exchange of situation is among possible events: that it may become probable by supernatural interference!"[63]

Alienation, dependency, deprivation, degeneracy, dissolution—these were the values assigned blackness and Indianness within racist scientific and political discourse. Eighteenth-century American evangelicalism provided almost nothing to counter these devastating negations of human worth and potential, except in its nominal egalitarianism, in its basic receptiveness to racial difference, and in the potential energies of its conversion theology. Especially in the Calvinist tradition, conversion was about change: the sovereign intervention of God, the abolition of the natural man, the overturning of sin, the regeneration of the soul, the establishment of a godly society. There was in this concept a capacity for overturning the degradation of enslavement, colonization, and racialization; it was, potentially, a means to the negation of negative racial formation and to the regeneration of American communities of color. A powerful group of black and Indian evangelists, many of them also pioneering published authors, rose up to claim these possibilities. African- and Native American literatures first emerged out of this commitment, as products and documents of their strivings for community redemption and regeneration.

Whereas negative racial construction held that blacks and Indians were socially dependent and degenerate, communities of color regenerated themselves by forming separate and independent religious bodies. Itinerancy and evangelicalism had pluralized American religion, establishing new venues and new modes of religious expression. Moreover, some elements of evangelical theology had been popularly interpreted to support the right of common people—regardless of education or ordination—to receive immediate revelation and to exercise spiritual gifts. With or without the sanction of the established churches, Native and black believers prayed, sang, shouted, testified, exhorted, preached, prophesied, and healed; when churches denied, repressed, or disciplined them, they walked out and formed their own congregations. These black religious movements sometimes gathered in a diverse range of African-descended peoples: men, women, and children; slaves, ex-slaves, and the freeborn; mulattoes and mistees; natives of Africa, the Caribbean, and America; Senegambians, Biafrans, and others. Similarly, Native Christian movements united members of different Algonkian- and Delaware-speaking tribes, which had suffered especially profound impacts under settler colonialism. Conversion and religious affiliation complemented the development of panethnic racial solidarity.

The racial and religious separatist impulse presented itself most dramatically during and after the War of Independence. The war caused significant disruption, dislocation, and resettlement for politically and economically vulnerable communities of color. From this chaos emerged new churches and new settlements with distinctive religious and racial identities. From 1774 to 1785, Samson Occom and other Indian evangelists led the exodus of hundreds of Christian Indians from Long Island and southern New England to a new intertribal settlement in upstate New York. Calling their settlement Brotherton, members of the Montauk, Mohegan, Niantic, Pequot, Narragansett, Farmington, and Stockbridge tribes forged a new common Christian Indian identity. In 1783, thousands of African-American Loyalists—including some ex-slaves who had won their freedom by fighting with the British—left the United States as exiles; more than a thousand founded the all-black township of Birchtown in Nova Scotia. Then estimated to be the largest independent settlement of free blacks outside of Africa, Birchtown was home to a remarkable concentration of pioneering black Baptist and Methodist preachers; they were joined by John Marrant, a fellow exile and ordained member of the Huntingdon Connexion, who preached a prophetic vision of black spiritual and political destiny. In Boston, on the eve of the war, the members of an Irish military regiment initiated an ex-slave named Prince Hall into Freemasonry; after the war, Hall founded a distinct and powerful order of black Freemasonic lodges promoting the spiritual and political strength of black communities. Finally, in Philadelphia, Richard Allen and Absalom Jones led a black walkout from the city's segregationist Methodist and Methodist Episcopal churches; Allen went on to found

"Mother Bethel," the African Methodist Episcopal church. Mother Bethel, Brotherton, Birchtown, and the African Lodge of Freemasons—among other religious and spiritual bodies of color taking shape in the postwar years—became sites critical to the formation of modern black and Indian political, religious, and cultural consciousness. Within these spaces, people of color claimed rights and powers denied them in the new nation's "public sphere," including the right to assemble independently and the right to exercise political authority. And while these spaces were not inviolate, nor were they free of racist, colonialist, sexist, or classist elements, they did allow people of color to develop a sense of self-possession, a sense of belonging denied them in their perpetual alienation.

Whereas negative racial construction declared their cultures barbarous or extinct, communities of color used the church to develop new rituals of regeneration. It cannot be denied that Christian evangelization—as an adjunct or component of colonialism—disrupted traditional African and Indian systems of belief and worship. But it also must be recognized that many Native and African-Americans appropriated and reinvested Christian worship with their own distinctive spiritual and cultural values. They developed religious rituals and practices that fostered community by uniting elements of indigenous African and Native cultures. A profound example of this recombination is the African-American practice of the ring shout, as described by Sterling Stuckey. At Brotherton, rituals of hymn singing renewed older tribal song practices and united the community in celebration of traditional harvest festivals. Other rituals sacralized the experiences of rupture, loss, and displacement shared by the members of aggrieved communities of color. Worship services in Birchtown were punctuated by episodes of fainting or "falling out," dramatic enactments of the experience of the death of the old and the birth of the new. Finally, within the space of the African Lodge, rites of initiation guided black Masons from chaos to community, from bondage to freedom, from death to life. All of these rituals had antecedents and parallels in non-Christian practices, but they were developed to answer the exigencies of life after colonization and the slave trade.[64]

Finally, whereas racist scientific and political writings declared African- and Native Americans to be without intelligent history, communities of color developed highly literate theologies that declared their unique and significant relationship to the divine. They transformed the profane construct of race into the basis for a covenant relationship with God. Black and Indian evangelists mastered Christian scripture: they had a powerful oral and literate command of biblical phrases, verses, typologies, and stories. Many were conversant with the dominant theological controversies of the time, and some were educated in the ancient languages of Hebrew, Greek, and Latin. They used their knowledge to develop new scriptural interpretations specific to the needs of their constituent communities. African-Americans found in the Old and New Testaments numerous references to African places and persons, including the Queen of Sheba, the Ethiopian eunuch Philip, and the Ethiopian Queen Candace; for Ethiopia and Egypt, pivotal sites for black identity, Psalms 68 foretold a glorious millennial destiny. African-Americans also found powerful support for their emancipation in the biblical stories of Joseph in Egypt, the deliverance of Israel from slavery, the resurrection of Lazarus, and many others. Native Americans at Brotherton turned for guidance to the Old Testament narratives of tribal gathering and government. Blacks and Indians alike rejected racist and colonialist interpretations of scripture and constructed an understanding of Jesus Christ as sympathetic to their sufferings under oppression. They also claimed the New Testament vision of the Christian church as a body of diversity. In developing their own relationship to scripture, neither black nor Indian religious communities were entirely bound by the orthodoxies and customs of the established church. Rather, as did so many separatist evangelicals and uniquely American sects, they promulgated theologies closely connected to their own values and experiences. Most important, black and Indian evangelists taught their followers to interpret their own lives and histories as the text of an unfolding covenant with God. They claimed for their communities a distinctive place within God's grand design for the redemption of humankind.

African- and Native American literatures of the eighteenth century document the processes of social, cultural, and textual regeneration through which communities of color developed positive and resistant corporate identities. More than documents, they are also intricate works of literature—sermons, conversion narratives, hymn texts, poems, and histories—which communicate through the richness of text the complexities of their contexts and concerns. The subsequent chapters will delve into their historical circumstances and literary substance, as well as their implications for our understanding of American literature and culture. These pioneering literary works challenge us to examine our assumptions about how authority happens, how meaning comes into being, and how chaos becomes order. Finally, these texts demand a new characterization of how American literature itself came into being: not out of fabled innocence as an American Adam, but rather out of the redemption of tragedy—as an American Lazarus.

2

Samson Occom and the Poetics of Native Revival

Mohegan, Connecticut; 1768

After completing a remarkable two-year tour of England, where he preached in the chapels of the kingdom's leading divines, dined with nobles, waited on the king, and was recruited for Anglican ordination by the archbishop of Canterbury, the Mohegan tribal leader and Presbyterian minister Samson Occom returned home to Connecticut in 1768 to find his family sick and starving. Occom had succeeded in raising thousands of pounds for Moor's Indian Charity School (now Dartmouth College), but the Reverend Eleazar Wheelock and his other American patrons had failed in their promise to support Occom's wife and thirteen children during his long absence. Moreover, Occom found that the Indian Charity School he had promoted to thousands of subscribers in England, Scotland, and Ireland was no longer an "Indian" school in earnest; Wheelock had moved the school from Lebanon, Connecticut, to Hanover, New Hampshire, and he was turning away Indian scholars seeking admission in favor of enrolling whites. Occom soon broke ties with Eleazar Wheelock and retreated from public life.

These were to be difficult years for Samson Occom. It was widely rumored that he had succumbed to episodes of public drunkenness. Hearing the news, Eleazar Wheelock wrote in January 1771 to express "pain & sorrow of heart" for Occom's "repeated & aggravated fall."[1] No healing balm, these words smacked of Wheelock's justification for abandoning the Indian Charity School. Occom responded a few months later with a withering condemnation of Wheelock's "grand design":

I am very jealous that instead of your Semenary Becoming alma Mater, she will be too alba mater to Suckle the Tawnees for She is already adorned up too much like the Popish Virgin Mary. . . . I verily thought once that your Institution was Intended Purely for the poor Indians—

with this thought I Cheerfully Ventured my Body & Soul, left my Country my poor young Family all my Friends and Relations, to sail over the Boisterous Seas to England, to help forward your School, Hoping that it may be a lasting Benefet to my poor Tawnee Brethren, With this View I went a Volunteer—I was quite willing to become a Gazing Stocke, Yea Even a Laughing Stocke, in Strange Countries to Promote your Cause. . . . Mr. Whitefield, just before I left England, in the hearing of Some gentleman—ah Says he, you have been a fine Tool to get Money for them, but when you get home, they wont Regard you, they'll Set you a Drift,—I am ready to believe it Now—2

Occom suffered profound losses on other fronts. In February 1771, his oldest son Aaron died at the age of eighteen, leaving a wife and small child.3 In June 1771, the colony of Connecticut decided a protracted and controversial land case against the Mohegan tribe and in favor of a white leaseholder named John Mason. Wrote Occom, "I am afraid the poor indians will never stand a good chance with the English in their land controversies, because they are very poor, they have no money. . . . The English have all."4 Then, on September 2, 1771, a Mohegan man named Moses Paul was executed for the murder of white merchant Moses Cook. A large crowd of whites and Indians gathered in New Haven to witness the execution, the first in that town in more than twenty years. Occom, a friend to both the victim and the accused, preached the execution sermon from Romans 6:23, "The wages of sin is death." His message was unsparing: Adam's fall meant that all were sinners—whether "criminal" or "innocent;" white, red, or black—and all were condemned to die. After this Calvinist exposition, Occom beseeched his "poor Kindred" Indians in particular to resist the sins of drunkenness which had brought so much sorrow, loss, impoverishment, and death to their communities.

If sorrow, loss, impoverishment, and death were the "wages of sin," they were also the consequences of English colonial occupation for the Indian communities of southern New England. For more than 150 years, tribal communities in the region had suffered wave after wave of colonial onslaught. War, settler population growth, land disputes, land seizures, missionary colonialism, disruption of traditional farming and fishing practices, the introduction of alcohol, and the importation of foreign illnesses caused tremendous population loss. Such pressures forced some tribes to abandon their ancestral homelands. Indeed, the very continuity of tribal societies, languages, and cultures came under threat, as many young Indian men and women left their home communities to be bound out as domestic servants, laborers, and sailors, or placed in boarding schools. Others met the fate of Moses Paul. If the people were to survive,

Samson Occom knew, then something had to change. Occom knew that a collective new birth, a resurrection, a revival was wanting for himself and his beloved Indian kindred.

Not long after the execution of Moses Paul, this change came for the Native peoples of southern New England as a powerful religious and political revitalization movement took shape. Like other American communities of color in the 1770s and 1780s, these American Indian communities used the resources of evangelical religion to create for themselves new identities and a new future. In so doing, they broke away from white missionary leadership to develop their own distinctive form of Christianity, which honored the rights of Indian people to independence, self-determination, and survival. On the basis of these shared values, they also developed a modern pantribal Indian identity and founded a separatist pantribal Christian settlement called Brotherton. The Brotherton movement took shape in early 1773, when members of seven New England and Long Island tribes—Mohegan, Pequot, Narragansett, Montauk, Niantic, Farmington, and Stockbridge—agreed to leave their traditional lands and to relocate themselves to upstate New York. The movement was led and facilitated by Occom and his fellow Moor's Indian Charity School alumni David Fowler (Montauk), Jacob Fowler (Montauk), and Joseph Johnson (Mohegan). During the 1760s, Occom, Johnson, and the Fowlers had itinerated among the New England and Long Island tribes as well as in upstate New York among the Oneida. Consequently, the four men were uniquely situated to accomplish negotiations crucial to the founding of Brotherton. Through their negotiations, the Oneidas allotted land to the New England tribes in January 1774 and welcomed them into the Iroquois Confederacy with the Cayugas, Nanticokes, Tuscaroras, Tutelos, Mohawks, Onondagas, and Senecas. An advance party of settlers traveled to Brotherton shortly thereafter, and a full migration began after the end of the American War of Independence.

In the shadows of the American Revolution, many Native Americans and African-Americans waged their own struggles for independence and freedom. They sought to collect and govern themselves, to provide physically and spiritually for their own aggrieved peoples, and to achieve politi-\ cal power independent of white oversight and regulation. Just as these dreams found a home in separatist black or Indian churches, religious societies, and settlements like Brotherton, they found a voice in early African-American and Native American literatures. This chapter will examine a literary work important to the Brotherton movement, the most extensive and influential project of Samson Occom's literary career: *A Choice Collection of Hymns and Spiritual Songs; Intended for the Edification of Sincere Christians, of All Denominations*. Occom published this collection of

109 hymns in April 1774, just as the Brotherton compact was being finalized. It set a precedent as one of the first interdenominational American hymnals; it also premiered hymn texts by leading British, American, and Native American hymn writers, including Occom himself. Consequently, the *Collection* enjoyed broad popularity and lasting influence: it was advertised for sale in Rhode Island, New York, and Connecticut, reprinted in several editions before 1800, and served as a template for popular nineteenth-century hymnals.[5] Its greatest influence, though, was at Brotherton, where the community united around Occom's hymnal and the rituals of hymn singing it inspired. Occom's *Collection* demonstrates the power of religion, literature, and performance in generating new communities, new identities, and new futures for Indian people in early America.

With his *Collection*, Occom contributed to a major, controversial, and democratizing shift in American religion and culture. This shift moved religious expression out of strict institutional control and toward more popular and pleasurable venues and forms; hymnody was an important element of this democratization. Until the Great Awakening, most American churches restricted congregational singing to the biblical psalms; the singing of original, nonbiblical hymn texts was condemned—and in some places criminalized—as an irreverent assertion of human authority. However, during and after the Awakening, New Light sects and revivalists popularized hymnody as a means of individual religious exercise, group worship, and theological elaboration. Whether committed to memory, hand-copied in personal tune books, or gathered in printed collections, hymns traveled across cultures, colonies, and continents; they crossed boundaries of denomination, race, class, and gender. Importantly, the orality of this textual form invited participation, innovation, and contribution even by semiliterate, nonliterate, or non-English-speaking worshippers. Thus, we find that hymns were an especially important part of the cultures of revival that attracted and enfranchised poor whites and people of color. Early African-American literature especially reflects and incorporates the power of hymnody: both Phillis Wheatley and John Marrant sampled from the works of Isaac Watts, and African Methodist Episcopal church founder Richard Allen published his own landmark hymnal in 1801.[6] Hymnody also played an important role in American Indian communities. From their first interactions with European missionaries, indigenous peoples throughout the Americas adopted Christian psalmody and hymnody into existing repertoires of religious expression. Introducing variations in performance style, rhythm, and instrumentation, Native peoples used hymnody to build on and extend existing musical traditions. As did Samson Occom, they also claimed authority in the production hymn texts that celebrated and promoted their own concerns and values.

This chapter examines Occom's *Collection* as an important document of the Brotherton movement and a revelatory work of early American Indian literature. This little-known, underacknowledged text is significant for the depth and complexity it adds to our understanding of Samson Occom. Occom is recognized as the founder of Native American literature for his unpublished life narratives and his best-selling 1773 execution sermon. However, his hymnal and his six original hymn texts establish him as a pioneering Native poet, a literary critic, an editor, an anthologist, and a theorist of Native Christian practice.[7] What did it mean to be Indian? What did it mean to be a Christian? These terms were undergoing significant revision during the 1770s, especially in southern New England's Indian communities, where colonial and protonational political pressures demanded a creative reformulation of Indianness. Samson Occom responded to these pressures by rearticulating Indianness as a distinctive and powerful religious identity.

The story of Samson Occom, his Native missionary colleagues, and the founding of Brotherton challenges us to reassess the relationship between Christian conversion and American Indian identity in early America. Two general models of American Indian Christian conversion prevail: the assimilationist model and the syncretist model. Assimilationists see conversion as a wholesale rejection or abandonment of older beliefs, practices, and identities; in their eyes, conversion is a concession—sometimes strategic, sometimes voluntary—to superior colonial power. Syncretists view American Indian conversion as protective cover for the continuance of indigenous faith practices. Recent scholarship on Samson Occom has proposed the terms *liminality*, *hybridity*, and *cultural mediation* as starting points for a more nuanced understanding of the situation of Indian converts. These accounts tend to position Occom and others like him as hovering "between white and Indian worlds," displaced by education and religious affiliation from simple tribal identity, but disqualified by race from full assimilation to white society. Yet another view comes from noted Native thinkers Jace Weaver (Cherokee) and Robert Allen Warrior (Osage), who position Samson Occom squarely at the head of a centuries-old Native tradition of intellectual sovereignty. Weaver and Warrior argue that even English-language literate Christian converts like Occom should not be viewed primarily as intercessors with the white world but as proponents of new and powerful definitions of Indianness.[8] Along with many contemporary Native theologians, they attest that Christianity is but another venue through which indigenous peoples continue their ongoing struggle for self-determination.[9] Neither the assimilationist, syncretist, or hybridity models fully appreciate Native conversion in this way: as an act of self-determination and an expression of sovereignty.

Recognizing Christian conversion as self-determination is especially important in the context of contemporary tribal sovereignty politics. As James Clifford's essay, "Identity at Mashpee," dramatically shows, competing views of historical Christian Indian conversion have contemporary consequences. Clifford rehearses these views as they emerged during 1976–77 court proceedings over the federal status of the Mashpee tribe of Cape Cod. In order to access the powers of political and economic self-determination enjoyed by federally recognized tribes, the Mashpee had to prove that tribal customs, structures, and identities had existed continuously through more than three centuries of aggressive colonialism. Their success depended on their ability to demonstrate their "Indianness" to non-Indian judges and jurors. One of the most critical issues in the case was the Mashpee history of Christian belief and practice. Mashpee plaintiffs argued that for more than two centuries a Baptist church had served as the center of tribal life. Judges and jurors, however, viewed conversion as a terminus for Mashpee culture. They failed to appreciate Christian practices as a venue for the maintenance, development, and expression of Mashpee identities. Consequently, they rejected the Mashpee petition.[10]

What Samson Occom discovered in Christianity was a venue for strengthening Indian communities and rearticulating tribal identities under siege by colonialism. His Mohegan community first demonstrated a significant interest in Christianity during the Great Awakening. Prior to the Awakening, ministers from the nearby town of New London, Connecticut, had seasonally visited the Mohegan. As Occom explains in his 1768 autobiographical narrative, the Mohegan responded with polite attention: "Not that they regarded the Christian Religion, but they had Blankets given to them every Fall of the Year and for these things they would attend." He continues, "When I was 16 years of age [in 1739], we heard a Strange Rumor among the English, that there were Extraordinary Ministers Preaching from Place to Place and a Strange Concern among the White People." Ministers and exhorters soon arrived at Mohegan. "These Preachers did not only come to us," Occom notes, "but we frequently went to their meetings and Churches." This revival season— which Occom calls "our Reformation"—initiated the first extensive adoption of Christianity among the Mohegan.[11] Other southern New England Christian tribal communities also responded favorably to New Light evangelicalism, which agreed with traditional tribal religions in emphasizing visionary experience, oral performance, and immediate spiritual authority.[12]

The Awakening also brought to the Indian communities of southern New England unprecedented missionary-education projects, which implemented more rigorous assimilation agendas. John Sargeant, a Congregationalist missionary among the Housatonic, or Stockbridge, Indians, insisted that English-language education was essential to religious education so that the Housatonics might be delivered from "their own imperfect and barbarous Dialect."[13] Eleazar Wheelock extended Sargeant's impulse in establishing Moor's Indian Charity School at Lebanon, Connecticut. Wheelock designed a program to prepare Indian boys to undertake missionary work among non-Christian tribes and to train Indian girls to serve in domestic capacities. Essential to his plan was removing Native children from the influence of their families and tribal communities; thus, Moor's Indian Charity School initiated the long and often dishonorable tradition of American Indian boarding schools. Wheelock viewed his work as the "domestication" of American Indians, and he promoted its benefits to English colonial interests. He claimed that converting Indians to Christianity and an agricultural lifestyle meant that vast tracts of wilderness could be reclaimed from Indian hunters for English settlement. Another outcome important to Wheelock's English sponsors was the inculcation in American Indians of an "attachment" to the British Empire. This language appears in instructions from the Society for Propagating Christian Knowledge (SPCK) to Wheelock-trained missionaries. For example, when Samson Occom and his Montauk brother-in-law David Fowler proselyted among the Oneida (1761–63), they received explicit instructions from the SPCK to "endeavour to attach" the Oneida to King George III and his subjects.[14] Wheelock himself adopted this usage when he promoted Moor's Charity School to Lord Dartmouth as a means of inducing an "attachment" between Native peoples and the "Civilish Interest" of the crown.[15] Additional benefits to the propertied interests of the British Empire were enumerated by Wheelock supporter John Smith: "What an increase of our Settlements! How great is the augmentation of ye Staple of these Dominions! What ye Increase of ye demand for British Manufactures to cloth the new Subjects! How important this to the Commerce of Great Britain & ye Colonies! And what a source of opulence to ye whole Empire!"[16] Of course, some of Wheelock's advisors and patrons disagreed with these aims. The ever-thoughtful, idiosyncratic Ezra Stiles judged that secular motives influenced Moor's Indian Charity School, and he recommended to Wheelock the more tolerant methods of Moravian missionaries. Wrote Stiles, "Perhaps it may be a mistake that civilizing is necessary towards Christianizing the Heathen."[17]

A very different mode of Indian Christianity emerged in institutions founded by Indian converts. Southern New England tribal communities fostered a distinctive regional culture of Christian Indian separatism, building around coherent elements of New Light and traditional belief. Native peoples exercised their individual spiritual gifts independently of church sanction; some separated from oppressive local churches to establish their own congregations. A Narragansett Indian named Samuel Niles established a separatist congregation when the local Congregational church excommunicated him for "exhorting in the Congregation." More than one hundred Narragansetts left Congregationalism with Niles, built their own meetinghouse, and arranged for his ordination by three Moravian Indians. Niles also pastored to residents of nearby Niantic, Pequot, Montauk, and Mohegan communities. Joseph Fish, a Congregationalist minister assigned to the Narragansett in the 1760s, repeatedly criticized Niles and his followers for their reliance "very Much upon the *Spirit* to teach him Doctrine and Conduct, he is in imminent danger of leaving *The Word*, for the Guidance of *Feelings, Impressions, Visions, Appearances*, and *Directions* of Angels and of Christ himself in a Visionary Way."[18] Conversely, Niles and his followers accused Fish of being a "Hireling" for taking money from his parishioners. The Narragansett church also developed religious practices distinct from English Christian congregations, including an annual church-sponsored harvest festival and funeral services for "backsliding" members. Many Narragansett separatists—including Samuel Niles—eventually joined Samson Occom in the pilgrimage to Brotherton.[19]

At Mohegan, Christian Indians resisted colonial efforts to use the church as a site of assimilation. James Fitch, the Congregationalist minister appointed to the community, was deserted by his Mohegan congregation when he introduced a primary school curriculum that would have abolished the native language. In the early 1740s Samuel Ashpo, a Mohegan tribal member who later attended Moor's Indian Charity School, established a separatist Indian church. This church remained an important seat of power for traditionalist members of the tribe, especially during the Mason land controversy of the 1760s. Samson Occom sided with the traditionalists in support of the Mohegan land claims; he also attended and ministered to the separatist congregation. Two white colonial appointees—schoolmaster Robert Clelland and Congregationalist minister David Jewett—tended to members of the opposing, pro-Mason tribal faction. In 1765, pro-Mason Mohegans accused Occom of doing "a great deal of hurt" to the tribe by his involvement in the controversy, his resistance to the leasing of tribal lands, his criticisms of white schoolmaster Robert Clelland, and his discouragement of tribal members from attending Jewett's church. Occom's sponsoring body, the SPCK Board of Correspondents in the Colony of Connecticut, conducted an official investigation and later cleared Occom of all charges—excepting his protraditional, anticolony agitation in the Mason case. It is clear that Occom viewed his political and spiritual roles at Mohegan as complementary, if not conjoined.[20]

Although New England Indians developed their own clergy, independent Christian communities, and distinctive modes of worship, white colonists continued to imagine violent opposition between "Christian" and "Indian" identities. The colonists' cognitive failure was visited heavily on the character and reputation of Samson Occom, especially as he prepared for his English fund-raising tour in 1765. Occom's impending travels ignited public debate over the probability and authenticity of Christian Indian ministers. Some thought an Indian preacher to be a curiosity or spectacle, easily duplicated. Rumor had it that Episcopal missionaries had found, imported, and ordained another American Indian "to ape & undermine Mr Occum." Although this decoy allegedly could not even speak English, Wheelock's London associates still urged him to send Occom immediately: "He must not stay to put on his wigg but come in his night cap."[21] Others thought it impossible that an Indian could be converted, educated, trained, and ordained in "a short space of time." On this basis, the SPCK Boston Board of Commissioners accused Wheelock of misrepresenting Occom's background and education. Adding to the contention was early tour publicity which incorrectly identified Occom as a Mohawk, a tribe most fearsomely associated with hostilities against the British during the late French and Indian War.[22] Occom reviewed the controversies in a December 1765 letter to Eleazar Wheelock: "They say it is a shame to send me over the great Water. . . . They further affirm, I was bro't up Regularly and a Christian all my Days, Some Say, I cant Talk Indian, others Say I cant read."[23] To answer these charges, he produced a short autobiography that affirmed both the "Heathenish" character of his upbringing and the quality of his conversion and education under Wheelock.[24] Even Occom's own word did not fully satisfy his critics, nor did it silence the hecklers who continued to mock him throughout his British tour.

This controversy impelled Samson Occom to confront again and again the conventional association of Christianity with European imperial "civilization." His travels in England also afforded him an opportunity to observe contradictions between these terms. The poverty of the English masses, the opulent pageantry of the English court, the customary and obligatory calls upon minor nobles—these convinced Occom that Anglo-American culture was descended from a parentage no less "heathenish" than his own. A diary entry dated February 10, 1766, records Occom's horror at the uncivil state of affairs in the streets of London:

Saw Such Confusion as I never Dreamt of—there was Some at Churches, Singin & Preaching, in the Streets som Cursin Swaring & Damning one another, others was hollowing, Whestling, talking gigling, & Laughing, & Coaches and footmen passing and repassing, Crossing and Cross-Crossing, and the poor Begars Praying, Cryin, and Beging upon their knees.[25]

Certainly no such state of "confusion"—anonymity, depravity, alienation—obtained at home in Mohegan, where even under the strain of colonial imposition tribal and familial relationships continued to anchor the community. His ethnographic observations of the English left a lasting imprint on his understanding of race, nation, religion, and culture. This imprint is strikingly legible in the pages of Occom's journal more than twenty years after his return from England. Writing in July 1786, he noted the church attendance of four Oneida men, "drest compleat in Indian way they Shind with Silver, they had large Clasps about their arms, one had two jewels in his Nose, and had a large silver half moon on his Breast; and Bells about their Legs, & their heads were powderd up quite Stiff with red paint." Observing that "one of them was white as any white man," Occom commented: "His appearance made me think of the old Britains in their Heathenism."[26] The English had no essential claim to Christianity or civilization. They too were but converts and latecomers to the faith.

Samson Occom, his Native clerical colleagues, and New England's Christian Indian communities also generated new discourses of "Indianness" at a time when older modes of identity were under tremendous strain. New England's indigenous peoples customarily understood themselves in relation to place, language, and ancestry; their identities were intricate, interlaced, historically sensitive, and narrative-based. Colonial imposition of the term *Indian* reduced these distinctive identities into a single racial category. Moreover, in the context of proto- and early national policy, the term *Indian* assumed legal status in connection with land purchases, disputes, and treaties. To colonists, the erosion of traditional Indian land bases meant the end of Indian communities and of Indians as such. But Native peoples developed new bases for continuance and identification: focusing on shared political, cultural, and spiritual values, they established new intertribal alliances and communities under the broad banner of "Indianness." The redefinition of Indianness as a *spiritual* identity was crucial to early revitalization movements. One such movement emerged in the 1750s and 1760s among the Delaware or Lenape peoples of the Susquehanna and Ohio River valleys, as a series of prophets preached Indian separatism and resistance as the will of God. The separatist Indian congregations of southern New England also cultivated a theological concept of Indianness. Samson Occom believed that he was Indian by the will—indeed, by the *grace*—of God. This belief emanates from a 1765 letter to Eleazar Wheelock, written on the eve of Occom's departure for England: "I have a Struggle in my Mind at times, knowing not Where I am going, I don't know but I am looking for a Spot of ground where my Bones must be Buried, and never to See my Poor Family again, but I barely believe I am Called of god by Strange Providence and that is Enough. . . . I want nothing but the Will of God, to be Wholly Swallowed up in it."[27] Despite his overwhelming sense of dislocation—his only certain resting place is the grave—Occom grounds himself in the "Will of God." He believes that he is "Called of god by Strange Providence" to occupy a peculiar position in an overarching design. That he was Mohegan was no accident; God designated his Indianness. Occom concluded his 1768 autobiography on the same note: "I am a poor Indian. . . . I Can't help that God has made me so; I did not make my self so—."[28] His pathetic tone cloaks but does not cancel his assertion of Indianness as a Godly identity.

The Brotherton movement gathered southern New England Christian Indians into an intertribal confederacy organized around common spiritual and political goals. A regional culture of Christian Indian separatism linked smaller tribal communities, as did the allied missionary efforts of Occom, the Fowlers, and Joseph Johnson. Still, there were significant cultural and linguistic differences among these communities as well. Occom's preaching to the Brotherton tribes offered scriptural models of diversity within gathered communities, particularly in the examples of the twelve tribes of Israel and the early Christian church.[29] But these efforts to forge pantribal Christian Indian unity were complicated by upheavals in colonial Indian policy. Brotherton was conceived at a critical point in American Indian relations, precisely one decade after the Treaty of Paris, which resolved the French and Indian War (1763) and one decade before the second Treaty of Paris (1783), which resolved the Revolutionary War. The 1763 treaty conceded all lands east of the Mississippi to English colonial control; a royal proclamation that same year established the Appalachians as a boundary between white and Indian lands. The 1783 treaty formally devolved on the new United States government responsibility for Indian policy. Indian affairs were quickly centralized, as the Articles of Confederation (1783) established federal powers for negotiating nation-to-nation with individual tribes.

These politics pressured the Brotherton community to maintain its "Indianness" in ways visible, recognizable, and meaningful to colonial and early national governments. Consequently, as Hilary Wyss observes in her study of Brotherton rhetoric, Occom and his fellows absorbed some of the racism and sexism inherent to colonial discourse. Occom discriminated between "our" Brotherton Indians and the "Wild Indians" of Iroquois country; community leaders also questioned the "Indianness" of mixed-race individuals. Moreover, the framing rhetoric of "Brotherton" projected a masculinist concept of the collective body. This masculinist conceit is especially revealing. First, it may signal a devaluation of women's roles within these Indian communities, which American Indian feminists like Paula Gunn Allen and Theda Perdue have linked to colonialism. Second, it constitutes a marked departure from the customary scriptural gendering of the Christian church as female, or the bride of Christ. It appears that Occom and his associates developed a poetic association between the tribes of New England and a suffering but transcendent Christ. Joseph Johnson preached to this theme at the Christian Indian town of Farmington, Connecticut, on April 25, 1773: "In vain the Britons boast of their brave Conquerors, our Captain is he who conquered when he fell forever."[30] Johnson rejected British imperial supremacy as worldly vanity, and he claimed the resurrected Christ as an emblem of Indian renewal and survival. His sermon reveals that members of the Brotherton community simultaneously negotiated with colonial expectations, developed an anticolonial Christology, and conceded to masculinist aspects of Christian evangelicalism.[31]

Sermons, narratives, letters, and journals from southern New England's Christian Indian communities show individuals and communities striving for renewal and revitalization. These texts do not support the conceptual reduction of Indian conversion to cultural or racial assimilation or even to hybridity. During the middle decades of the eighteenth century, Mohegan, Narragansett, and neighboring tribal communities were occupied with a set of concerns about the maintenance and promotion of community welfare against persistent colonial pressures. Individual and community redemption and revival were also key elements of New Light evangelicalism. Through their adoption of Christianity, Native people developed new venues for addressing tribal issues, new ways to articulate the spiritual value of Indianness, and new pantribal identities and affiliations. With these considerations in mind, then, how do we reimagine American Indian conversion as something other than assimilation, hybridization, or cultural extinction? A compelling image comes to us in a story attributed to Samson Occom, by one who heard him preach in 1776. Occom related "an anecdote of an old Indian, who had a knife, to which as he wore out blade or handle he annexed a new one to the remaining part 'till the knife had half a dozen blades and as many handles." "Still," Occom insisted, "it was all the time the same knife."[32] The "old Indian" did not compromise the integrity of his knife by "annexing" new implements, nor did he sacrifice old blades or old handles in order to take on the new. His ownership, maintenance, and use of the knife made it "all the time the same." Read as a parable for Native conversion, Occom's anecdote asserts the value and integrity of Indian Christianity as an expression of religious self-determination and spiritual sovereignty.

The old Indian knife with many blades and many handles is also a fitting analogy for the history of American hymnody, which emerged in the eighteenth century from a confluence of controversies and cultural forces. Among these were a noted declension in the quality of Congregational psalmody, the rise of "regular singing" and singing schools, the ascendance of British hymn writers such as Isaac Watts, the Moravian exodus to America, the integration of folk tunes into sacred music tune books, and the liberalization of religious expression in the Great Awakening. The redevelopment of American congregational song was in fact intertwined with the Great Awakening. Jonathan Edwards noted his own congregation's improved singing as an evidence of the "surprising work of God" at Northampton in 1735: "Our congregation excelled all that ever I knew in the external part of the duty before, the men generally carrying regularly, and well, three parts of music, and the women a part by themselves; but now they were evidently wont to sing with unusual elevation of heart and voice, which made the duty pleasant indeed."[33] In *Some Thoughts Concerning the Present Revival* (1742), Edwards weighed in on emergent forms and customs of hymnody. He defended the use of hymns by modern authors; his own congregation had recently adopted the works of Isaac Watts. According to Edwards, modern hymnody was more appropriate to the present evangelical dispensation than psalmody; psalmody was bound up in Old Testament usages, praising God and Christ "under a veil," or "hid under the name of some type."[34] As for the more controversial practice of mass hymn singing in the streets, Edwards urged caution and restraint. Nothing in scripture prohibited such a public demonstration, but custom militated against it. To persist in such practices was, according to Edwards, like "putting new wine into old bottles," "as if it were with no other design than to burst them directly."[35] Both the Great Awakening and the emergence of American hymnody challenged and even threatened the "old bottles"—old customs, old forms, and old venues—of religious practice. As Stephen Marini observes in his study of the hymn controversy, both phenomena were sites of social and cultural tensions between young and old, rural and urban, conservative and progressive, Arminian and Calvinist; both generated public debate over the proper expression of religious experience; and both resulted finally in the development of a new American religious vernacular. Like the Great Awakening, the shift from psalmody into hymnody also opened new, non-institutional venues for authoritative literary, cultural, and religious expression by African-Americans and Native Americans.

Native Americans especially were positioned to make a significant contribution to the development of American hymnody, as they were better-educated and more versatile singers than many of their Anglo-American contemporaries. From the time of colonization, psalmody and hymnody were staples of Native-missionary interaction. In 1661, John Eliot produced an Algonkian-language Psalter; later, Cotton Mather praised Eliot-affiliated Indians as "Notable Singers" who excelled over his own "English Assemblies."[36] Eliot was not alone in this enterprise: Anglicans, Moravians, Dutch Reformed, and Catholics introduced, translated, and published Psalters, hymnals, and catechisms for northeastern tribes from the Delaware-Lenape to the Mohawk. John Sargeant introduced the works of Isaac Watts to the Stockbridge Indians in the 1730s, long before Watts was accepted into Congregational usage. Watts, who took a special interest in the evangelization of American Indians, raised seventy pounds to support Sargeant. Sargeant's contemporary David Brainerd noted in 1746 that the Lenape had "taken pains, and appeared remarkably apt in learning to sing psalm-tunes, and are now able to sing with a good degree of decency in the worship of God."[37] Sacred music was also taught at Moor's Indian Charity School, where student performances drew praise even from skeptics of the Wheelock plan. A 1764 visitor to the school wrote: "I reached his House a little before the Evening Sacrafice & was movingly Touched on giving out the Psalm to hear an Indian Youth set the Time & the others following him, & singing the Tenor, & Base, with remarkable Gravity & Seriousness. . . . They unmoved seemed to have nothing to do but to sing to the Glory of God."[38]

Native hymn singing seemed to impress Anglo-American colonists more convincingly than any other performance of piety. If audiences believed that sacred song was a mode of divine communion, then harmonious psalmody signified the singer's whole submission to God. Or, if they believed it to be a species of regenerate emotion, then Native singers appeared to be effectually in a saving way. To colonists' eyes, Native hymn performance spectacularized the bodies, the lungs, and the mouths of American Indians as well-trained vessels of the Spirit.

How colonists viewed and interpreted Native hymn singing should not be confused with how Native people valued their own participation in this medium. American Indians were not passive vessels for psalmody and hymnody, nor were they musical instruments dependent on spiritual animation. Rather, Native peoples adopted hymnody and psalmody as modes of religious expression. They exercised agency and creativity in adapting, stylizing, and implementing sacred music into their individual and communal religious practices. In a gracious study of hymn singing among the White Earth Ojibwa, Michael McNally parallels Native hymnody and Native Christianity: neither are simply "translations" of Christianity; instead, they are a matter of "transposition and performance in the context of an entirely different religious idiom."[39] McNally suggests that hymn singing is an especially vital and demonstrative example of how American Indians adopt Christianity into their lives, their communities, and their religious repertoires while maintaining their distinctiveness as Native peoples. Tribes members actively revised, translated, and reorganized hymn and psalm texts; they substituted indigenous for European instrumental accompaniment; they introduced structural variations such as repetition and choral refrains; they developed new styles of inflection, embellishment, and vocalization. Most important, they adopted hymns into the existing contexts of Native religious life. New contexts for performance and new ritual usages redetermined the value of hymnody.

Hymnody was a particularly effective medium for negotiating the circumstances and pressures of colonization. It mediated between traditional contexts and Christian practices, between native languages and phonetic English, and between orality and text. Indeed, Occom's hymnal—a text written to be vocalized—challenges us to rethink the intersections of oral and written Native American literatures. Craig Womack (Creek) has argued that Native books be viewed "as a *complement* of oral tradition rather than a *replacement*."[40] Hymnals produced for and cherished by Christian Indian communities exemplify the potency of printed text not only as a "complement" but also as an *instrument* in the continuation of oral traditions. Rather than a substitute for indigenous traditions, hymnody was adopted into an expanding repertoire of Native religious expression. We find instances of this creative adoption and adaptation throughout the colonial period, from Canada to Mexico. In the sixteenth century, Nahuatl scholars laboring under the direction of Fray Bernardino de Sahagun compiled a Nahuatl-language *Psalmodia christiana* (1558–60; pb. 1583). Sahagun hoped the *Psalmodia* would eradicate and replace traditional festival songs; however, the scribes stylized and adapted the psalmody to their own tastes and traditions.[41] Similarly, Algonkian tribes of Canada's eastern woodlands manipulated text and tune selections to create native-language hymnbooks that helped preserve and perpetuate oral traditions.[42] Massachusetts Algonkians proselytized by John Eliot restyled hymn performance to suit their own aesthetic sensibilities. In August 1651, a visitor to John Eliot and the Natick people wrote: "There was a psalme sung in the Indian tongue, and Indian meeter, but to an

English tune."[43] Some Native peoples believed that hymnody did not belong primordially and exclusively to Europeans. Thomas Commuck, a nineteenth-century Brotherton Indian and the author of a hymn tune book called *Indian Melodies* (1845), recorded the following Narragansett tradition: tribe members had heard a hymn tune "in the air" before the first arrival of colonists; when churchgoers at Plymouth sung the tune during Sunday services, native peoples "knew it as well as the whites."[44] This story reflects the extent to which native peoples assumed proprietorship and authority in the practice of Christian sacred music.

The Native practice of hymnody also signaled a developing aesthetic and theological independence from Anglo-American traditions. Their ready adoption of hymnody signaled tribes members' rejection of dominant Congregational custom and their alliance with more radical Protestant sects. Many southern New England Indians were converted by separatist Congregationalists and Baptists, who encouraged a freer use of sacred song. For example, James Davenport, who was influential in Samson Occom's conversion to Christianity, was arrested for leading hymn singing crowds through the towns of rural eastern Connecticut. Occom later developed his own hymnodic liturgy as a preacher among the Montauk on Long Island. He described his Wednesday and Sunday night worship meetings as follows: "We begin with Singing; we generally Sung Dr. Watts's Psalms or Hymns. I distinctly read the Psalms or Hymn first, and then gave the Meaning of it to them, after that Sing, then Pray, and Sing again after Prayer."[45] It appears that Occom sometimes substituted psalms and hymns for scriptural text in his preaching. This advantageous medium allowed him to negotiate more effectively differences among his students in language, literacy levels, and book ownership. Occom's brothers-in-law, Montauk tribe members, and fellow Wheelock alumni David and Jacob Fowler established a singing school among the Oneida in the 1760s. "They take great pleasure in learning to sing," Fowler reported to Wheelock. "We can already carry three Parts of several tunes."[46] In November 1766, Jacob Fowler wrote that "we have got the Indians so, that we can sing good many Tunes with all three Parts."[47] Mohegan tribal member and Wheelock alumnus Joseph Johnson joined the Fowler brothers at Oneida in the winter of 1766, with the express purpose of learning "David [Fowler's] Art in teaching the Natives."[48] When Johnson became the Oneida schoolmaster in February 1768, he too kept "Singing School every Evening very full meetings."[49] Samuel Niles and his fellow Narragansett Christians—who split from white Congregationalists in the 1760s—established their own singing meetings each week on Tuesday, Thursday, and Saturday evenings; according to Joseph Fish, the local Congregationalist minister, the Narragansett also developed their own

"Way" with hymnody, a performance style and sound unique from Anglo-American congregations.[50] By the late 1760s, Native clergy of the Occom-Wheelock connection had instituted singing schools and singing meetings in tribal communities from Long Island, across Connecticut, and to upstate New York. From the Montauk to the Oneida, diverse tribal peoples learned English language hymnody as an intertribal lingua franca.

Samson Occom developed an authoritative interest in hymnody during his preaching tour of the British Isles, from 1766 to 1768. As the fundraising emissary of Moor's Indian Charity School and the special guest of George Whitefield, he preached in England, Scotland, and Ireland; attended King George II; dined with Lord Dartmouth and Selina, countess of Huntingdon; visited Westminster Abbey and the Tower of London; and was invited to consider ordination by Anglican church leaders. Occom also found himself in close company with leading English hymn writers. He preached to the congregations of Martin Madan, Phillip Dodderidge, and John Wesley. John Newton—the famously converted slave-trader, author of "Amazing Grace," and coproducer with William Cowper of the *Olney Hymns*—extended special courtesies to Occom and welcomed him as a houseguest. During his travels, Occom amassed an impressive personal collection of hymnals by Isaac Watts, John and Charles Wesley, George Whitefield, Lady Huntingdon, Martin Madan, and John Mason. Other well-wishers honored Occom by donating hymnals and tune books to Moor's Indian Charity School. The English tune writer William Knapp donated copies of his *A Sett of New Psalm Tunes* to David Fowler and the Oneida. A London singing-school master and tune book compiler named Thomas Knibbs dedicated a new tune composition—named "Lebanon," in honor of the school's location—to Eleazar Wheelock. Knibbs also took a personal interest in the musical enterprises of David Fowler and Samson Occom. To Fowler, Knibbs addressed and sent a copy of his *Hymns of Universal Use*. As for Occom, Knibbs extended this invitation on February 8, 1768: "Understanding by the Rev. Dr. Whitaker that you know Music I here Present you with upwards of Six Score Tunes amongst which there are several of the Modernest & some of the Pleasantest that are us'd amongst the Methodists & if at any time it should suit your conveniancy to call & Drink a Dish of Tea at my House should be glad to sing a few of them over together."[51] When Occom returned from England in 1768, he brought home to Mohegan not only a substantial musical library but also an advanced appreciation for the emergent art of hymnody.[52]

These musical resources became crucial to the tribal communities of southern New England in the 1770s, when a wave of religious revivalism intersected with the nascent Native revitalization movement that culminated in the founding of Brotherton. Singing meetings in particular functioned as sites for community fellowship, interpersonal reconciliation, independent religious development, and political organization. Journals from this time period show that Mohegans gathered for hymn singing several times a week: in addition to Sunday worship services, Occom himself hosted Tuesday night singing meetings at his house. Hymn singing was also a feature of tribal meetings and weddings; female tribal elders made regular Sunday night house visits, to fellowship in song and prayer.[53] As rituals of hymnody became established, demand for hymnals and tune books far outpaced supply. The shortage impelled Occom to seek donations. On March 4, 1771, he wrote to an English benefactor, thanking him for an earlier shipment of hymn books and Psalters:

> I have dispos'd of them all among the poor Indians, and them most thankfully receiv'd, and they have been of great Use and Benefit to the Indians, and they Continue to Come to me from all Quarters for Books, even to the Distance of 60 miles. The Indians are greatly Delighted and edified with Singing, it is Judg'd by the White People in this Country, that the Indians have most Melodious Voices of any People . . . The Indians in their Religious Meetings round about here, Sing more than any Christians and they have frequent meetings in all Indian Towns.[54]

Evidently, the singing meeting phenomenon had spread beyond Mohegan to "all Indian Towns" in the region—Niantic, Stonington, Farmington, Groton, Stockbridge, and others. Occom requested from his English patron more copies of the most popular hymnbooks: he cited the "Little Hymn Book Design'd for the Negroes, Printed by John Oliver in Barthomew Close near West Smithfield" and John Mason's "Songs and Penitential Hymns" as "very Pleasing to the Indians." Just one day later, on March 5, 1771, Occom asked a similar favor of his friend and correspondent, Susannah Wheatley: "Madam, I have a favour to beg of you, that is, to get me a Singing Book, I think it was Printed at Salem lately[,] price, I was told 8. My Children are much Inclin'd to Singing and I would Encourage them in Time."[55]

The demand for hymnals and tune books was so intense in some native communities as to induce Native missionaries to make these materials by hand. As a schoolmaster and minister among the Christian Indians of Farmington (1772–73), Joseph Johnson instituted a vigorous program of community sings. In addition to hymn singing at Sunday services, the tribe also convened a twice-weekly singing meeting to be held at the home of Johnson's fellow Mohegan and Wheelock alumnus Samuel Ashpo. However, few among the impoverished Farmington Indians owned hymnals or instructional tune books, called "gamuts." Johnson wrote on December 3, 1772: "The indians are all desireous of having Gamuts, but I am in Continual hurry. Nevertheless, I purpose to furnish them with Singing books as Soon as time will admit."[56] Johnson's plan for furnishing the community with "Singing books" meant weeks of painstaking handicraft, binding gamuts and printing, or "pricking out," tunes. Johnson would finish a heroic eight gamuts during his ten-week stay in Farmington. The rhythms of this steady work soon took shape in Johnson's daily journal. Writing on December 17 about a disturbance and the Farmington School, Johnson breaks into rhymed common meter: "I Spoke freely to all the rest—that they a warning take—for I assure them that I will no Distinction make—." What follows is an incredible and emotive patchwork of hymn references:

Keep them in they womb O Mohegan, till thou dost hear the Voice of God—O Mohegan give up thy Dead—then no longer Prisoners Shall they be unto thee—the joyfull hour is Approaching. *My Soul Come Meditate the Day and think how near it stands when you must leave—this house of Clay and fly to Unknown Lands.*—Hast my beloved fetch my Soul up to thy blest aboad fly for my Spirit longs to see—my Saviour and my God—Mohegan is a lonsome place, oft have I sighed—but sighed in vain—desired, but desired in vain—Cast down—but no one to Comfort me—in destress—no one to relieve me—no friend to open my heart and vent my Sorrow. Thus o Mohegan have you treated me—and thinkest thou—I can forget thee—or thy inhabitants—thinkest thou—or thine inhabiters that I am desirein to be on thee or with them—far far from me be such a thought—but Still there is a precious few in thee, which Causes my mind often to Meditate of thee—[57]

The discourse of psalmody and hymnody allows Johnson to express the difficulties of his work and the loneliness of his removal from his native Mohegan. Here, he recites a full two verses of Isaac Watts's funeral hymn "My Soul Come Meditate the Day" as a meditation on the fragility of human relationships and endeavors. Johnson also adapts portions of Psalms 137, substituting "Mohegan" for "Jerusalem" as his spiritual and physical homeland. The example of Joseph Johnson shows that the practice of hymnody was neither bound nor determined by Anglo-American orthodoxy but adopted into public and private usage by Christian Indians.[58]

The absorption of hymnody into southern New England Christian Indian culture, the dire need for more hymnals, and the emergence of the Brotherton movement motivated Samson Occom to compile and publish his own hymnal. It was to be his most ambitious literary undertaking, exceeding in scale, scope, and longevity his *Sermon at the Execution of Moses Paul*. It was also a work that allowed Occom to exercise a new degree of literary authority as a judge, editor, and compiler of hymn texts. He advertised his project in the New London, Connecticut, *Gazette* on December 24, 1773:

> Mr. Occum, having some time since intimated to many of his friends, his intention of publishing a Collection of Hymns and Anthems, from the most approved modern authors—he now informs them that the Collection is nearly compleated and ready for the press. It already consists of above one hundred and twenty Hymns, &c. And in order to render this publication as beneficial as possible, the editor requests the favour of gentlemen and ladies who have in their hands any valuable and approved Hymns or Anthems, that they would without delay, send them to him.

The following section turns to a close examination of the hymnal, its contents, its design, and its implications as a pioneering work of American Indian literature and American religion.

Samson Occom's *A Choice Collection of Hymns and Spiritual Songs; Intended for the edification of sincere Christians, of all denominations* includes a two-page preface by Occom, 109 numbered hymn texts (without tunes), five doxologies, a first-line index, and a two-page poem, "The Unknown World: Verses occasioned by hearing a Pass-Bell." Its publication in 1774 positioned the *Collection* and Occom at the forefront of American hymnody. Until 1760, American hymn singers relied primarily on imported and reprinted editions of English hymnals; the publication of James Lyon's *Urania* (Philadelphia, 1761), Francis Hopkinson's *Collection* (Philadelphia, 1763); Josiah Flagg's *Collection* (Boston, 1764); Samuel Hall's *Hymns and Spiritual Songs* (place, 1766); and William Billings's *New England Psalm-Singer* (Boston, 1770) marked the beginnings of domestic hymn production. Most of these works emerged in response to the hymnody-psalmody controversy, in connection with particular congregations, or in association with amateur singing schools. They focused primarily on musical technique, introducing original hymn texts incidentally. Occom's *Collection* redirected the priorities and energies of American hymnody away from technical virtuosity and theological contest, focusing instead on hymn texts as instruments of personal and communal renewal. It includes neither tunes nor musical instructions; it does not apologize for its inclusion of modern authors; it serves no single denomination. Rather, the *Col-*

lection frees hymn texts from customary Euro-American contexts and contests and offers them up to new usages and new users.

Occom rejected the conservative, formalist views that dominated contemporary debates over sacred music. Partisans in the psalmody-hymnody debate vested the text and form of sacred music with supernatural power. Defenders of psalm singing believed that the individual should conform her own expressive impulses to the text of the psalms, for to sing the words of scripture was to harmonize with the mind of God; likewise, advocates of "regular singing" and musical literacy emphasized discipline and virtuosity as expressions of devotion. But in his preface to the *Collection*, Occom warns against an exclusive occupation with "Form" and "Method":

> People ought not to be contented with the outward Form of Singing, but should seek after the *inward* Part.—There are two Parts of Singing as St. Paul informs us, in 1 Cor. 14. 15. (*I will sing with the Spirit, and I will sing with the Understanding also.*) To sing without the Spirit, (though with good Method) is like the Sound of a musical Instrument without Life. To sing with the Spirit, I understand Paul further to mean, [is] to sing with spiritual Matter: And thus when we sing with the Understanding or Method, and with spiritual Matter, by the Influence of God's Spirit, we sing agreeable to God's mind.[59]

Here, he generates a set of paired terms—"outward" and "inward," "understanding" and "Spirit," "method" and "spiritual matter"—to represent the basic elements of hymnody. "Outward" forms depend on an "inward" presence; without the "Spirit," music is instrumentation "without Life." Occom's formulation takes on additional richness in the multiple meanings of the word *Spirit*. Having studied ancient languages, he knew that in the Greek of the New Testament "spirit" was "pneuma" or breath. Hymns, then, are instruments to be enlivened, filled, and animated by breath—both the human breath of respiration and the sacred breath of inspiration. Further, by characterizing "Spirit" as "spiritual matter," Occom reorganizes the conventional opposition of matter and spirit. By his view, form is insubstantial, a husk, a shadow, words and notes on paper; spirit is material force, power, presence, breath, and life. Thus, spirit *matters*; it matters more than the text, more than the tune, and more than the technique of the singers. What matters is that the community breathes life into its religious practices; what matters is the presence of the Holy Spirit commingling with the breath of the singers. What matters is the harmonious collaboration of human and divine agents. Inspired human activity, not formal virtuosity, sacralizes music.

Occom's theories of hymnody reflect on his views of Native Christianity in general. It is as though he conceived of hymnody as a perishable body to be inhabited, enlivened, and actualized by a spirit that precedes and survives it. What implications did this view bear for other Christian forms, identities, and beliefs adopted by Native peoples? Were not all of these immaterial shapes given force, power, and meaning by the Indian peoples who breathed life into them? Occom's counsel about the "inward" and "outward" components of singing invokes another biblical text germane to these questions. In Romans 2:28–29, Paul distinguishes the "outward" marks of religious affiliation from the "inward" signs of the spirit: "For he is not a Jew, which is one outwardly; neither is that circumcision, which is outward in the flesh. But he is a Jew, which is one inwardly; and circumcision is that of the heart, in the spirit, and not in the letter." Paul criticized the assumption that birthright inheritance and physical conformity to law and custom distinguished one in the eyes of God. To Paul as to Occom, what mattered was the spirit that inhabited the form. It would be a mistake, then, to imagine that Occom viewed Christian Indians as passive vessels to be filled by Euro-American Christianity and hymnody. Rather, they adopted the forms of Christianity and filled them with the concerns, hopes, joys, and sorrows they shared as Indian people. Christian Indian communities sacralized hymnody by using it to renew their individual lives and common bonds, to replenish the tribal repertoire of religious practices, and to revive community relationships.

That Christian Indians did not bring to hymnody the strictures of Euro-American dogma and custom afforded Samson Occom greater latitude in the design of his hymnal. He designed the *Collection* to appeal to a broad range of denominational affiliations, aesthetic sensibilities, spiritual conditions, and emotional states. This internal diversity empowered individual singers and independent religious communities to choose hymns that most pleased them or best served their spiritual needs. By virtue of its internal diversity, the hymnal is also a textual template for the negotiation of difference within Christian communities. This connection materializes in Occom's prefatory invocation of 1 Corinthians 14; here, Paul addresses the practice of speaking in tongues and the problems of communicating spiritual experience among the people at Corinth. Paul acknowledged the value and the difficulty of negotiating difference within the church: "There are, it may be, so many kinds of voices in the world, and none of them is without signification. Therefore if I know not the meaning of the voice, I shall be unto him that speaketh a barbarian, and he that speaketh shall be a barbarian unto me" (v. 10–11). He also believed that God might make instruments of barbarians, or speak in foreign lan-

guages. Meaningful religious experience required negotiation, reciproca-
tion, and exchange.

To this end, an important feature of the hymnal is its interdenominationalism. The very title page of the *Collection* announces its broad inclu-
sivity in the subtitle—*Intended for the edification of sincere Christians, of all
denominations*—and in Occom's description of himself as a "Minister of
the Gospel" at large. In his preface, Occom explains, "I have taken no
small Pains to collect a Number of choice Hymns, Psalms, and spiritual
Songs, from a Number of Authors of different Denominations of Christians, that every Christian may be suited."[60] He built the *Collection* by se-
lecting works from his own library of hymnals, as well as by soliciting favorite hymns from the public at large. By enfranchising individual
believers in the construction of the hymnal, Occom demonstrated his respect for independent religious activity and expression. Implicit also in
this process is a new concept of ministerial authority as a power located in
the cultivation of consensus rather than the protection of tradition and
the promulgation of doctrine. This democratic appeal vests the hymnal
with a communal authority. It also ensured the *Collection* a broad audience, lasting popularity, steady reprints, and numerous emulators. Other
early American hymnals—including Joshua Smith's much reprinted *Divine
Hymns, or Spiritual Songs for the use of religious assemblies and private Christians* (1784) and Richard Allen's *A Choice Collection of Hymns and Spiritual
Songs* (1801)—relied on Occom's *Collection* as a model and a source text.[61]
Finally, the interdenominationalism of the hymnal was important to
American Indian Christian communities, which had developed their own
eclectic hymn repertoires. Decades of colonial proselytizing exposed individual tribal communities to a wide variety of faith traditions and modes
of sacred song; additionally, Christian Indian communities culled their favorite hymns from the cast-off, remnant, secondhand hymnals given them
by European and American donors. In order to serve the tribes uniting at
Brotherton, the *Collection* had to incorporate the various hymns most
cherished by individual tribes and tribes members. The editorial compila-
tion of the hymnal thus parallels and textualizes the social formation of
the Christian Indian community at Brotherton.

The *Collection* includes works by English and American authors, Anglican and dissenting, Methodist and Baptist, known and unknown. (Occom
did not attribute individual hymns, but it is possible to identify authors for
a majority of the collected works; see appendix 1.) Isaac Watts is the clear
favorite, with twenty-eight hymns selected; the Wesleys follow with
twenty-two. From Baptist Samuel Hall's *Hymns and Spiritual Songs* (1766),
Occom chose six hymns for republication. Another six belong to the
seventeenth-century Anglican John Mason, whom Occom cited as a par-

ticular favorite among the Christian Indians of southern New England. Eighteenth-century English hymnodist John Cennick (a Methodist convert to Moravianism) contributes four hymn texts, while the seventeenth-century Anglicans Samuel Crossman and George Herbert both contribute two. Alexander Pope, Phillip Dodderidge, Joseph Hart, John Newton, and Nahum Tate are also represented with one hymn each. Occom also published one of his own compositions as hymn 77, "Throughout the Saviour's Life We Trace."[62]

The variety and quality of these collected hymn texts shed new light on the literary career of Samson Occom. Assessments based solely on his short autobiography and his execution sermon tend to reduce Occom to an autoethnographic confessor or an apologetic purveyor of Puritanism. The hymnal, however, reveals him to be much more accomplished, sophisticated, and versatile; a poet as well as a prose writer; an editor and critic as well as an author. His own hymn, "Throughout the Saviour's Life We Trace," establishes Occom as the first Native American to write and publish poetry in English. Occom also can be credited with introducing new hymns by leading English writers to American audiences: these hymns include his friend John Newton's "Come, ye Sinners, come to Jesus" (hymn 71); John Mason's "So foolish, so absurd am I" (hymn 9); George Herbert's "Come to Judgment, come away" (hymn 75); "Who can have greater Cause to Sing" from George Whitefield's *Collection* (hymn 82); and Charles Wesley's "Jesus, friend of Sinners hear" (hymn 85). As an editor, Occom revised hymn texts to better reflect his own theological values. He rejected in his maturity the fire-and-brimstone teachings of Eleazar Wheelock in favor of a gospel emphasizing mercy, forgiveness, love, and affection. This new emphasis comes through in hymn 74, a revision of the Wesleys' "He comes! he comes! the Judge severe." Occom softens the Wesleys' stern characterization in a new first line, "He comes! He comes! the Saviour dear." Hymn 81, "Come to Jesus, come away," revises George Herbert's "Come to Judgment, come away" along similar lines. Occom retains the five stanzas, metrical format (7 7 7 7 7 7), trochaic rhythms, and rhyme scheme (*aabbcc*) of the original but completely changes the content. Herbert's original call to "Judgment" is transformed into a more merciful call to "Jesus." Herbert gives a forbidding description of moral and metaphysical decay: "Dust," "instant Doom," "Atoms" "disperst," "Order hurl'd," and "broken Concert." Occom instead opts for invitation and welcome:

Come, and all the Sweetness prove,
Of the Holy Ghost and Love; [. . .]
Jesus laid aside his Robes,

That you may lay aside your sobs; [. . .]
Come away, come to thy Home,
Come away to thy Bridegroom.

Occom felt enough freedom from the conventions of proprietary authorship and enough confidence in his own authority to create a hymnal appropriate to the spiritual needs of his community.

Occom also demonstrated editorial independence and creative vision in
publishing a large number of new hymns. More than one-quarter of the
collected hymns—29 of 109—have no known author and no known previous publication (see appendix 2.) Certainly, most were of American origin, written by minor hymnodists and collected by Occom during his domestic missionary travels. It is also possible that a few were written by
Samson Occom himself, or by other members of the Occom-Wheelock
missionary connection. We know that Occom authored at least one hymn
in the *Collection*: "Throughout the Saviour's Life We Trace."[63] David
Fowler, Jacob Fowler, and Joseph Johnson also demonstrated avid interest
and aptitude in hymnody. A letter written by Johnson to a British colonial
officer in July 1774 strongly suggests that Johnson "composed" two hymn
texts for the *Collection*: "I Send to your Honor two Small Pieces, which I
composed, and got Printed, which may perhaps give little Satisfaction to
the Curiousity of Some of the Gentlemen that Resort to your Honors
house."[64] It is difficult to prove or disprove that Johnson, or the Fowlers,
or Occom himself authored some number of the twenty-nine anonymous hymns. Known manuscript sources—journals, letters, and other
papers written by Occom, Johnson, and the Fowlers—provide little solid
evidence to go on. Moreover, an unknown number of Occom, Johnson,
and Fowler manuscripts have been lost to posthumous dispersal and
physical destruction. Still, it is possible that Native authors wrote several
hymns in the collection. If so, then the *Collection* houses a cache of early
Native American poetry—in fact, the earliest known body of English-
language poems by Native American authors.

We can be certain that Occom did incorporate hymns designed specifically to appeal to the musical tastes and traditions of Native peoples.
In his preface to the *Collection*, Occom explains that he had included a
number of hymns "of uncommon Measures, for new Tunes and new
Singers."[65] Several hymns feature ten or more stanzas, longer line lengths,
unusually bracing rhythms, choral refrains, and rapturous conclusions.
These compositional features contribute to a more involved, extended,
and transformative hymn-singing experience; their style is especially appropriate to the long, communal singing meetings held in southern New
England Indian towns. This style is exemplified in the unattributed hymn

104, "Farewell to My Pain and Farewell to My Chain." Whereas typical hymns observed long meter (LM; eight syllables per line; 8 8 8 8) or common meter (CM; alternating eight and six syllables; 8 6 8 6), this hymn features two eleven-syllable lines and a two-line repeating chorus (11 11 11 11). Its metrical lines also diverge from the conventional hymnodic iambs, consisting of one iamb and three anapests. In ten rollicking stanzas, singers address a catalog of mortal fears and perils. Here are stanzas two and three:

> The earthquakes may quake, and the Mountains may break;
> Yet never a jot of my Confidence shake. [. . .]
> Old Ocean may Rage, and fierce Tempests engage;
> Yet none of them all shall my Courage asswage.

These lines match the "Confidence" and "Courage" of the believer against chaos and destruction, which are characterized and even personified as natural forces. The choral refrain subdues fears and dangers with faith:

> My Sins and my Sorrows, farewell evermore;
> My soul and all in me, Jehovah adore.

The hymn gains momentum as it moves through the stanzas, a momentum matched in the progress of the narrator. In stanza eight, the narrator ascends from the "World" to a higher plane:

> World it shall die, and expire with a sigh;
> But I, as an Eagle, shall tower to the Sky.

Stanza ten culminates in transcendence:

> amazing it is! What an Extasy this!
> I'm swallow'd, I'm lost in an Ocean of Bliss!

This hymn does not merely represent spiritual transformation; it vicariously and performatively effects it, as singers are transported from the "pains" and "chains" of the opening line to the "extasy" and "bliss" of the final stanza.

Occom also favored hymns structured in antiphonal, "call and response" verses—a style traditional to northeastern tribal societies. John Heckwelder, an eighteenth-century Moravian missionary, observed that the Lenape (relatives to the Mohegan) sang "in chorus; first the men and then the women. At times the women join in the general song, or repeat the strain which the men have just finished. It seems like two parties singing in questions and answers, and is upon the whole very agreeable and enlivening."[66] Three antiphonal works appear in Occom's *Collection*: hymn 39, the unattributed "Tell Us, O Women Travellers"; hymn 46, the unattributed "What Poor Despised Company"; and hymn 93, "Tell Us, O Women, We Would Know," by John Cennick. All three alternate stanzas of questions and answers; two of these engender the verses, assigning questions to men and answers to women. In hymn 39, male voices ask:

Tell us, O Women Travellers,
Unto what Place ye go?
And why ye do not seem Content
To stay on Earth below?

Women answer by reminding the men that "We're Pilgrims here, Earth's not our Home" and that the "Sight of Jesu's Love" makes worldly things "Appear as Dung and Dross." Similarly, in hymn 93, men ask the women if their "native Country" is "the place of your abode," while women respond that they "seek a better Country far," in a "City built by God."

Textual motifs featured prominently in the collected hymns also appealed to Christian Indian communities. Chief among them was the motif of the spiritual journey or trail. This image was a Christian commonplace, an impending reality for the Brotherton tribes, and a key element of Algonkian spiritual tradition. As Mohegan tribal historian Melissa Fawcett explains, the trail motif represents different phases of the soul's progress—"the Path of the Sun," "the Trail of Life," and "the Beautiful White Path"—as well as the connections between generations. Trail patterns recur in Mohegan beadwork, basketry, regalia, and carving, including a birch-elm box sent from Brotherton back to Mohegan by Samson Occom and other pilgrims.[67] Occom also incorporated this image into the preface to the *Collection*: Occom dedicates the hymns as a "comfort" "in your weary Pilgrimage; I hope they will assist and strengthen you through the various Changes of this Life, till you shall all safely arrive to the general Assembly Above, and Church of the First-Born, where you shall have no more need of these imperfect Hymns; but shall perfectly join the Songs of Moses and the Lamb."[68] Nine hymns feature this imagery. Those compiled from known sources include hymn 4, "Hail! happy Pilgrims, whence came ye?" from Samuel Hall's *Collection*; hymn 28, John Mason's "I sojourn in a Vale of Tears"; and hymn 45, Samuel Crossman's "Farewell vain World, I must be gone." The unattributed hymn 39, "Tell us, O Women Travellers," reveals the "pleasant Path, / That Worldlings love so well" to be an "open Road to Hell" and the "rugged thorny Maze" to be the only "Road, / to Salem's Happy Ground." In hymn 40, "Lo! We are journeying home to God," singers assume the roles of pilgrims:

> We walk a narrow Path and rough,
> and we are tired and weak:
> Yet soon shall we have Rest enough,
> In those bless'd Courts we seek.

The unattributed hymn 49, "Now has the Ever Rolling Year," tells of a "Bright Center of united Praise" to which "pious Tribes of heavenly Line" will gather, while "pastures fair" and "Canaan's Milk and Honey Land" await Christ's followers in hymn 96, "Companions of the Little Flock." Finally, the trail motif forms the backbone for Occom's own composition, hymn 77, "Throughout the Savior's Life we Trace." I will examine this hymn—and introduce others written by Samson Occom—in the following section.

Samson Occom's hymn composition "The Sufferings of Christ," or "Throughout the Savior's Life we Trace," establishes him as the first Native American to publish English-language poetry. At least five other Occom compositions were published in the late eighteenth and early nineteenth centuries: "The Slow Traveller," or, "O Happy Souls How Fast You Go"; "A Morning Hymn," or, "Now the Shades of Night are Gone"; "A Son's Farewell," or, "I Hear the Gospel's Joyful Sound"; "Conversion Song," or, "Wak'd by the Gospel's Pow'rful Sound"; and "Come All My Young Companions, Come." (For full texts, see appendix 3.) Written by Occom during the 1770s, these hymns circulated among the evangelical singing meetings of the Norwich-New London-Mohegan, Connecticut area. There, they were learned by a young Norwich native named Joshua Smith (1760–95), who later became a Baptist itinerant and published the hymns in his highly popular *Divine Hymns, or Spiritual Songs* (1791). Two other natives of Norwich, the brothers Asher Miner (1777–1841) and Charles Miner (1780–1865), obtained copies of Occom's hymns when they apprenticed at the printing shop of Thomas Green in New London, Connecticut, where Occom's *Collection* was produced. More than twenty years later, after migrating to Wilkes-Barre, Pennsylvania, the Miner brothers published *Divine Hymns, or, Spiritual Songs For the Use of Religious Assemblies and Private Christians; Being a Collection by Joshua Smith, Samson Okcum* [sic], *and Others* (1802).[69] The Smith and Miner collections restore Occom's name to the title page of Smith's hymnal and introduce previously unpublished hymns by Occom. Subsequently, Occom's hymns appeared in dozens of New Light, Congregationalist, Baptist, Methodist, Lutheran, Mennonite, and Moravian hymnals published from Vermont to North Carolina. At least two—"A Morning Hymn," or, "Now the Shades of Night are Gone" and "Throughout the Saviour's Life We Trace"—remain in contemporary usage.[70]

Taken together, these six original hymns by Samson Occom reveal a major new dimension of Occom's literary career, Native American literature, and early American literature. They establish Occom as a pioneering Native American poet. They also establish the beginnings of Native poetry in English in the late eighteenth century, rather than in the nineteenth century as is now commonly thought. Occom's hymns demonstrate that even the earliest Native authors did not write for white audiences alone; intercultural mediation was not their highest calling. Rather, in the spirit of Jace Weaver's "communitism," they wrote to serve Native communities. The forms and themes of Occom's hymns reveal his commitment to Native peoples' spiritual needs as well as his recognition of the power of sacred song to unite and transform Indian people.

Occom selected the Mohegan spiritual motif of the trail or beautiful path to structure his hymn "Throughout the Saviour's Life We Trace." This hymn follows the path Christ walked from his intercessory prayer in the Garden of Gethsemane to his crucifixion. Its rhythms are steadily iambic; its six sextain stanzas (8 8 6 8 8 6) halt slightly, as alternating trimeter lines interrupt the narrative. Occom focuses on physical details of suffering—the "cold Ground" of Gethsemane, the "chilly sweat" and "Blood-drops" "through eve'ry open'd Pore," the "pricking Thorns" placed on his head, the "Lashes" doled out by Roman soldiers "Till one the Bones might see"— which evoke an intimacy with the embodied, persecuted Christ. Also provocative is Occom's description of the way to Calvary:

Mocking, they push'd him here and there,
Marking his Way with Blood and Tear,
Press'd by the heavy Tree.

Christ's path encompasses experiences familiar to tribal communities: criminalization, forced displacement, and state-sponsored violence. "What Tongue his Grief can Tell?" asks Occom in stanza five. The question indicates the unspeakable depths of Christ's sorrows. However, it also premises the final stanza of the hymn, which exhorts:

Shout, Brethren, shout in songs divine,
He drank the Gall, to give us Wine,
To quench our parching thirst.

Occom positions his "shouting" singers as the vicarious voice of the suffering Christ. Moreover, he parallels hymnody with redemption in its power to "quench" the "parching thirsts" of silent suffering.

The trail of life or beautiful path is also incorporated in "The Slow Traveller," or "O Happy Souls, How Fast You Go." This common-meter hymn affectionately addresses deceased members of the community; its tone is unmistakably hopeful and its iambic rhythms are upbeat. Characterizing the dead as "fast" travelers on the trail to heaven, singers comfort and encourage them to relinquish their earthly attachments. "Don't stop for me," sing the living; "Go on, go on, my soul says go, / And I'll Come after you." Death does not sunder relationships, nor isolate souls from their communities of origin. Rather, souls remain present in the spiritual life of the tribe: as guardians of the living, in visionary experience ("You are not out of Sight"), and in the rituals of hymnody ("Tho' I'm behind, yet I can find, / I'll sing Hosanna too"). This hymn thus resounds a theme important to Occom: the power of hymnody, like other rituals of worship and condolence, to raise the dead and regenerate the community. Hymn singing punctures the linear time of the profane world, to bring memory and expectation, past and future, dead and living, into a gathered presence. The chorus for "O Happy Souls" not only emphasizes but also enacts through repetition—an important feature of American Indian song and poetry—the "togetherness" of the community in song and praise:

> There all together we shall be,
> Together we will Sing,
> Together we will praise our God,
> And everlasting King.

"Come all my Young Companions, Come" also acknowledges and implements the community-building powers of hymnody. This ten-stanza, common-meter hymn opens with an assonant and alliterative invitation—"Come all my Young Companions Come / And hear me boldly tell"—which establishes mutuality and reciprocity amongst the singers, positioning them individually and collectively as both "tellers" and "hearers." In stanzas two through six, singers narrate and vicariously experience a vision of damnation. "Nothing but hell and dark Disgrace / Lay plain before my face," the narrator recounts; "Nothing but Jesus Crucified, / Could save a wretch like me." (Here Occom samples with appreciation a line from his friend John Newton's anthem "Amazing Grace.") The vision terminates with a view of "mount Calvary" and Christ on the "Cursed Tree." Then, in stanzas seven through ten, the narrative shifts away from the medium of sight to emphasize the power of sound. If sight convicts, then sound liberates, celebrates, and consoles. Having viewed damnation, the narrator internalizes the promise of salvation as a "Blessed Sound" and a "pleasant" "ring." Song also provides the means to celebrate this promise:

> And while I dwell on Earth below
> I'll praise my Jesus here,
> And then go to yonder World
> And praise my Jesus there.

Sound is a key thematic feature of two original Occom hymns: "A Son's Farewell," or, "I Hear the Gospel's Joyful Sound" and "Conversion Song," or, "Wak'd by the Gospel's Pow'rful Sound." Perhaps Occom's best-known composition, "Wak'd by the Gospel's Pow'rful Sound" shares the 8 8 6 8 8 6 structure of his hymn "Throughout the Saviour's Life We Trace." Its first five stanzas resound the message "The sinner must be born again" as an internalized chorus. Each stanza also narrates a stage in the conversion process, delineating the contours of Occom's theology: "relief" comes not from "the law" but in the dispensation of "free grace" and the experience of being "born again." The final stanza joins the redeemed singer with a heavenly chorus:

> Now with the saints I'll sing and tell,
> How Jesus sav'd my soul from hell,
> And praise redeeming love.

Both figuratively and performatively, in the text and in its performance, sound assumes the power to transport and transform the individual in his or her relationship to the divine and the community.

Although its title closely follows "Wak'd by the Gospel's Pow'rful Sound," "I hear the gospel's joyful sound," or "A Son's Farewell" tells a different story of personal transformation. Its five common-meter stanzas voice the internal conflicts of a young man called to the ministry. In stanza one, the narrative subject declares his "call" to be an "organ" of the "gospel's joyful sound" and "to sound forth redeeming love / And sinner's misery." Subsequent stanzas reveal the narrator's struggle to relinquish ties to home and family. Stanza three relates:

> With due affections I'll forsake
> My parents and their house,
> And to the wilderness betake,
> To pay the Lord my vows.

The word *forsake* suggests that this missionary's departure from home involves a profound relinquishment of the familiar and the customary. But the "wilderness" he enters is not the profane "desert" of the Puritan imagination; rather, it is a space of freedom, memory, and comfort. Here is stanza five:

> Then through the wilderness I'll run,
> Preaching the gospel free;
> O be not anxious for your son,
> The Lord will comfort me.

The convert does not wander through the wilderness but rather "runs" through it, unbounded in his mission to communicate the "joyful sound." This hymn is important for its resignification of "wilderness" as a space of freedom for Native missionaries and converts. It reverses the express aims of colonialist missionary activity to use Christianity to domesticate and settle indigenous peoples so as to obtain Native land tracts for colonial exploitation. It also reveals the hopes of New England Christian Indians for new settlements such as Brotherton, which brought them away from encroached ancestral lands.

In addition to these known Occom compositions, other hymns that suggest the authorial or editorial influence of Samson Occom appear in the 1802, 1803, and 1804 editions of *Divine Hymns, or, Spiritual Songs For the Use of Religious Assemblies and Private Christians; Being a Collection by Joshua Smith, Samson Okcum* [sic], *and Others.* The 1803 and 1804 editions of this hymnal were published in Albany and Troy, New York, less than a hundred miles from the Brotherton settlement and Oneida territory. The restoration of Occom's name to the title page of this volume also suggests that publishers Asher and Charles Miner remembered Occom and that they knew his name would be significant to their intended audiences. It is thus likely that these editions of *Divine Hymns, or Spiritual Songs*, contain hymns designed by and for Christian Indians. One of these is "The Minister's Song." The structure of this hymn—sixteen stanzas of anapestic eleven-syllable lines—matches the "uncommon measures" of Occom's 1774 *Collection.* So too are its themes familiar—conflict between family devotion and religious calling, physical hardship, contention within the church, and ridicule from without:

> The church oft neglects in times of distress,
> The world they despise his humble address;
> He's a fool, and impostor in infidels' eyes.

The hymn finds resolution in comparing the trials of the minister to those of ancient prophets, who had "goat-skins and dens" for their "reward," and to the apostles who had "dungeons and gibbets," or gallows, for their "pay":

> We labor much less, but have better fare;
> Then banish complaint and all anxious care;
> Confide in that God who hears young ravens cry—
> Be stedfast in duty, till death shall draw nigh.

This striking description of God as the one "who hears young ravens cry" recalls several biblical texts, including Psalms 147:9, Job 38: 41, and Christ's teaching that his disciples "Consider the ravens: for they never sow nor reap; which neither have storehouse nor barn; and God feedeth them" (Luke 12:24). It also signifies on an old and unfriendly custom of racial address: New Englanders called Indians "ravens" because, like the ravens of the Bible, they were poor, they appeared not to work, and they were dark.[71] But here "young ravens" claim a specific trust in Providence and an exclusive audience with God.

Another provocative hymn appears in the 1803 edition of *Divine Hymns, or, Spiritual Songs For the Use of Religious Assemblies and Private Christians; Being a Collection by Joshua Smith, Samson Okcum [sic], and Others.* "Lord, when shall we mount up to thee" describes a God who is neither white nor red. Here is stanza one:

> Lord when shall we mount up to thee
> Upon the wings of grace,
> And see thy bright and lilly white,
> And ruddy, rosy face—

This text and others by Samson Occom demonstrate the power of hymnody as a venue for the creation, articulation, and elaboration of Christian Indian liturgy, imagery, and theology. They incorporate older Mohegan images such as the path or the beautiful trail, transform racialized figures like the raven, reclaim the wilderness for Christian Indians, and declare the "ruddy, rosy" complexion of God. In structural features such as repeated choruses and numerous stanzas, these hymns also facilitate the rituals of group singing that would forge and strengthen community bonds among Indian converts. Credit goes to Samson Occom for his vision as a poet and hymnodist, and for ushering into print this emergent strand of Native poetics.

The importance of hymn singing to the fledgling Christian Indian community at Brotherton is documented in Samson Occom's journals. When Occom finally arrived in Brotherton on October 24, 1785, as the leader of a group of emigrants, he was welcomed by a chorus of hymns:

> As I approach'd [David Fowler's] House I heard a Melodious Singing, a number were together Singing Psalms hymns and Spiritual Songs: We went in amongst them and they all took hold of my Hand one by one with Joy and Gladness from the greatest to the least, and we sot down awhile, and they began to sing again, and Some Time after I gave them a few words of Exhortation, and then Concluded with Prayer,— and then went to Sleep Quietly, the Lord be praised for his great goodness to us.[72]

Later journal entries show that Brotherton residents sang at Sunday worship services, weeknight house meetings, and traditional festivals. During the annual corn harvest—an event important to Mohegan community life—Occom wrote, "The Huskers Sung Hymns Psalms and Spiritual Songs the bigest part of the Time, finish'd in the evening, and after supper the Singers Sung a while, and then dispersed."[73] Ritual cycles of planting, harvesting, and preparing corn, or "yokeag," connected generations of Mohegan; these rituals continued at Brotherton, incorporating new community members and new songs. Five days after the corn harvest, Occom conducted Brotherton's first wedding. The ceremony was concluded with a "Marriage Hymn," number 106 from Occom's *Collection*; after dinner, Occom wrote, the wedding party "Spent the Evening in Singing Psalms Hymns and Spiritual Songs—and after that every went home Peaceably without any Carausing or Frollicking."[74] In hymnody, the community celebrated its bonds, old and new, tribal and Christian, ancient and elected. Like other rituals of work, worship, celebration, and condolence, hymn singing had a tremendous power to gather, transform, and incorporate. It conveyed singers beyond the constraints of conventional time into a sacred space where memory and hope, past and future, dead and living existed together.

Who would declare these Lazarus spaces exclusively Christian or Indian? Do denominations and racializations exist outside of human time? Occom did not presume to assign colonialist motives to God, or Godly motives to colonialism. Rather, he believed that a "strange providence" beyond human comprehension made him an Indian and then made him a Christian too. He was determined to live out these dictates and dedicated to the survival and renewal of his Christian Indian community. Through these labors, he found comfort when embraced by a strangeness full beyond his conception. One such comfort came to the sixty-three-year-old Samson Occom in a dream, which he recorded on April 2, 1786:

> Last Night I had a remarkable dream about Mr. Whitefield, I thought he was preaching as he use to, when he was alive, I thought he was at a certain place where there was a great Number of Indians and Some White People,—and I had been Preaching, and he came to me, and took hold of my wright Hand and put his face to my face, and rub'd his face to mine and Said, I'm glad, that you preach the Excellency of Jesus Christ yet, and Said, go on and the Lord be with thee, we Shall now Soon be done, and then he Stretched himself upon the ground flat on his face and reach'd his hands forward and made a mark with his Hand, and Said I will out doe and over reach all Sinners, and I thought he Barked like a Dog, with a Thundering Voice,—and I thought Some People Laugh'd Some were pleased, and Some were frightened. . . . This Dream has put me much upon thinking of the End of my Journey.[75]

Although he had dissolved his relations with most white ministers, Occom remembered with affection his late friend George Whitefield, who had once warned him of Eleazar Wheelock's mercenary designs. Now, in the space of dreams, Whitefield returns from the dead like Lazarus to comfort Occom: he gives him the right hand of fellowship, kisses him affectionately, and encourages him to continue in his faith. "I'm glad you preach the Excellency of Jesus Christ yet," says Whitefield, acknowledging the real discouragements that beset Occom's path. And then, the grand evangelist falls to his hands and knees and barks like a dog. Strange comfort, indeed. But such dreams were a vital part of Mohegan spiritual life, a fact recorded by colonial missionaries from David Brainerd to the Moravians, and attested to by contemporary Mohegan tribal historians Gladys Tantaquidgeon and Melissa Fawcett. In addition to conveying guidance, hope, and comfort, dreams were also important venues for the revelation of guardian spirits. Sometimes these spirits took human form, sometimes they appeared as animals, and sometimes a human spirit revealed its animal aspect at dream's end. To the Mohegan— the Wolf Clan of the Delaware tribal family—dogs held special power as spiritual intermediaries and protectors. In the sacred space of Samson Occom's dreams, grand evangelists become dogs: white Christians take on Mohegan shapes, just as Mohegans take up Christianity. Evidently, Occom's God spoke fluently and interchangeably in Mohegan and Christian forms, choosing the most appropriate instruments to uplift the faithful.[76]

In the last decades of the eighteenth century, African-American and Native American communities were developing new cultural and religious strategies for collective regeneration and emancipation. As a spiritual leader of the Mohegan and Brotherton Indians, it was Samson Occom's responsibility to choose the most appropriate instruments to uplift, encourage, and renew the community. He was as the "old Indian" of his own anecdote, adding new "blades" and new "handles" to an "Indian knife" that remained Indian still. More than the pained logic of his execution sermon, or the strained ethnographic confessions of his autobiographical narrative, Occom's *Collection* of hymns demonstrates how Indian people took up and breathed new life into Christian practices. It promulgates a new understanding of tradition not as the preservation of culture but as a constitutive, generative force in the community. Rituals of hymn singing allowed Native communities to engage with changing historical circumstances and transcend the chaos of everyday life. For contemporary readers as well, Occom's hymns have transformative potential. They challenge us to reimagine conversion in colonial Indian communities as an act of self-determination, creativity, power, and grace. They help us glimpse Occom's world in its inspiring vitality and providential strangeness: a ruddy-faced God; a sacred wilderness; guardian dogs; spirit trails; Indian knives with new blades and new handles; new tunes, and new singers.

3

John Marrant and the Lazarus Theology
of the Early Black Atlantic

Birchtown, Nova Scotia; November 1785

Just weeks after Mohegan minister Samson Occom joined his Christian Indian settlement at Brotherton, New York, another providential reunion was about to take place several hundred miles to the north, in the British Maritimes. The black Loyalist exile and evangelist John Marrant (1755–91) landed in Nova Scotia in November 1785, after an eleven-week sail from Gravesend, England. Marrant traveled with the blessing of the renowned Selina Hastings, countess of Huntingdon, who had hosted his ordination at her chapel in Bath on May 15, 1785. As an emissary of the Huntingdon Connexion, he was sent to Nova Scotia to preach the Connexion's brand of evangelical Calvinism, do battle against "free-thinkers" and Wesleyan Arminians, and serve the province's indigenous and black populations. The Huntingdon Connexion—and especially the late Reverend George Whitefield—had long demonstrated an interest in the religious welfare of blacks and Indians. Publicly, the ordination of John Marrant was a commitment to this end. Privately, Marrant was not motivated by patronistic or charitable but rather by more radical views: he believed himself a prophet, sent to Nova Scotia to initiate the redemption of scattered Africa. Thousands of African-Americans had been exiled to the province at the end of the War of Independence, in 1782. Fifteen hundred free black Loyalists established their own township at Birchtown. It was the largest community of free blacks outside of the continent of Africa.

Birchtown was one of several black Atlantic religious communities to take shape after the War of Independence. War produced massive dislocation and resettlement among African-Americans. Out of the chaos emerged new churches and new settlements with distinctive religious and racial identities. From Philadelphia's African Methodist Episcopal church to the First African Baptist church on the Kentucky frontier, from the

Huntingdonians of Birchtown, Nova Scotia, to the First Baptist Church of Kingston, Jamaica, these "citadels of African evangelism"—as historians Sylvia Frey and Betty Wood call them—were cells crucial to the formation of modern black political, religious, and literary culture. "As the only form of organized communal life available to slaves," Frey and Wood write, "evangelical institutions came to constitute important loci wherein African peoples could develop a sense of belonging and assert a cultural presence in the large society through the creation of their own moral and social communities."[1] It is important to note that these communities by and large did not rely on the dominant political discourses of the era as bases for their collective organization. Unlike the founders of the United States, they did not assume the "natural" and "self-evident" character of their societies. Rather, they gathered as a consequence of unnatural barbarity—the inhumane and arbitrary removals of the slave trade—and as an expression of supernatural faith. Through their reinterpretations of evangelical Christianity, black Atlantic communities like Birchtown sought to redeem the gross violence of enslavement, the confusion of diaspora, and the arbitrary imposition of race. They gathered in a diverse range of African-descended peoples: men, women, and children; former slaves, impressed sailors and soldiers, indentured servants, and freeborn; African, Caribbean, and American natives. Out of these differences, communities forged new common identities and envisioned new common destinies. They developed rituals of worship that dramatized the radical disruption and regeneration of their lives; they created theology and literature that sacralized their shared experiences of rupture, loss, and displacement. Together, they pieced together a narrative of community regeneration, which would lead some of these black Atlantic Christians— hundreds of Birchtowners among them—to emigrate to Sierra Leone in pursuit of an Africanist Zion.

The thirty-year-old Marrant knew intimately Birchtowners' experience of displacement and exile. Born free in New York in 1755, Marrant passed through a childhood "unstable as water" in Florida, Georgia, and South Carolina. After a corrupting apprenticeship to a worldly musician in the black-majority city of Charleston, South Carolina, the thirteen-year-old Marrant experienced a dramatic conversion under the ministrations of George Whitefield; years later, he himself would preach the gospel, first to Cherokee Indians, then to plantation slaves. The War of Independence interrupted his preaching activities: Marrant was impressed into the British Navy, wounded in battle, and hospitalized in England.[2] Denied a sailor's pension on his discharge, he remained in London and worked for three years. He also resumed his preacherly avocation as an occasional exhorter at the Spa-Fields Chapel of the countess Huntingdon. "During this time," Marrant recalled in his autobiographical *Narrative*, "I saw my call to the ministry fuller and clearer, had a feeling concern for the salvation of my countrymen: I carried them constantly in the arms of prayer and faith to the throne of grace, and had continual sorrow in my heart for my brethren, for my kinsmen according to the flesh."[3] Among these longed for "kinsmen" were relatives who had joined the black Loyalist exodus. A letter from his brother in Birchtown alerted Marrant to the community and its needs for religious leadership.[4]

Although his three-year Nova Scotian ministry touched whites, Indians, and blacks, Marrant selected Birchtown as the seat of his mission. There, he established a Huntingdonian church, appointed pastoral assistants, and organized a school. He also promulgated a powerful black Atlantic theology specific to the community's needs and experiences. Marrant's theology combined traditional Calvinist tenets such as predestination, absolute depravity, and justification by grace with more updated Edwardsean and New Divinity perspectives on dispensationalist history. Significantly, Marrant also restored the abandoned Calvinist concept of the covenant community as a site of regeneration, and he redeveloped this covenant theology for the black Atlantic. God had gathered Birchtown to advance the liberation and redemption of all black people, he preached; they were as the hidden "leaven," described in Luke 13:21, which would transform the whole.[5]

These teachings are documented in *A Journal of the Rev. John Marrant, From August the 18th, 1785, to The 16th of March, 1790.*[6] Published in London in 1790, the *Journal* is the most extensive black-authored account of evangelism and community life in the eighteenth century. It includes Marrant's seventy-five-page record of his North American mission, notes for about one hundred sermons preached, two full sermons, a list of subscribers, and letters, including one from the countess of Huntingdon.[7] In addition to its value as a documentary history of Birchtown and as an intellectual history from the early black Atlantic, the *Journal* is a consciously crafted account of a covenant community struggling to realize its prophetic destiny. What would their world look like after chattel slavery? Where were they to go? What were they to become? This chapter will examine the way race and faith took shape within historical narrative, and how the exigencies of black experience and the contours of black religion demanded and engendered new narrative forms. Marrant encouraged his Birchtown followers to view their daily lives as scripture, to attend carefully to their own thoughts and experiences as potentially revelatory. Likewise, in his *Journal*, Marrant compiles scriptural citations with dramatic accounts of his own travails in Nova Scotia, his parishioners' struggles for economic survival, and their shared experiences of the Spirit as it was manifest in religious meetings. From this interweaving of theological, personal, communal, and ecclesiastical histories emerge patterns or structures of feeling that reveal the shape of the community's covenant with God: separation and reunion, "falling out" and revival, death and resurrection. Like the tricksters of African and African-American folklore, and like the biblical Lazarus, the community had been chosen to outlive death as a witness to powers overruling the worldly, the rational, and the natural. The story of Lazarus is thus a key prototype for John Marrant's *Journal*, as it was for other early African-American narratives, and as it continues to be in black church culture today. It is a story that honors experiences of alienation, displacement, and loss even as it counters normalized assumptions about subjective control, coherence, and continuity. It is a narrative model appropriate to Birchtown, Marrant's *Journal*, and the broader black Atlantic as, in Paul Gilroy's words, a "counterculture of modernity."

Thousands of enslaved African-Americans won their freedom during the War of Independence, not in colonial secession from Britain but in siding with the failed Loyalist cause. The British hoped that by promising freedom for black Loyalist volunteers they might destabilize the slave-dependent domestic colonial economy, humiliate elite slave-owning colonists, incite slave rebellions, and recruit more soldiers. On November 7, 1775, John Murray, earl of Dunmore and royal governor of Virginia, issued the first such proclamation, declaring "all indented Servants, Negroes, or others, (appertaining to Rebels,) free that are able and willing to bear Arms, they joining His MAJESTY'S Troops as soon as may be." Several hundred slaves left their masters on the force of this declaration; under the direction of Dunmore, they formed an eight-hundred-member "Ethiopian Regiment" and wore uniforms emblazoned with the words "Liberty to Slaves." Similar effects followed General Henry Clinton's "Philipsburg Proclamation" of June 1779, which promised black defectors "full security to follow within these Lines, any Occupation which [they] shall think proper." Some slaves won their freedom by joining the British. Others were impressed into British military service, or taken as plunder by victorious British forces. Still others fled slavery during British raids on Boston, Philadelphia, Savannah, and Charleston, using the chaos and confusion as cover for their escape. At the end of the War of Independence, in 1782, the British evacuated almost three thousand free blacks from Savannah, Charleston, and New York, a move protested vigorously but unsuccessfully by the United States Congress.[8]

In order to answer American complaints of slave plunder, British officers supervising the Loyalist evacuation from New York to Nova Scotia carefully documented each black Loyalist emigrant. The three-volume

Book of Negroes they compiled contains the names, ages, birthplaces, and physical descriptions of almost three thousand black Loyalist emigrants, and it reveals a tremendous diversity among them. The emigrants were freeborn, former indentured servants, and ex-slaves; they were African-Americans, Afro-Native Americans, black Britons, native Africans, and French-speaking West Indians; and their birthplaces ranged from Massachusetts to Georgia, Antigua, Grenada, Jamaica, Barbados, Montserrat, and Guinea. A few wore traditional Gambian scars or "country marks" on their cheeks and brows: Pompey Linden, twenty-seven, formerly a slave in Rhode Island, had "cuts in each cheek"; Fanny, thirty-three, had "3 scars in each cheek"; and Bristol, forty, wore "3 marks between his eyes." Others came bearing the injuries and insults of slavery, including gouged eyes and crippled limbs. Many emigrants traveled in female-headed family units. Women too had won their freedom by joining the British forces: Peggy Croaker, twenty-four, and Peggy White, forty, left their masters in South Carolina to join British troops at Savannah in 1779. Hundreds of women emigrated with young children, including one remarkable ex-slave named Hannah Whitten, age thirty, who brought with her five children ages "8, 7, 6, 5, & 1 years old." The youngest of the evacuees was Peter Van Sayl, two months old, born free "within the British lines" to his escaped slave mother; the oldest were Ben Elliot and Mary Brown, ex-slaves, both sixty-nine years old. Ex-slaves with famous former owners included Deborah, twenty, and Harry Washington, forty-three, who escaped General George Washington, and Pompey Fleet, twenty-six, formerly enslaved to the Boston printer Thomas Fleet.

Once in Nova Scotia, this diverse emigrant population banded together to form all-black settlements. Birchtown, the largest, was established on the harbor shore opposing the port city of Shelburne and named in honor of British Brigadier General Samuel Birch, whose signature authorized the emigrants' certificates of passage. Although settlers hoped to clear lots, build homes, and put in crops before the onset of winter, forces natural and political conspired against them. The land at Birchtown was rocky and the growing season short; the provincial government failed to provide promised supplies and tools; and local whites delayed, reapportioned, and reduced land grants promised black Loyalists. Consequently, most of the emigrants found themselves still homeless at the onset of winter; those who did receive grants found their lands to be but a tiny fraction of those allotted white Loyalists. Many enrolled as laborers in the "black Pioneer Corps" and survived the snows in army barracks or tents, subsisting on "meal and molasses." Continuing economic hardship forced residents into tenant farming, perpetual indebtedness, or indenture. These difficulties were compounded by antiblack violence in the region, including a month-long riot by whites against the free blacks of Shelburne and Birchtown in July 1784. Elective affiliation as well as shared suffering formed the basis of Birchtowners' identity.[9]

The black Loyalists also shared in the intensity of their religious beliefs. Many had been affiliated with pioneering black Christian separatist movements in the colonies, and they established their own independent religious bodies in Nova Scotia. The province was generally friendly to separatist sensibilities, thanks to the ministrations of Henry Alline, a Rhode Island–born charismatic who itinerated successfully during the 1760s and 1770s. Alline preached to his fellow Yankee migrants that they were a chosen remnant of New England Congregationalism—"a people on whom God had set His everlasting Love"—charged with the preservation of the gospel in the wilderness.[10] His example helped prepare the way for similarly powerful black preachers and distinctive black churches. David George, an ex-slave who founded a pioneering Baptist congregation in Silver Bluff, South Carolina, in 1773, established another black Baptist congregation in Shelburne; among his fifty communicants were several former Allinites.[11] A black Anglican lay preacher named Joseph Leonard pastored the black Loyalist community at Digby. Although he had not been ordained, Leonard independently baptized children and converts, performed marriages, and administered communion; confronted by the bishop of Nova Scotia, he demanded ordination and explained that his congregation wanted "to be entirely independent and separate from the whites, and to have a church of their own."[12] The drive to establish separate black Nova Scotian churches was an essential component of the broader movement toward self-determination. It coincided with similar religious independence movements taking place around the black Atlantic, from the black Baptists of Kingston, Jamaica, to the black Methodists of Baltimore and Philadelphia.

Methodists maintained an influential presence at Birchtown, but they struggled to accommodate residents' strong separatist impulses. John Wesley himself recognized Birchtown's potential when he visited the region in 1784: "The little town they have built is, I suppose, the only town of negroes which has been built in America—nay, perhaps in any part of the world, except only in Africa. I doubt not but some of them can read. When, therefore, we send a preacher or two to Nova Scotia, we will send some books to be distributed among them; and they never need want books while I live."[13] American Methodist itinerants Freeborn Garrettson and John Oliver Cromwell came to Birchtown in August 1785, and they requested that the African-American exhorter Harry Hosier join them. Garrettson wrote to Francis Asbury: "There are several thousand coloured people in this province, and the greater part of them are willing to be instructed. What do you think of sending Harry here this spring? . . . I have no doubt but the people will support their preachers in this country."[14] Hosier never arrived. In his stead, Garrettson appointed two black Birchtowners—Moses Wilkinson and Boston King—to serve as local pastoral assistants. Both King and Wilkinson, who was described as "blind & lame" in the *Book of Negroes*, won fame for their fervent preaching.[15] Neither man, however, could independently lead the Birchtown Methodist church. Their appointment as pastoral assistants with limited power conformed to a wider pattern of racial discrimination within the hierarchy of the Methodist Episcopal church, which restricted the authority of its African-American lay preachers. The church did not ordain a black man until 1799, when African Methodist Episcopal church founder Richard Allen was made a deacon.

John Marrant's arrival in Birchtown in 1785 posed a significant theological, ecclesiastical, and political challenge to the Methodists. As an emissary of the Huntingdon Connexion, Marrant represented the opposing faction in a bitter Calvinist-Arminian debate. In 1783, the Connexion defended its Calvinist belief in predestination and formally disassociated itself from the Arminianism of Wesleyan Methodists. The Huntingdonian Connexion also differed from the Methodists in the degree of autonomy it afforded local churches and in its more progressive attitude toward black ordination. As early as 1774, the Connexion had educated and ordained a black Briton named David Margate, who subsequently served a controversial mission in the American South, where he declared himself "called to deliver his people from slavery." In Charleston, Margate met with hostility and threats of violence from enraged whites, and a local friend of the Connexion arranged for Margate's immediate transport to England. "His Business was to preach a Spiritual Deliverance to these People, not a temporal one," James Habersham advised the countess. "He is, if I am not mistaken, very proud, and very superficial, and conceited, and I must say it's a pity, that any of these People should ever put their Feet in England, where they get totally spoiled and ruined, both in Body and Soul, through a mistaken kind of compassion because they are black."[16]

The short-lived career of David Margate did not deter the Huntingdon Connexion from extending its endorsement to another black preacher who would also capitalize on his ecclesiastical authority and independence. John Marrant came to Birchtown with full pastoral authority: he was the only black man independently authorized to perform baptisms, marriages, and communions. For three years, he battled fiercely and publicly with "the Arminians" Moses Wilkinson and Freeborn Garrettson. Garrettson advised John Wesley: "A negro man, by the name of Morant, lately from England, who says he was sent by lady Huntingdon, has done much hurt in society among the blacks at Burch town. I believe that Satan sent him. Before he came there was a glorious work going on among these poor creatures, now . . . there is much confusion."[17] To Francis Asbury, the American Methodist bishop who played a crucial role in establishing the society among blacks in the American South, Garrettson wrote, "In and around Shelburne there are between two and three hundred members, white and black. Much hurt has been done by a black man sent by Lady Huntingdon."[18] In July 1786, Garrettson visited Birchtown, intending to dissolve the Huntingdonian congregation. But Marrant's followers rebuked him and sharply castigated him for calling their leader a "devil." One Huntingdonian elder said, "I can testify, and several others who are now in the congregation, that God made him the instrument of our souls conversion, for the devil never converted a soul in his life, nor never can he."[19] Curiously, Garrettson claimed success in having put Marrant out of town, reporting to John Wesley in September 1786 that "most of the coloured people whom Morant drew off have returned."[20] In fact, Marrant did *not* leave Birchtown, except for short stints of itinerancy, until January 1789.

What was at stake in these clashes between John Marrant, Freeborn Garrettson, and Moses Wilkinson was more than sectarianism. It was the distinctive identity and destiny of Birchtown itself. If the Methodist circuit riders saw Birchtown as just another whistle-stop, John Marrant came to Birchtown with a specific vision for the community's future. He embodied the emergent role of the preacher in black Atlantic Christian communities, which surpassed the limited denominational leadership opportunities then available to black men, exceeded conventional orthodox religious offices, and assumed political, cultural, and social powers. In short, Marrant was not a preacher, but a prophet. In his first sermon at Birchtown, on Sunday morning, December 20, 1785, he initiated his ministry by preaching from Acts 3:22–23: "For Moses truly said unto the fathers, A prophet shall the Lord your God raise up unto you of your brethren, like unto me; him shall ye hear in all things whatsoever he shall say unto you. And it shall come to pass, that every soul, which will not hear that prophet, shall be destroyed from among the people." His chosen text bore several powerful implications for the Birchtown community. First, it posits blackness as a marker of chosenness. The fact that God "raises up" prophetic leadership from within the black community—"of your brethren"—indicates that black people have a specific covenant relationship with God. Second, Marrant's declaration implies that membership in this black covenant community is not predicated on the accident of skin color but rather on faithfulness: "Every soul, which will not hear that prophet, shall be destroyed from among the people." Thirdly, by referencing Moses, this scripture positions black people as a latter-day Israel and suggests that the content of their covenant with God is liberation. It was Marrant's responsibility as a prophet to articulate and advocate this covenant relationship, to call the community to recognize and to realize its chosenness.

Especially within a community of black exiles and dissidents, the language of prophecy also carried a strongly oppositional political charge. Its emphasis on human authority, group distinction, and divine intervention set prophecy culture against the politics of republicanism. The antimony between the politics of prophecy and the politics of republicanism manifested itself within the sphere of early national culture as antipathy toward Islam. Newly made American citizens viewed the Islamic declaration of faith in the prophet Mohammed as typifying the dangers of submission to human authority. American newspapers in the 1770s carried ethnographic reports of despotic Islamic "prophets" from the conflict-ridden Middle Eastern colonies of the British Empire. Susanna Rowson's novel *Slaves in Algiers* (1794), Royall Tyler's *The Algerine Captive* (1797), and popular captivity narratives dramatized the cruelties of "Algerian" (Muslim) captors toward American sailors. Finally, some abolitionists blamed Islamic traders for the African component of the transatlantic slave trade. These popular notions of Islamic culture and civilization constructed slavery, tyranny, and fanaticism as the consequences of prophecy culture.[21]

Marrant's declaration of prophecy also challenged the religious residue of American exceptionalism. Was America a nation founded by the will of God? Was it the product of a divinely appointed exodus, a gathering? Was it possible that God might initiate other gatherings, other covenants, with other modern peoples? If so, could Americans still stake an exclusive claim to divine favor? White American theologians like Jonathan Edwards taught that the modern era was an age of evangelicalism but not prophetic activity. John Marrant declared that black people were on their own divine timetable and that prophecy had not passed away among them. He modified the view of slavery developed by Edwards' New Divinity school descendents, who held that slavery was a sinful albeit providential mode of introducing Christianity to Africa. Marrant flipped the script, repositioning blacks not as the passive and unfortunate objects of this design but as actors in their own divinely intended history. What role would the blacks of Birchtown—a gathered people, to be sure—play in this history? What did this history look like from the viewpoints of its true subjects? How was God manifest in their individual lives and common struggles? What shape would their history take? It was up to John Marrant and his Birchtown congregants to discover the forms, patterns, and contours of their collective story.

It is no simple project to conform the textures of human narrative to the designs of God. First, there are the basic problems of accuracy in reporting, given the partiality and limitations of human apprehension. Then, there are more intricate problems endemic to the medium: the strictures of syntax and narrative, sequence and sequentiality, causes and effects, beginnings and endings. These problems profoundly concerned the Congregationalists of the Massachusetts Bay Colony throughout the seventeenth century. Individually and collectively, they believed themselves participants in a Godly design, and they struggled to commemorate and realize that design through narrative confessions of faith and common histories. Meanwhile, Africans in America initiated a distinctive but parallel quarrel with God and narrative. Over the course of more than one hundred and fifty years, from the oral conventions of slave worship to the poetic reckonings of Phillis Wheatley, African-Americans confronted the challenges of using text as a medium for discovering the will of God in history. Compounding the general problems of representation were historical circumstances specific to the black Atlantic, which called into crisis the organizing assumptions—essential identity, subjective autonomy, sequential continuity, centripetal force, and temporal progress—of modern narrative and narrative history. Consequently and conscientiously, as agents of what Paul Gilroy calls "a counter-culture of modernity," black Atlantic authors like John Marrant developed narrative modes more responsive to their shared experiences of alienation, depersonalization, and displacement. Their narratives also constructed a distinctive concept of how God manifested and intervened in human affairs.

The first historians of Puritan New England attempted the weighty undertaking of writing scripture in real-time. Proceeding from the divinely appointed origins of their American settlements, they immediately augured events natural and supernatural, personal and impersonal, private and social for indications of their continued good standing with God. The paramount example of this approach to history is William Bradford's *Of Plymouth Plantation*. Bradford attempted to write the history of Plymouth as it was unfolding, to correctly place discrete events within the larger framework of heavenly intention. However, as the population grew beyond its original plantation, Bradford found it harder to maintain a unified story. Rather than falsely impose his own human desires on holy history, he conscientiously elected to abandon the project in 1647. Bradford's heirs were not so scrupulous or rigorous in their methods. Increase Mather attempted to salvage the providential concept of New England history by abandoning narrative for the methods of natural philosophy. Rather than analyze events in sequence, Mather concentrated on only the most remarkable experiences. As he explained in *The Doctrine of Divine Providence*

Opened and Applyed (1684): "There are some events of providence in which there is a special hand of Heaven ordering of them. There are *Magnali Dei*, things wherein the glorious finger of God is eminently to be seen . . . in plain legible characters."[22] These only were selected for systematic documentation, organization, and analysis in his *Essay for the Recording of Illustrious Providences* (1684). From the ruins of his father's scholasticism, Cotton Mather built the *Magnalia Christi Americana* (1702). The younger Mather's sweeping, protonationalist summary of American providences and judgments resuscitated and propelled forward William Bradford's abandoned thesis. It reconstructed American providentialism not as a day-to-day experiment but as a predetermined conclusion, an artfully crafted master narrative of self-evident force. The writing of the *Magnalia* preserved the innocence and integrity of its collective subject, which, like R. W. B. Lewis's "American Adam," remained essentially "untouched and undefiled."[23] If this kind of history emancipated the first New England generations from the darker, more complicated aspects of their experience, it also devolved on subsequent generations the perpetual responsibility for maintaining the story and keeping up appearances. This was the narrative economy of privilege and, incipiently, whiteness.

Early African-American narrative proceeded from radically different premises. Its earliest published instances—*A Narrative of the Uncommon Sufferings and Surprising Deliverance of Briton Hammon, a Negro Man* (1760) and *A Narrative of the Lord's Wonderful dealings with John Marrant, a Black (now going to preach the gospel in Nova Scotia)* (1785)[24]—reflect in form and content the constituting experiences of the black Atlantic. They depict a world of cruelty and instability. Their storylines are ruptured, episodic, and nonteleological. Their subjects confront a series of impossible circumstances—captivities, mortal dangers, near-death experiences, dead ends—from which there is no rational escape. Due to their unconventional, unresolving plot structures, neither Marrant's narrative nor Hammon's conforms to dominant autobiographical genres like the captivity narrative, the conversion narrative, or even the picaresque. Consequently, both have been criticized—by readers then and now—as underdeveloped, unrealized, and incomplete. In November 1785, London's *Monthly Review* snidely observed that Marrant's *Narrative* was "embellished with a good deal of *adventure*, enlivened by the *marvellous*, and a little touch of the *MIRACULOUS*."[25] Contemporary critics have sometimes construed Hammon and Marrant as mere tale-tellers, dependent on the manipulations and improvements of white amanuenses.[26] But such interpretations fail to recognize that these deceptively incomplete stories contain a profound commentary on power, experience, and agency. Just like the African and African-American trickster tales to which they are surely related, these narratives suggest that human history cannot be mastered. What Lawrence Levine observed of the trickster tales also applies to Marrant and Hammon: "Their eternal and inconclusive battle serve[s] as proof that man is part of a larger order which he scarcely understands and certainly does not control."[27] There is no principled movement, no sure arc from chaos to order, perdition to redemption, separation to reunion. Rather, these early narratives begin and end in uncertainty.

Marrant and Hammon convey these traditional trickster forms and themes into the context of Christianity. Both authors ascribe their survival to providence or divine intervention, suggesting that God is mindful of the precarious life-and-death struggles that characterized both slave and free black existence. Significantly, both narratives index the New Testament story of Lazarus. In John 11, Jesus raised the brother of Mary and Martha from the dead after four days in the tomb; Lazarus was reclaimed from death to become a story, an emblem of the resurrection, and a witness to the divinity of Jesus. By cross-referencing their own tricksterlike experiences with the story of Lazarus, Marrant and Hammon successfully communicate and assign meaning to the discontinuity and impossibility of their lives. What was life on the black Atlantic but a series of deaths and births? For the enslaved, it was involuntary relocation, separation from family, deprivation of name, loss of native language—in sum, as Orlando Patterson has compellingly argued, slavery was social death. Free blacks hardly experienced more secure circumstances. In addition to inheriting the alienation inflicted on their enslaved ancestors, they were subject to states of being approximating slavery—indenture, military impressment, criminal incarceration, perpetual indebtedness; nor did their nominally "free" status protect them from the dangers of kidnapping and resale.[28] As Patterson writes: "The essence of slavery is that the slave, in his social death, lives on the margin between community and chaos, life and death, the sacred and the secular. Already dead, he . . . can cross the boundaries with social and supernatural impunity."[29] Like Lazarus, African-Americans lived in a liminal state where redemption, rebirth, and resurrection were not hopeful abstractions but existential imperatives. Their lives were more closely communicated and interpenetrated with the materiality of a sovereign God and a delivering savior.

The autobiographical narrative of Briton Hammon begins as the enslaved Hammon leaves his master John Winslow to ship himself on an ill-fated English vessel. Shipwreck, Indian captivity, and forced servitude to a Caribbean colonial governor follow, then impressment, imprisonment, illness, and indenture. Finally, thirteen years later, Hammon unexpectedly meets his master on board a ship at sea: "My good master was exceeding glad to see me, telling me that I was like one arose from the dead, for he thought I had been dead a great many years."[30] Indeed, like Lazarus, Hammon had been miraculously recovered from death not once but several times during his thirteen-year hiatus. His mute response to his master conveys the irony of his situation: these death-defying experiences allowed him more movement and freedom than life with Winslow. The *Narrative* of John Marrant also incorporates the figure of Lazarus, in connection with the story of Joseph in Egypt. After his dramatic conversion at age fourteen, John Marrant fled into the wilderness to escape the scorn of his unconverted family. His wanderings brought him into contact with several Indian tribes—Cherokee, Creek, Housaw, and Catawa—to whom he preached Christianity and from whom he adopted a new manner of appearance: "My dress was purely in the Indian stile; the skins of wild beasts composed my garments; my head was set but in the savage manner, with a long pendant down my back, a sash round my middle, without breeches, and a tomohawk by my side."[31] Returning home months later, Marrant discovered that his family believed that he had been "torn in pieces by the wild beasts," nor could they identify him through his new "Indian stile" appearance. Wrote Marrant, "I was overcome, and wept much; but nobody knew me." Finally, a younger sister recognized and embraced him. "Thus the dead was brought to life again; thus the lost was found."[32] This anecdote closely recalls the Old Testament story of Joseph, who was betrayed by his brothers, sold into slavery, and reported to be dead—as Jacob thought, "an evil beast hath devoured him"; eventually, he rose to favor in the Egyptian courts, where he experienced a dramatic reunion with his brothers (Genesis 37:29–25; Genesis 45:1–5). Joseph was a powerful model for many early black and white abolitionist writers.[33] In relating his own story to both Lazarus and Joseph, Marrant forges an Old Testament–New Testament correlation paralleling the Moses-Jesus connection so critical to emancipatory black religious thought. By reworking this association from the viewpoint of the captive rather than the viewpoint of the deliverer, Marrant can elaborate on the sufferings of slaves and captives. In particular, the link between Joseph's restoration to family and Lazarus's restoration from the grave indicates that slavery is an alienating and depersonalizing form of social death. Thus, his story also addresses the distress felt by many African-Americans who feared that their removal from Africa made them permanent aliens, doomed to wander after death rather than return home.[34] It forges a link between death, social death, and the Israelite sojourn in Egypt, with promises of resurrection and redemption.

The Lazarus pattern develops through a number of life and death scenarios in Marrant's *Narrative*. First, Marrant represents conversion as a physical experience of death and rebirth. His own dramatic conversion took place at a George Whitefield–led revival in Charleston. Marrant entered the meeting daring to disrupt it with his French horn but was stopped in his tracks by Whitefield's declaration, "Prepare to Meet thy God o Israel." These words struck him "speechless and senseless" for almost half an hour; he could not stand on his own strength, and had to be carried out of the meeting: "Every word I heard from the minister was like a parcel of swords thrust into me."[35] Doctors were called to rescue him, but Marrant refused the medicines and sunk into a convulsive state for three days. His sister worried that "the lad will surely die."[36] But a Baptist minister forcibly prayed over him. "I asked him if he intended to kill me?" 'No, no, said he, you are worth a thousand dead to me."[37] These prayers finally liberated Marrant from his soul pains, and on the fourth day—like Lazarus—he returned to life.

Marrant also represents mortal danger as a chosen space where one can access "clearer views into the spiritual things of God."[38] For example, after his conversion and persecution by his family, Marrant resolved that "it was better for me to die than to live among such people."[39] Carrying only a Bible and an Isaac Watts hymnbook, he set out into the "wilderness," where he faced wolves and bears, searched vainly for food or water, was reduced to his knees by weakness, and prayed that God would "command the wild beasts to devour me, that I might be with him in glory."[40] Although these days were "much chequered with wants and supplies, with dangers and deliverances," Marrant remembered, "the Lord Jesus Christ was very present, and that comforted me."[41] Years later, as an impressed sailor on board the British vessel the *Scorpion*, Marrant experienced this same presence at sea. He was washed overboard three times, nearly devoured by sharks, and "covered" with "blood and brains" during fierce naval engagements. These dangerous episodes were to Marrant's mind the means for his spiritual redemption: "a lamentable stupor crept over all my spiritual vivacity, life, and vigour; I got cold and dead . . . [but God] roused me every now and then by dangers and deliverances. . . . These were the means the Lord used to revive me, and I began to set out afresh."[42] Entering into the wilderness, whether voluntary or involuntary, on land or at sea, forces the narrator to confront death and to find in that confrontation a new orientation toward life.

Finally, in the authoritative fourth edition of his *Narrative*, Marrant represents black religion as an enterprise itself fraught with mortal dangers. Under the oppressive conditions of slavery, even the practice of faith was liable to swift and cruel retribution from white owners. Marrant established an evening school for about thirty slaves on a South Carolina plantation, where he was employed as a carpenter. The school was soon discovered and its participants brutally punished, at the behest of their slave-mistress Mrs. Jenkins. Marrant remembers:

They caught them, and tied them together with cords, till the next morning, when all they caught, men, women, and children were strip'd naked and tied, their feet to a stake, their hands to the arms of a tree, and so severely flogg'd that the blood ran from their backs and sides to the floor, to make them promise they would leave off praying, &c. though several of them fainted away with the pain and loss of blood, and lay upon the ground as dead for a considerable time after they were untied.[43]

Because he was a free man, Marrant did not receive punishment but instead charged the slave-owner, Mr. Jenkins, that "the blood of those poor negroes which he had spilt that morning would be required by God at his hands."[44] The scene constructs the slave worshippers as types of the crucified Christ, "strip'd naked," hung arms outstretched on a "tree," "flogged," and left for dead. It offers a dark and sober parallel to Marrant's own conversion story. If he had "fainted away" "as dead," passing through a kind of death to prepare for the new birth, what was the daily life of slaves but an extended preparation? If he had passed episodically through the valley of the shadow, they lived in the shadow of death every day. By virtue of their unthinkable sufferings and improbable survivals, black slaves were then material witnesses to resurrection and revival.

Thus, the character constructed by early African-American narratives is not an American Adam but rather an American Lazarus. Lazarus embodies the imposed discontinuities, cruelties, and mortalities of black Atlantic life, as well as an elective orientation toward change. The figure of Lazarus also indicates the challenges of representing black experience by conventional narrative means; the improbability, or irrationality, of life as a series of near-death experiences defies modern assumptions about narrative, agency, and subjectivity. As an emergent figure within and a symbol of early African-American culture, Lazarus represents the drive to claim life from death and meaning from chaos, to honor through stories shared experiences of loss, and to witness to the possibility of redemption. Willing confrontation with death indicates the depth of black alienation as well as a radical commitment to what Paul Gilroy has called the "politics of transfiguration." As Gilroy argues, in early African-American literature, death is a commentary on freedom:

It supplies a valuable clue towards answering the question of how the realm of freedom is conceptualised by those who have never been free. This inclination towards death and away from bondage is fundamental. It reminds us that in the revolutionary eschatology which helps to define this primal history of modernity, whether apocalyptic or redemptive, it is the moment of jubilee that has the upper hand over the pursuit of utopia by rational means. The discourse of black spirituality which legitimises these moments of violence possesses a utopian truth content that projects beyond the limits of the present.[45]

It was this prophetic vision of utopia that John Marrant would pursue in his ministry at Birchtown, this Lazarus theology that he would extend to an entire community.

John Marrant arrived at Shelburne, Nova Scotia—the port city neighboring Birchtown—on December 16, 1785. At first, he found Shelburne to be a disappointment and wondered if "God had some people in this place." His prayer was answered the next morning at breakfast, when an old friend came into his lodge and sat down at his table. At first, this man did not recognize Marrant, then "burst into a flood of tears" when he did. He soon after conducted Marrant to Birchtown, where they met more familiar souls and "talked about old times, which made us shed many tears."[46] As a close parallel to the "Joseph in Egypt" homecoming in his 1785 *Narrative*, this scene establishes Marrant's arrival in Birchtown as a reunion. It also inaugurates one of the key narrative patterns—separation and reunion, death and resurrection, "falling out and revival"—which would resonate throughout his Birchtown ministry and his *Journal*. These patterns took their shape from the hardships Marrant and his parishioners experienced in Nova Scotia, as well as within a theological context that prophesied regeneration for black covenant communities.

His Nova Scotian ministry exposed Marrant to extreme hardship, both at Birchtown and in the surrounding areas that he serviced as an itinerant. In accordance with the Huntingdon Connexion's mandate that its ministers preach constantly and itinerantly, he visited small settlements of impoverished blacks, Indians, and whites scattered along the southeastern coast between Shelburne and Liverpool. In these places—Green Harbor, Ragged Island, Sable River, Cape Negro, and Jordan River—as at Birchtown, the people struggled to maintain themselves by subsistence farming and fishing. Long winters, short growing seasons, deep snows, rocky soils, and rough seas frustrated their efforts. Famines and smallpox epidemics afflicted the region. When he was able, Marrant took part in community relief efforts. In May 1786, when Birchtown found itself abandoned by its appointed colonial officer—the black "colonel" Stephen Blucke—residents asked Marrant to petition the Halifax government on their behalf for badly needed supplies, including "tools, spades, hoes, pickaxes, hammers, saws and files . . . and blankets."[47] He successfully accomplished the task. He also contributed to efforts to build chapels at Birchtown and Preston, another black Loyalist community. But certainly his missionary status did not shelter him from the hardships endemic to the region, and his extensive itinerancy exposed him to the additional dangers of traveling through swamps, deep snows, icy rivers, and rough seas. By the spring of 1787, Marrant found himself in increasingly dire circumstances: a famine afflicted the region, he contracted smallpox, his funds expired, he had even been forced to pawn his jacket, and still the Huntingdon Connexion failed to respond to his requests for support. An unusually long winter, poor lodging, and meager diet protracted Marrant's illness. His *Journal* records:

> Although the people did all that they could, and gave the best attendance that laid in their power, yet that was very poor nourishment for a sick person in the state I was then in; for I must inform my readers, that in my greatest illness, my chief diet was fish and potatoes, and sometimes a little tea sweetened with treacle, and this was the best they could afford, and the bed whereon I laid was stuffed with straw, with two blankets, without sheets; and this was reckoned a very great advantage in these parts of the globe; for in some places I was obliged to lay on stools, without any blanket, when the snow was five and six feet on the earth, and sometimes in a cave on the earth itself.[48]

Marrant's parishioners looked to him for relief despite his poor condition. While he was confined by smallpox at Birchtown, Marrant wrote, "[I] had many distressing objects before me, who were continually coming begging, and were really objects of pity, and were perishing for want of their natural food for the body."[49] Shortly after he recovered from his illness, traveling on the road to Birchtown, he discovered two black women—one dead in the snow, one standing over her weeping. "They had both been over to Shelburne, to beg something to eat, and were then returning back to Birch Town, and had got a little Indian meal, but had not strength to reach home with it," Marrant explained.[50] He started back on the snowy road to Birchtown with the living woman—"sometimes we both fell down together, I being so weak after my late illness"—and he officiated at the burial of the deceased. Several times during this season, Marrant was called to small villages in the region to conduct funerals. Not surprisingly, death is a major concern in his *Journal*. It shadows the daily experiences of Marrant and his parishioners, and it informs the theology Marrant developed for them.

Marrant was an evangelical Calvinist, an ordained member of the Huntingdon Connexion, which had split from Wesleyan Methodism in 1783 in reaction to Methodist Arminianism. In Nova Scotia, Marrant taught the absolute depravity of humankind and justification by grace alone. During one exemplary encounter with "free-thinkers" at Jones Harbor in January 1786, he asserted that "they could not think any good thing of themselves; but some said they never had any bad thoughts, and I insisted upon it they never had any good ones."[51] This brand of Calvinism would have been considered both conservative and radical by late-eighteenth-century standards. Whereas mainstream American Protestantism was moving ever closer to a universalist view of salvation and a republican conception of holy society, Marrant preached predestination and regeneration within covenant communities. His vision of the plan of salvation—almost narrative in its movement from predestination before time to gathering at the end of time—also reflects the influence of the New Divinity school. The hallmark of the ultra-Calvinist New Divinity, which emerged in the mid eighteenth century among students of Jonathan Edwards, was absolute providentialism: God overruled sin by using it to fulfill the grand design. New Divinity men like the Reverend Samuel Hopkins attempted to closely reckon human history to sovereign intention. Hopkins in particular developed a highly influential providentialist view of slavery. As the pastor of the First Congregational Church in Newport, Rhode Island, he had witnessed firsthand the wages of the slave trade as it was carried out on the city's docks, and he subsequently founded the African Union Society, an organization for free and enslaved blacks. He argued that the slave trade, albeit sinful, was an appointed means to the Christianization of Africa. Among whites, this understanding of slavery was put in the service of colonizationist schemes to resettle African-Americans in Africa, and Hopkins himself pursued this end by training Bristol Yamma and John Quamine, two members of his African Union Society, to serve missions in Africa. Although many blacks did not share in this enthusiasm for expatriation, some—notably the Reverend Lemuel Haynes—did value the historical and theological value the New Divinity assigned to the modern oppression of black people.[52] Similarly, it appears that John Marrant selectively adopted elements of New Divinity belief. He did not assume the ultimate benignity of human sins such as the slave trade and slavery: his own experience as a lay preacher among slaves in South Carolina led him to condemn slaveholders that God would "require" a "blood" atonement from them. Nor does it appear that Marrant assumed Africa to be the foreordained destination for American blacks; nowhere in the *Journal* does Marrant refer to or preach from the most heralded biblical texts about Africa, such as Psalms 68:31. He did develop a New Divinitylike historical view of black slavery as a meaningful part of God's design, but he particularized the significance of black suffering to the covenant relationship between God and his modern black Israel.

Combining elements of providentialism, predestinarianism, and covenant theology, Marrant preached that God had chosen the enslaved and oppressed descendents of Africa as special witnesses to and emblems of his overruling power. Just like the resurrected Lazarus, they had been called forth to manifest the power of God to emancipate and regenerate. Moreover, just like another New Testament Lazarus—the outcast beggar taken into the "bosom of Abraham" (Luke 16:20–31)—they would know God as an opponent to worldly relations of oppression. In heaven, Lazarus found comfort, while his oppressors found torment. The theology of Lazarus was a theology of overturning, revolution, and transformation. It sanctified the paradoxes of black Christian life as indices to the "contrariety" of God. These teachings provided Marrant's followers with a new understanding of the hardships they survived under slavery and encountered in Nova Scotia. No good works, according to Marrant's Calvinist theology, could have overcome the evils of this world; oppression was not the consequence of insufficient efforts but rather the evidence of their covenant with God.

The *Journal* textualizes this covenant relationship as it interweaves scripture with remarkable incidents from the lives of Marrant and his congregants. As John Saillant observes, "With nearly one hundred biblical references, Marrant imbued his *Journal* with a text beyond the chronicle of his itinerary—a text narrating the divine design given for black people in the Bible. The biblical references in his *Journal* set the sufferings, triumphs, and hopes of his audience in God's providential design."[53] This design emerges especially in the scriptures Marrant selected for his sermons at Birchtown. His introductory sermon, preached on the morning of December 20, 1785, from Acts 3:22–23—"For Moses truly said unto the fathers, A prophet shall the Lord your God raise up unto you of your brethren, like unto me; him shall ye hear in all things whatsoever he shall say unto you. And it shall come to pass, that every soul, which will not hear that prophet, shall be destroyed from among the people"— established Birchtown as a covenant community, a latter-day Israel, complete with active prophets. For his second sermon, preached later that afternoon, Marrant chose his text from John 5:28–29: "Marvel not at this: for the hour is coming, in which all that are in the graves shall hear his voice, and shall come forth; they that have done good, unto the resurrection of life; and they that have done evil, unto the resurrection of damnation."[54] As a sequel and complement to the morning's preaching, this sermon communicated a sense of timeliness and urgency to the design. "The hour is coming," Marrant preached, "in which all that are in the graves shall hear his voice, and shall come forth." Here, Marrant compares the gathering of Birchtown to the answering of a divine call and to the resurrection of Lazarus. It was God's will that black people should come forth from the mortifications of chattel slavery and be gathered into regenerate covenant communities. As one of the first all-black postslavery communities in the New World, Birchtown was an important part of this design.

Marrant's most extensive elaboration of God's design for Birchtown took place on December 25, 1785. Christmas day was important both as a commemoration of the birth of Jesus and as a traditional holiday for slaves. Some black communities—especially in North Carolina—used Christmas to celebrate the West African-descended festival of John Kunering.[55] For his part, Marrant used Christmas as an opportunity to perform religious rites that the community's lay preachers were not empowered to do, including ten baptisms and four marriages.[56] Then, in the evening, he preached from Isaiah 60. The chapter does not reference the birth of Jesus but rather announces the coming of Zion: "Arise, shine; for thy light is come, and the glory of the LORD is risen upon thee" (v. 1). It prophesies for God's chosen people a "gathering" of "sons" and "daughters" "from far," an amassing of worldly wealth, the establishment of political power, as well as "beauty," "glory," "light," "righteousness," and peace (v. 4–18). In the spirit of Lazarus, this glorification follows a season of oppression and suffering. "In my wrath I smote thee, but in my favour have I had mercy on thee" (v. 10). It also indicates a righting of past injustices and a dispensation of punishment on the unjust:

> The sons also of them that afflicted thee shall come bending unto thee; and all they that despised thee shall bow themselves down at the soles of thy feet; and they shall call thee, The city of the LORD, The Zion of the Holy One of Israel. Whereas thou hast been forsaken and hated, so that no man went through thee, I will make thee an eternal excellency, a joy of many generations. (v. 14 – 15)

The chapter concludes by foretelling the appointed emergence of a "strong nation" (v. 21). It was a vision that must have resonated powerfully with Marrant's audience members, committed as they were to their own freedom and to the founding of an all-black settlement. Such a prospect justified their sufferings under slavery and their hardships in Nova Scotia as a preparatory episode to a remarkable transformation, the transfiguration of scattered and oppressed black people into a righteous nation.

This Lazarus theology recurs more subtly in subsequent sermons as an emphasis on the paradoxical nature of power. On July 7, 1786, Marrant preached from the Beatitudes: "Blessed are the poor in spirit: for theirs is the kingdom of heaven. Blessed are they that mourn: for they shall be comforted" (Matthew 5:3–4). Months later, in December, he preached twice from Psalm 73, which exposes the false power of the worldly and prosperous. The psalmist admits to having envied their ease but in a moment of visionary radicalization—described as "a dream when one awaketh"—comes to recognize the bondage and barbarity of privilege: "Pride compasseth them about as a chain; violence covereth them as a garment" (v. 6). The scripture also prophesies that when God "awakest" worldly powers will be overturned. "Surely thou didst set them in slippery places: thou castedst them down into destruction" (v. 18). Both this psalm and the Beatitudes criticize the arrogance of power. They also assign to the poor and oppressed a superior spirituality, a capacity for vision, and a glorious future. Birchtown's impoverished population surely appreciated this teaching.

The *Journal* also includes the full text of a funeral sermon, preached on October 27, 1787, which advocates courage in the face of death as an exercise of faith. The deceased was a recent convert named John Lock, Jr., an impoverished, illiterate man who lived with his family in the village of Jordan River. For more than "twenty years," no clergy had visited the Lock household; Marrant found John Lock, Jr., to be "ignorant of God and himself." "I asked him what he thought would become of his wife and three children, if they should die in that state," Marrant remembered. "He answered nothing but cried; so after supper I went to prayers with them, and he continued sobbing the whole night."[57] Some months after his conversion, while suffering a fatal bout with smallpox, Lock requested that Marrant preach his funeral sermon from Philippians 1:21: "For me to live, is Christ; and to die, is gain." Marrant opened his address by acknowledging the toll the epidemic had taken on the region: "Death has late been walking round us, and makes breaches upon breach upon us, and now has carried away the head of this family with a sudden stroke."[58] Marrant used the occasion to expound on the Calvinist tenet of "weaned affections," or detachment from worldliness as a necessary precondition for justification. He preached that a proper understanding of death would foster a rejection of worldly values and a "correspondent" disposition of one's life to the glory of God.[59] Improving on the sociopolitical aspects of this doctrine, Marrant argued that their hardships better qualified the poor and the oppressed for salvation: "The doctrines of Christ and his interest, are not calculated to gratify the pride, and carnal reasonings of the polite world, in the present age; the instances of the great, and noble that are called are very rare."[60] Those who did not fear death or love the world too much were, like Paul, more emboldened to resist "principalities and powers."[61]

Conviction and courage still did not diminish the hardships of this world. This Marrant acknowledged, and he promised that death would deliver the elect from their "houses of clay."

Death will put an end to all the weakness and miseries they have groaned under in this life. . . . There is nothing to break the thread of their peace, and intense pleasure to endless ages. "God shall wipe away all tears from their eyes." Rev. xxi. 4. not only relieve all their sorrows, but entirely remove them, absolutely and eternally banish all things uncomfortable, and sin the cause of them, to the remotest distance.[62]

Not only would physical and spiritual sufferings find relief in heaven, but God would also comfort the faithful with a complete and wholly satisfying understanding of their sufferings in life. Marrant did not subscribe to the New Divinity conceit of the intelligibility of God's will in human history. "God often hides the sensible signs of his favour from his dearest friends, and leaves them in such inextricable windings, that they know not what course to steer," he preached.[63] "Some things are so variable, or mixed in providence, that we are ready to say, 'wherein does the holiness and glory of God appear in them?'"[64] Death, however, would remove the mediate "obscurity" of the "word," resolve "seeming contradictions," introduce a more "familiar knowledge," and reveal the "grand design."[65] In this context of understanding, satisfaction, and relief would the ideal of the holy community be fully realized:

When death let them out of these dark cottages of flesh, they have such clear views of the glories and grace and of the Lord Jesus Christ, exemplified in the saints in light, and at the same time are divested of self, as to be entirely united in one indissoluble bond of love, without any mixtures of envy, or shadows of ill will, they have one heart and one soul and are entirely as well pleased with the blessings conferred upon each other, as upon themselves.[66]

Marrant taught his followers to expect an overturning of worldly relations of domination in heaven, just as Lazarus the beggar had found comfort and understanding in the bosom of Abraham. This teaching was not meant to pacify his listeners, but rather to embolden them. It confirmed the contrariety between the ways of the world and the ways of God, and it honored the paradoxes they lived as God's chosen people. It encouraged them to confront fearlessly hardship, oppression, and even death.

These teachings are also reflected in the narrative content of the *Journal*, which interweaves dramatic conversion stories with equally dramatic episodes from Marrant's itinerancy. Marrant represented his own ministry as a physical and sometimes violent struggle with death. In February 1786, he proselyted at the home of an "abandoned woman," a former prostitute, "one that had been on board a man of war" during the War of Independence. Although his traveling companions warned him not to approach her house, Marrant insisted because "it was impressed upon my mind to go in and see them."[67] The woman cursed him, then beat him with a pair of fireplace tongs, drawing blood from wounds to the head and hands, and finally drove him from her house by beating him with a broom. Marrant took refuge in a barn and prayed, "lifting my hand up which was then bleeding, and the blood trickling all over my face, begging the Lord to search my heart, whether I had lost these drops of blood for the gospel of Christ, and the good of souls. . . . [I said] If it is his will that I should spill more blood, in his cause, I was willing."[68] He was "strengthened and encouraged" to return, confront, and subdue the woman. As Marrant went to prayer on her behalf, she "fell off from the bed, as though she was shot, and screamed out with a loud voice, and stretched herself off, as though she was going out of the world."[69] Two days she remained in this state, faring "worse and worse," growing "pale as death," while a "frightened" multitude gathered outside her home; Marrant preached to them from Luke 13: 5, "Except ye repent, ye shall all likewise perish." Finally, on the third day, she "got up" and "praised God in a remarkable manner." Recognizing the wounds in Marrant's hands, she "begged" his forgiveness. Wrote Marrant, "I told her that Christ had pardoned her and [that] I had nothing against her."[70] Continuing important themes and patterns from Marrant's 1785 *Narrative*, the scene depicts conversion as resurrection. For this woman, as for John Marrant, the new birth entailed a physical if virtual passage through death, taking place over a three-day time frame paralleling Jesus' death and resurrection. The violence, bloodletting, and crucifixion imagery in this episode also recall the brutal punishment of Marrant's slave catechists in South Carolina. It locates the exercise of faith in the confrontation with death and establishes the wounded as emblems of Christ.

Death was also a more quotidian concern for Marrant, as his itinerancy put him, in the language of 2 Corinthians 11:26, "with Paul, in peril at sea, in peril in the wood, in peril in the city."[71] During the spring of 1787, Marrant suffered a severe bout of smallpox that turned his pulpit into a spectacle of morbidity. Preaching on April 25 at Birchtown, he "began to bleed in the pulpit and was taken out."[72] Months later, after another round of illness, which confined him to his house with "the spitting of blood" for seven days, he attempted to return to his Birchtown pulpit to preach the regular Sunday service. "About the middle of the discourse I found myself pretty warm, had much liberty, so exerted myself, forgetting my former illness," Marrant writes, "but before I concluded I was nearly strangled with blood. The blood came running out at my nose and mouth, so that the people were all frightened. They took me out of the pulpit and carried me into my house."[73] In addition to illness, his travels exposed him to the dangers of icy river crossings and rough seas. False reports of his demise by drowning circulated constantly, vesting his homecomings with a sense of the miraculous. Marrant was often received by his parishioners as a man returned from the dead.

Beyond these false alarms, his *Journal* records two instances when Marrant was miraculously delivered from near fatal circumstances. In November 1787, Marrant lost his way while wandering through a Nova Scotia swamp. Exhausted, he laid himself down to rest, in the snow. Twice he "felt something push" him; twice he ignored the prompting. He writes:

> I was touched again in the former manner, but more powerfully, which was accompanied with a voice which I thought said arise, why sleepeth thou in a dangerous place? I arose with surprise, and searched all about for a quarter of a mile round, and fancying that there was some human person laid by, but had hid himself; but after a little while it came into my mind that it was the Lord, then I wept, and was full of trouble, because of my slothfulness in going to sleep in a wilderness, where I was certain I had lost my way.[74]

Only a few weeks later, Marrant once again found himself alone and lost in the woods, as a snowstorm descended. He wandered for two days— "sometimes reading, sometimes praying, and sometimes crying"—and slept in a bear's cave at night as "the God who saved David and Paul from the mouths of the lions and bears" prevented its erstwhile inhabitant from entering.[75] On the third day of wandering, famished and exhausted, Marrant laid down "with my bible under my head, and commended my spirit to God who gave it."[76] Soon after, he was discovered by two women in a search party: "One was rather frightened and started back, the other came and laid her hand upon me, perceiving life was still in me; she said to the other, he is alive, so they raised me up, and two men came and took me away."[77] In his *Journal*, Marrant celebrates this restoration: "Here we see the amazing and boundless love of God, in delivering his people from the jaws of death."[78] Both of these stories assume a parabolic value. In the first, the effective interposition of an invisible hand and a divine voice place Marrant's rescue in the liminal space between physical and spiritual, heavenly and human realms. The second bears clear resemblance to scripture, in the story of Lazarus and the story of Christ's resurrection, as indicated by the women who discover the dead to be alive. It is this symbolic convergence that marks a covenant relationship: for chosen people, life and scripture blend and merge indefinitely.

It comes as no surprise, then, that the key patterns that connected black experience to Lazarus theology—sleep and awakening, death and resurrection—found expression in the bodies of Marrant's followers. Indeed, within the space of worship, their very bodies became texts, manifesting the overturning and reviving powers of God. Marrant's *Journal* consistently records these significant acts. They include vocal expression: "singing," "groans and sighings," "weeping," and "crying" so loud that it overwhelmed the preacher's own voice.[79] For Marrant himself, the outpouring of the Spirit had an inverse effect, leaving him unable to speak for five minutes or more.[80] Other worshippers expressed themselves in bodily syntax. They fainted and had to been "carried out," or were "struck down on the floor, apparently dead."[81] At one revival, sixteen people had "fallen to the ground," so Marrant "took the bason" and "baptised them on the floor."[82] At another meeting in Birchtown, Marrant records, "Here I stood astonished to hear the shouts of the people, and the groans of poor sinners, God's word went as a two-edged sword, and poor sinners were slain. I concluded the discourse, and came out, leaving several of them lying on the floor stretched out as though they were dead."[83] Those who were not struck down by the Spirit were elevated and invigorated beyond the natural reach of sleep. Marrant frequently reports that worshippers stayed up until four or five in the morning, singing hymns, exclaiming praises, but refusing to return to their homes.

Around the black Atlantic, and especially in its separatist religious communities, the act of worship was being imprinted with a distinctive black style. Marrant's report from Nova Scotia corroborates others from America and the Caribbean in documenting visions, trances, shouts, and "falling out" as elements of black revival worship. By 1800, these performative elements took their place within a broader culture of American evangelicalism, but noted historians from Melville J. Herskovits to Mechal Sobel agree that they were introduced to our religious idiom by African-descended peoples, who remembered and reinterpreted traditional rites within a New World context.[84] Whatever these behaviors came to mean to white revivalists, among black worshippers, their significance was inextricably connected to and determined by black experience. Distinctive black worship rituals must not be viewed only as relics of African culture, but as creative responses to New World conditions. Take, for example, the black Protestant emphasis on immediate conversion, aptly described by Sylvia Frey and Betty Wood as "the principle motif of their pilgrimage, the key to their religious transformation."[85] If this overwhelming and instantaneous conversion experience descended from African spirit possession rituals, as has been suggested, its meaning to black religionists was also determined by their experiences of possession and repossession, disruption, alienation, transport, and transformation under slavery. The performed elements of immediate conversion—shouts, trances, loss of consciousness—echoed and expressed the discontinuities and liminalities imposed by the slave trade. To undergo such a conversion, then, was to enact the spiritual content of slave experience, to radicalize the relationship between past and present, and to negate the assumed finality of enslavement and white domination. It was to witness with voice and body, against the cool and ghostly facades of worldly privilege, to the reality of an unstable, convulsive, unmasterable higher power. Finally, as a collective and even collaborative social performance, like water baptism and the ring shout, the performance of immediate conversion marked a passage from African ethnic to modern black identities.[86]

The immediate conversions remembered in Marrant's *Journal* powerfully complement his articulate Lazarus theology and its episodic fulfillments in narrative. Indeed, reading the bodies of black worshippers not as passively represented entities but as active social texts disrupts the modern notion of written language as authoritative and final. It suggests that early black narratives do not take shape along assumptions of linear progress but rather, like trickster tales and Lazarus stories, around moments of interruption and transformation. Describing the expressive aspects of the "politics of transfiguration," Paul Gilroy writes, "This politics exists on a lower frequency where it is played, danced, and acted, as well as sung and sung about, because words, even words stretched by melisma and supplemented or mutated by the screams which still index the conspicuous power of the slave sublime, will never be enough to communicate its unsayable claims to truth."[87] Or, as John Marrant wrote after his improbable, even miraculous restoration from death in the snows of Nova Scotia: "I assure thee, Reader, I am at a loss for words; but this I know, experience goes beyond expression."[88]

Because the *Journal* of John Marrant takes shape around moments of transformation, in the interstices between scripture and experience, it does not give readers the detailed personal history featured in many eighteenth-century autobiographies. The *Journal* provides little information about Marrant's closest relationships or his family. [89] It affords us neither the satisfaction of strict daily discipline nor that of teleological accomplishment. John Marrant struggled through his final months in Nova Scotia. His health was poor, his destitute parishioners could scarcely afford to maintain him, and the ailing countess Huntingdon did not answer his requests for support. Depleted by illness and devoid of funds, Marrant sailed for Boston in January 1789. There, he would come into the considerable sphere of influence commanded by Prince Hall, the founder of black Freemasonry, a visionary theorist of black identity, and a tireless community organizer. Under Hall's tutelage, Marrant joined the African Lodge of Freemasons and served as lodge chaplain. On June 29, 1789, at the lodge's St. John the Baptist Day commemoration, he delivered a keynote sermon from Romans 12:10: "Be kindly affectioned one to another, with brotherly love, in honour preferring one another." Marrant would preach to his black brethren, and before an invited audience of white dignitaries, that they were the descendents of a noble African line, that God had endowed them with an inalienable inheritance of arcane wisdom and insight. Some months later, still seeking contact with his sponsoring connection, Marrant returned to London, where he died in April 1791. He was thirty-five years old.

Back in Birchtown, the Huntingdonian congregation continued to pursue Marrant's vision of a regenerate black community. Marrant had taught them that such a community must be responsive to the callings and leadings of God, that they must always "face Zion forward."[90] Now, after years of preparatory exile in the proverbial wilderness of Nova Scotia, the community was faced with a new prospect for their future. Representatives of the Sierra Leone Company, including John Clarkson, brother to famed abolitionist Thomas Clarkson, traveled to Nova Scotia in November 1791 to recruit voluntary emigrants from among the province's free black population. An estimated two thousand black Nova Scotians embarked for Sierra Leone in January 1792.[91] Not surprisingly, almost every one of Nova Scotia's black evangelists—including David George, Boston King, and Moses Wilkinson—joined the company. So did the whole of John Marrant's Birchtown congregation. Led by his two appointed successors, Cato Perkins and William Ash, they disembarked at Sierra Leone singing this selection from the Huntingdonian hymnal:

Ye slaves of sin and hell,
Your liberty receive;
And safe in Jesus dwell
And blest in Jesus live.
The year of jubilee is come;
Return, ye ransom'd sinners, home![92]

Its troubled modern history has since shown Sierra Leone to be no Zion. However, this does not disprove the strength of John Marrant's vision or the faith of his followers. The real power of Lazarus theology was in the space of radical change, at the edge of the tomb, in the hands of God, where life merged with scripture and prophecy with history.

4

No

Prince Hall Freemasonry:
Secrecy, Authority, and Culture
Boston, Massachusetts; February 1789

On February 1, 1789, celebrity black Atlantic preacher John Marrant landed in Boston. Financial hardship and physical exhaustion induced the thirty-four-year-old Marrant to abandon his three-year mission in Nova Scotia and his congregation of black Loyalist exiles; now he found himself, as he remembered in his *Journal*, like Abraham, "in a strange country knowing nobody."[1] Carrying letters of introduction from his sponsor, the renowned Selina, countess of Huntingdon, Marrant called at the homes of several Boston ministers. He was soon conducted to the home of Prince Hall, whom Marrant described as "one of the most respectable characters in Boston."[2] Hall (1738?–1807) was a tireless, visionary organizer of Boston's emergent black community. He had been manumitted from slavery in 1770; in March 1775, six months before the battle of Lexington and Concord, he and fourteen other free blacks were initiated into the Masonic Order by members of Irish Military Lodge # 441. After the war, Hall served as grandmaster of Boston's African Lodge of Freemasons. From the shops where he ran his catering and leather-tanning businesses—under the sign of the Golden Fleece on Water Street, and later, near the Quaker Meeting House on Quaker Lane—Hall nurtured the organizational beginnings of what would become a major force in African-American community life.[3]

John Marrant lodged with Prince Hall during several turbulent months of preaching to large crowds in Boston's West End. During the spring of 1789, Marrant was initiated into the African Lodge of Freemasons. He kneeled—perhaps blindfolded, torso partially exposed, the point of a blade at his throat—before Prince Hall and African Lodge officials; he repeated secret passwords and performed signal gestures. These secrets Marrant swore to uphold on penalty of death. To celebrate this making of a new brother, African Lodge members ceremonially reenacted the death and resurrection of Hiram Abiff, architect of Solomon's Temple and founder of the first Masonic fraternity. They also recounted the history of their order: its divine origins, its Egyptian and North African anciency, its scattering into modernity. Now, this ancient wisdom had come home to the brethren of African Lodge #459 in Boston, Massachusetts.

How this curious alchemical attraction between free northern blacks and Freemasonry came into being is something of a mystery. Some scholars have suggested similarities between the Masonic Order and West African traditional secret societies, particularly the Poro of Sierra Leone.[4] Others see the initiation of Prince Hall and his fellows as an accident, or as a strategic attempt to gain insights into the secrets and powers of white men. Once initiated, however, Hall demonstrated both an authentic commitment to the principles of the order and a real aptitude for developing a distinctly African-American brand of Freemasonry. Seventeenth- and eighteenth-century Freemasonry lent itself to such adaptations and developments. It fostered a variety of confraternal enterprises: learned societies, mystical cabals, and political cells; the Royal Society of England and the Library Company of Philadelphia, as well as the Jacobin clubs of France.[5] Hermetic alchemy, Newtonian science, cabalistic mysticism, neo-Platonism, Jacobinism, republicanism, materialism, pantheism, natural religion, and universalism—all of these were articulated, explored, and negotiated within the social and textual venues of the order. Many lodges came to forsake arcana and ephemera for the polite *lingua franca* of the bourgeois Enlightenment. And yet, as Masonic historian Margaret Jacob has argued, there was in late-eighteenth-century Freemasonry a significant "porosity" towards local settings and concerns.[6] A Masonic lodge, according to Jacobs, was a potential "exit from the Enlightenment," a space for mystical, subversive, or resistant activities.

It is this mystical and subversive potency that Prince Hall and his fellows cultivated within the African Lodge. Like the independent black churches emergent in the same era, Freemasonry provided a precious venue for the development of fellow feeling, the exercise of black political authority, and the discussion of spiritual principles; members enjoyed the pleasures of ritual, the pride of corporate distinction, and the powers of secrecy. This element of secrecy secured social bonds and demarcated boundaries between insider and outsider, sacred and profane; African Lodge officials were obliged to guard these boundaries by regulating membership and meeting attendance. Consequently, the lodge enjoyed a rare degree of freedom from white oversight and interference. Its official chartering in 1787 furnished the African Lodge of Boston with a declaration of independence: it established an autonomous "African" cultural, political, and ritual space in America.[7] Prince Hall and his fellows turned the secrets of the Masonic temple into a template for racial consciousness. Within this space, members learned to criticize white supremacist narratives of the history of civilization and to claim for black peoples a central role in that history. They recollected from Masonic source-texts an ancient and noble African history, reconstructed a corporate identity through the formulas of the Masonic order, and reclaimed an empowering sense of interiority by regulating access to lodge rituals and membership. This chapter examines three foundational texts in the history of Prince Hall Freemasonry: John Marrant's *Sermon to the African Lodge of the Honourable Society of Free and Accepted Masons* (1789) and Prince Hall's *Charges* to the lodge at Charlestown (1792) and Menotomy (1797).[8] Hall and Marrant delivered these speeches at public celebrations of Masonic holidays. There, before audiences of black and white Bostonians, they revealed that the legacy of ancient Egypt and the biblical destiny of Ethiopia belonged to African-Americans. And, according to Hall and Marrant, this destiny was already unfolding.

W. E. B. Du Bois once speculated that "the tale of Ethiopia the Shadowy and Egypt the Sphinx" was a remnant of "Egyptian" and "African" ideas preserved by the diaspora's "scattered" "tribes."[9] Early African-American cultural formation and historical consciousness have continued to intrigue and vex scholars, from St. Clair Drake and Martin Bernal to Mary Lefkowitz and Molefi Asante.[10] Time has not demystified the origins of blackness; indeed, scholars continue to affirm its "veiled" origins in "instinct," "ideology," or "experience."[11] One recent and helpful study— Michael Gomez's *Exchanging Our Country Marks: The Transformation of African Identities in the Colonial and Antebellum South* (1998)—represents the transition from ethnic African identities to a racial African-American identity not as a process of attrition but rather as a conscientious collective undertaking. Gomez writes, "This basic dialectic—the adoption of an identity forged by antithetical forces from both without and within the slave community—is itself emblematic of the contradictory mechanism by which the African American identity was shaped."[12] Although his research focuses on southern slave and free populations, his dialectical approach is a welcome corrective to dichotomous readings of black culture as *either* African survival *or* European borrowings. This dialectic view challenges us to denaturalize our assumptions about the birth of culture, to suspect meaning in apparently coincidental or accidental events. It demonstrates that African-Americans did exercise creative, politicized, and principled agency in the development of new identities, new cultures, and new discourses. This principle is critical to the study of early African-American literature, which yields up its secrets only to faithful, suspicious, and vigilantly inductive readers.

A strictly historicist approach to the problem of early literate African-American cultural formation inevitably fails to fully appreciate the extent, creativity, and resourcefulness of black authority. This is because historical forces such as imperialism, slavery, and racism have impacted the representational quality of the historical record. Important factors here include the differential documentation of African-American lives in government, church, business, and private records; differential access to political representation, literacy, publication, and preservation; and the politicized assumptions guiding the composition of "official" state histories. This last problem especially has been addressed by members of the subaltern studies group, who correctly point out several limitations in statist and imperialist historical narratives: these limitations include the assumption of history as a sequential narrative of progress rather than as a series of confrontations and cataclysms; the denial of agency to insurgents; and the failure to account for signification as a site of historical contention and negotiation. All of these material and immaterial forces have shaped contemporary understandings of African-American intellectual history, its points of origination, and its modes of development.

The literature of eighteenth-century Prince Hall Freemasonry provides new insights into this history. It challenges the long-held assumption that black political discourses first emerged in the shadows of nineteenth-century white abolitionism. Scholars have long cited two texts published in 1829—Robert Alexander Young's *Ethiopian Manifesto* and David Walker's incendiary *Appeal to the Colored Citizens of the World*—as the first print instances of Ethiopianist or black nationalist discourse. Wilson Jeremiah Moses defines black nationalism as "the ideology that argued for the self-determination of African Americans within the framework of an independent nation-state"; Ethiopianism is described by St. Clair Drake in his landmark *Black Religion and the Redemption of Africa* (1970) as an empowering view of black identity based in the biblical text Psalms 68:31, "Princes shall come out of Egypt; Ethiopia shall soon stretch out her hands unto God."[13] One strictly historicist account of the sources of Ethiopianism argues that African-Americans "got the idea" of a powerful African past from eighteenth-century historical and scientific writings by European-Americans—including Samuel Stanhope Smith's *Essay on the Causes of the Variety of Complexion and Figure in the Human Species* (1787) and the comte de Volney's *Ruins; or Meditation on the Revolutions of Empires: and the Law of Nature* (1789; published in the United States in 1802)—which were excerpted in the American Colonization Society's *African Repository* and reprinted in *Freedom's Journal* (1827–28).[14] Speeches by Prince Hall and John Marrant document the lively presence of Ethiopianist ideas within the black community almost three decades before

Young and Walker. They also challenge the notion that black discourses about Africa were wholly borrowed from, dependent on, and mediated by white texts. Rather, they reveal a dialectical process of creative elaboration in the development of African-American culture and identity.

African-Americans did not have to wait for the nineteenth-century publications of the American Colonization Society or for the more emancipatory *Freedom's Journal* to access and participate in eighteenth-century discussions of Africa. Indeed, during the 1780s and 1790s, the relationship of black peoples to Africa and America was a subject of intensive political, theological, and natural-historical consideration by both whites and blacks. In February 1787, the British-sponsored Sierra Leone project embarked, resettling hundreds of American and British blacks in this West African colony. The project also revived American interest in colonization, which some whites viewed as potential remedy for the slave trade and as a prophylactic for the threat of racial amalgamation. The resettlement of black slaves in Africa was a key component of Philadelphia publisher Mathew Carey's "Philosophical Dream" (*Columbian Magazine*, October 1786)—an utopian vision of the United States in 1850. Imagined Carey, "Very few blacks remain in this country now: and we sincerely hope that in a few years every vestige of the infamous traffic carried on by our ancestors in the human species, will be done away."[15] More extended considerations of the subject included Thomas Clarkson's *Essay on the Slavery and Commerce of the Human Species* (1785) and Thomas Jefferson's *Notes on Virginia* (1787). Observing with alarm the high growth rate of the slave population, Jefferson asked, "Will not a lover of natural history, then, one who views the gradation in all the races of animals with the eye of philosophy excuse an effort to keep those in the department of man as distinct as nature has formed them?"[16] One such "effort" suggested by Jefferson was the removal of African-Americans to a territorial possession of the United States. William Thornton, later a Jefferson appointee to the Patent Office, traveled the New England lecture circuit in the late 1780s to promote his own African colonization scheme. Thornton found an interested audience with the Reverend Samuel Hopkins, pastor of the First Congregational Church and founder of the African Union Society in Newport, Rhode Island. A New Divinity man, Hopkins adhered to an Edwardsean-dispensationalist view of history and accordingly held slavery to be a providential instrument for the millennial Christianization of Africa. In the 1770s, Hopkins imagined that black members of his African Union Society might serve this heavenly design as missionaries in Africa, but Thornton convinced him of a more ambitious and sweeping colonizationist plan. In Hopkins's words, this plan would "gradually draw off all the blacks in New England, and even in the Middle and Southern States, as fast as they can be set free," thereby absolving America of the sin of slavery.[17] Hopkins and Jefferson differed sharply on many points of racial ideology—indeed, Hopkins would have considered Jefferson's polygenism to be heretical—but they agreed that America would be redeemed in the resettlement of its black population.

Among black people themselves, there was no uniformity of opinion about the relationship between geographical Africa and black liberation. Hopkins successfully recruited African Union Society members Bristol Yamma and John Quamine to train for missionary service in Africa, but he was rebuffed by Phillis Wheatley. "How like a Barbarian Should I look to the Natives," Wheatley opined. "I can promise that my tongue shall be quiet for a strong reason indeed being an utter stranger to the Language of Anamaboe."[18] Her ironic response inverts the paradigms of savagery and civilization which framed the Hopkins missions, and it pokes fun at the reductive racialized thinking which failed to recognize the cultural and linguistic divides between Africa and African-Americans. Wheatley's black literary contemporaries—American and British—shared her ambivalence. Consequently, in their writings, they adopted a range of personas, autobiographical devices, and representational strategies to position themselves in relationship to Africa. Some like James Albert Ukawsaw Gronniosaw and Olaudah Equiano presented themselves as African princes, remembering their early years in Africa as fantastic or Edenic. Wheatley assumed an iconic "Ethiopian" persona, and her writings rehearse the passage "from Africa to America" more frequently than they recall Africa itself. Finally, American-born black authors like John Marrant articulated little or no native connection to Africa, instead characterizing themselves as types of the transformative biblical character Lazarus.

Africa did figure significantly as a *keyword* in the postemancipatory political development of northern black communities. Beginning with Pennsylvania in 1780, northern states moved slowly to establish legal bases and pass legislative measures to enact a gradual emancipation of African-American slaves and indentured servants. Despite the painfully slow and partial character of these emancipation acts, a measurable migration of newly freed blacks to northern cities began in the 1780s and 1790s. There, in urban centers such as Philadelphia and Boston, they organized mutual-aid associations, establishing a new domain for the conception and articulation of black and African-related identities, politics, and theologies. Boston's African Lodge of Freemasons played a signal role in developing a black public presence. The lodge relied on the scaffolding of Masonic customs such as parades, feasts, and meetings and Masonic values such as public "propriety" and "dignity" to construct its public character. Both appearances and perceptions were carefully monitored by Prince Hall. For example, on December 30, 1782, Boston's *Independent Ledger* reported the African Lodge celebration of St. John the Evangelist's day. According to the report, "Saint Black's Lodge of Free and Acc-pt-d M-s-ns" proceeded "dressed in their aprons and jewels," "up State-Street, and thro' Corn-hill, to the house of the Right Worshipful Grand Master, in Water-Street, where an elegant and splendid entertainment was given upon the occasion."[19] Soon after, Hall filed a correction with the printers:

> Our title is not St. Black's Lodge; neither do we aspire after high titles. But our only desire is that the Great Architect of the Universe would diffuse in our hearts the true spirit of Masonry, which is love to God and universal love to all mankind. These I humbly conceive to be the two grand pillars of Masonry. Instead of a splendid entertainment, we had an agreeable one in brotherly love.[20]

It is noteworthy that Hall lead his complaint with a point of nomenclature. He wanted the fraternity to be known by its chosen name—the African Lodge—rather than by the false name—"St. Black's"—assigned by satiric observers. Africa dignified; the fictional "St. Black" did not.

The African Lodge also utilized high-profile petition drives to establish its political presence in the state of Massachusetts. Its petitions reflect a consistent concern with the needs of black Bostonians and evolving strategies and attitudes toward Africa. In January 1787, on the eve of the Sierra Leone project, Hall and seventy-three other African-American men petitioned for assistance in emigration, explaining that conditions in Boston "induce us to return to Africa, our native country, which warm climate is more natural and agreeable to us; and for which the God of nature has formed us; and where we shall live among our equals and be more comfortable and happy, than we can be in our present situation; and at the same time, may have a prospect of usefulness to our brethren there."[21] Although the petition was unsuccessful, its text documents influential elements of early black political thought. The petitioners combined natural historical and New Divinity arguments for colonization: both the "God of nature" and the God of providential history intended them for Africa, an environment which afforded them a more natively "comfortable" climate as well as opportunities for "usefulness" as missionaries, teachers, and Christian exemplars. Just ten months later, in October 1787, Hall returned to the Massachusetts legislature with a radically different set of demands. He and his fellow petitioners demanded that the state provide public education for black children. Arguing that the tax dollars exacted from black workers should not be withheld from their families, Hall claimed for African-Americans the "no taxation without representation" logic of the American Revolution and implicitly the full rights of citizenship. This petition was also rejected by the legislature, but again it marks an important change in early black political thought: a swift and thorough rejection of the logic of colonization, which held Africans in America to be perpetually alien. The petitions of January and October 1787 reveal a striking revision in the community's concept of itself and its future. They demonstrate a revaluation of the roles of geography and nation, Africa and America, birthright and citizenship. Sometime during the spring or summer of 1787, Prince Hall recognized that the welfare of Boston's black community rested immediately with its domestic political power.

What caused this marked change in African Lodge polity? Perhaps the increasing popularity of colonizationist ideas among whites spurred Hall and his fellows to a critical reexamination of their premises. We can be certain that Prince Hall carefully monitored newspapers and periodical writings about issues affecting the black community; had he read, for example, Mathew Carey's "Philosophical Dream" of an "unspotted," African-free America, he would have discerned readily the antiblack prejudices undergirding colonization. Events internal to the African Lodge also factored into this ideological shift. On April 29, 1787, the lodge received its official charter from the Grand Lodge of England, thereby securing its independent operating authority. For almost a decade, the lodge had operated under provisional permits from Irish Military Lodge #441 and from Provincial Grand Master John Rowe. Both racial and national politics complicated the chartering process: first, there were delays associated with the Revolutionary War, then deferrals by American lodges unwilling to sanction black Freemasonry. Finally, in March 1784, Prince Hall wrote a letter to William Moody, master of a London Masonic Lodge, who had received two members of the African Lodge traveling to London. Hall enlisted Moody to present the lodge's petition for a charter to the Grand Lodge of London. "Though we have been importuned to send to France for one," Hall explained, "yet we thought it best to send to the Fountain from whence we received the Light for a Warrant."[22] African-Americans perceived the British to be more friendly on race matters, and many had sided with the Loyalists during the Revolutionary war. They found no cause for disappointment in the conduct of the English Grand Lodge, which overrode American Masonic authorities to directly charter Boston's African Lodge. Although the charter was issued in early 1785, financial and organizational mishaps delayed its arrival in Boston by almost two years. Not since the post-Restoration intrigue of the Bay Colony had an English charter been so anxiously awaited in Massachusetts. This charter secured to the African Lodge of Freemasons the authority to claim and regulate an autonomous venue for black thought, speech, and activity. No longer was Africa the only conceivable habitat for Prince Hall and his fellows: they had established a physical, ritual, and social space for themselves in Boston.

Rejecting colonization did not mean turning away from Africa. Rather, it meant a freedom to establish a more imaginative, historical relationship to Africa unbounded by the narrow rigidity of nativism and "natural" identities. Freemasonry furnished Prince Hall and his fellows with a functional model of a community founded in textually reconstructed history. Masons emphasized the historicity or "anciency" of their order as a measure of its legitimacy. This emphasis emerged in the seventeenth century, when English guilds of practicing stonemasons opened their fraternity to nonartisans. With this shift from "operative" to "speculative" Masonry, the basis for affiliation shifted from practical craftsmanship to metaphysical principles, secret passwords, and rituals. Freemasons self-consciously inscribed this profound transformation within a historical narrative of revelation or recovery: practical Masons had been entrusted through the ages with the knowledge of geometry; modern Freemasons were the recipients of that ancient and holistic wisdom and participants in its restoration. Initiation into Freemasonry meant admission to a transhistorical fraternity of wise men, magi, philosophers, scientists, and mystics. To emphasize the transhistorical character of the order, modern initiation rituals centered around the recitation of Masonic genealogy—the so-called proof of "anciency."

The basic narrative of Masonic "anciency" recounted the development and propagation of building or civilizing knowledge from the Garden of Eden to Solomon's Temple. But these narratives were also elastic texts, subject to revision by individual lodges. According to one late-seventeenth-century version, the principles of geometry were inscribed onto a pillar by Jubal Cain, discovered there after the flood by the Egyptian magus Hermes, received in turn by Abraham, Euclid, and "Aymon," "master of Geometrie and the chiefest master of all his masons" at work on Solomon's Temple.[23] Eighteenth-century editions of this history—including James Anderson's standard-setting Masonic *Constitutions* (1723)—distanced Freemasonry from occultish associations by removing references to Hermes Trismegistus and oriented it more closely to Judeo-Christian traditions by rerouting the narrative directly through Noah. Still, these organizational impulses toward orthodoxy did not discourage individual Freemasons from antiquarian fascinations with Egyptian magi, Pythagorean mystery cults, Jewish Gnostics, and Druids. Through creative elaboration and encyclopedic accretion, in private notebooks, circulated manuscripts, and published writings, variant crypto-Masonic fragments continued to accumulate and circulate.

During the late seventeenth and eighteenth centuries, English Freemasons adapted the lore of anciency to suit their own ethnic, religious, and political sensibilities. Isaac Newton and archeologist William Stukeley celebrated the cabalistic kernels of Freemasonry; moreover, they claimed that Druids were but displaced Semitic peoples—a lost tribe of Israel, who carried Abrahamic religion and Masonic tradition to Northern Europe. Irish freethinker John Toland (1670–1722) rejected this Judeo-Christian orthodoxy and instead asserted the Celtic pagan origins of Freemasonry. His *Pantheisticon* (1720) proposed a Druidicial Masonic rite, and his *History of the Druids* (1722) located parallels to Druidism in Egyptian antiquities and Pythagorean mysteries. For Toland and his fellow republicans, these Freemasonic-Celtic researches served distinctly political purposes: they discovered in indigenous paganism a "natural" religious antidote to the king-making regimes of the Anglican and Catholic churches, and they identified Freemasonry as a prime venue for the development of an antimonarchical morality. As Margaret Jacob observes, this Druidical Freemasonry maintained its popularity among the English and Anglo-American partisans of the radical enlightenment, including Thomas Paine.[24]

Claims of "anciency" were also used to challenge exclusionary practices within the Masonic order. In the 1720s, working-class Irish Masons living in London were barred from entry to the city's more aristocratic English lodges. English officials claimed that Irish Masonic rituals were irregular and that the Irish lodge itself was "clandestine"; the Irish countered, claiming to be the "Antient" practitioners of the craft and therefore not subject to "Modern" English regulation. Under the leadership of Irish-born grand secretary Laurence Dermott, they established their own "Grand Lodge of Ancients" in 1751. Dermott authored a new constitution for the Ancients, *Ahiman Rezon*, which served as a primer in Masonic lore and lodge organization. Published and distributed widely in Britain and its colonies, *Ahiman Rezon* furnished upstart lodges with a Freemasonic manual and, more important, with a means of self-legitimation. By 1771, there were more than 140 Ancient lodges. Ancients were especially active in chartering military lodges, for the benefit of rank-and-file soldiers excluded from participation in elite officer class gatherings.[25]

Political tensions between Ancients and Moderns replicated themselves in early American Freemasonry. During the 1730s, the Modern English Grand Lodge appointed provincial masters to regulate Freemasonry in the American colonies. But the colonies already sustained a number of operating lodges—in Philadelphia, Savannah, Boston, New York, Charleston, and Cape Fear, North Carolina—independent of English sanction. Attempts to coordinate far-flung, locally organized, and self-authorizing colonial lodges under a single metropolitan authority inevitably floundered. Moreover, the metropole-identified, elitist character and Tory political culture of the Modern lodges fell out of favor among American Freemasons, who imagined themselves to be (and to some extent were) a more populist fraternity of artisans and merchants. By the end of the Revolutionary War, Modern Freemasonry had all but disappeared from the former colonies, and American lodges emphasized their independence from Britain by establishing an Ancient-identified national grand lodge.

American Masonic primers adopted and then adapted the English lore of Freemasonic anciency. *A candid disquisition of the principles and practices of the most antient and honourable society of Free and Accepted Masons*, published in Boston in 1772, asserted that "Freemasonry was introduced in Britain by the first inhabitants" and cultivated by Anglo-Saxon kings from Athelstone onward.[26] This Celtic indigenism was deemphasized in manuals published after the Revolutionary War, which instead attributed the advent of English Freemasonry to Continental influence. Pennsylvania Grand Lodge's edition of *Ahiman Rezon* (1783) claimed that the first Freemasons were sent to England "at the request of Saxon Kings, by Charles Martell, King of France, more than one thousand years ago."[27] The lodge also reprinted a fabled Masonic document: a fifteenth-century catechism entitled "The Mystery of Maconrye," originally attributed to King Henry VI, but allegedly transcribed in 1696 from a Bodleian Library manuscript by the philosopher John Locke and addressed to the earl of Pembroke. The late-middle-English-styled document traces the history of Freemasonry through one "Peter Gower, a Grecian," who "journeyedde ffor Kunnynge yn Egypte, and yn Syria, and yn everyche Londe whereas the Venetians hadde plauntedde Maconrye; Wynnynge Entraunce yn al Lodges of Maconnes, he lerned muche."[28] Returning to Greece, this "Peter Gower" established lodges, from which Freemasonry was transmitted to France and, finally, England. Notes attributed to John Locke identify "Peter Gower" as a mistranscription of the name "Pythagoras" by an "unlearned Clerk." This elaborate document—first published in the *Gentleman's Magazine* in 1753—has been judged a forgery by contemporary scholars. Still, it is a striking example of how the lore of Masonic anciency was remodeled and revised to suit new political sensibilities, national allegiances, and cultural identities. The document connects Pythagoras and Locke; Egypt, Greece, France, and England; mystery and philosophy; mathematics and politics; ancient and modern. As reprinted by the Pennsylvania Grand Lodge, it confers on American Freemasons a privileged access to all of these.

The principle of "anciency" was essential to the founding and development of Prince Hall Freemasonry. The first black Freemasons were initiated by an *Ancient*-affiliated Irish military lodge stationed in Boston on the eve of the American Revolution. The Irish Ancients were among the most egalitarian of Freemasons, and their extension of fraternity to black men invites speculation about revolutionary-era alliances between colonial subalterns—Irish Continental Army soldiers and African-Americans. As Prince Hall Freemasonry grew beyond its chartering moments, the African Lodge established its own rituals and its own version of the narrative of Masonic anciency. Every time Prince Hall and his fellows recited the standard proof of anciency, at every initiation, they heard praise for the ancient wisdom of Egypt. Masonic history specified that the building trade and its attendant wisdoms originated in North Africa and did not arrive in northern Europe until many centuries later. This no doubt did not fail to impress the African Lodge, to vest lodge members with a new discursive means to articulating historical consciousness, racial pride, and claims to equality if not superiority. That the black Freemasons quickly moved to reclaim and reorient the Masonic narrative of anciency is clear from the first extensive published accounts of African Lodge activity. In 1788, Philadelphia publisher Mathew Carey's *Columbian Magazine* filed a somewhat satirical report of an African-American Masonic lodge, which, though denied legitimacy by white Masons, nonetheless defended its ancient rights to the order. The *Magazine* published a versified version of the lodge's "proof of anciency," translated from the "*Mandingo* language" and translated into "English doggeral" by "a gentleman, formerly concerned in the African commerce."[29] The African lodge orator claimed that the ancient wisdom of Freemasonry belonged first to black peoples, emphasizing the role of Cain in Masonic genealogy: Cain "buil[t] the FIRST city—Ergo, then / This ground we safely rest the case on, / That brother Cain was the first mason." This proof of African primacy also serves as a basis for an oratorical challenge to polygenism and a defense of the legitimacy of modern black Freemasonry. The orator does acknowledge that he has taken some creative license with Masonic genealogy— "where 'tis short to give it length'ning, / Or where 'tis weak to give it strength'ning."[30] If Carey intended this as a satirical jab at the fraudulence of the African lodge, it was instead a fairly accurate reflection of the textual inventions and revisions—shortenings and lengthenings, weakenings and strengthenings—fundamental to the character of eighteenth-century Freemasonry. The *Columbian Magazine* report partially glimpsed the African lodge's particular claims to anciency. The fullness and potency of this story would soon be publicly revealed.

On the festival of John the Baptist, June 24, 1789, Masons celebrated with parades, speeches, and feasts. This was the day Prince Hall selected for a public exposition of African Lodge–style Freemasonry, an exposition he carefully organized and produced. Earlier that spring, Hall had initiated John Marrant into the African Lodge and invited him to serve as lodge chaplain; he engaged this black Atlantic celebrity preacher as featured speaker. Hall also invited leading white and black Bostonians to attend the public rites, and he enlisted printers and prominent Freemasons Thomas and John Fleet to publish and distribute a commemorative edition of Marrant's *Sermon*. The title and frontispiece design of this published edition— *A Sermon Preached on the 24th Day of June 1789, Being the Festival of St. John the Baptist, at the Request of the Right Worshipful the Grand Master Prince Hall and the Rest of the Brethren of the African Lodge of the Honorable Society of Free and Accepted Masons in Boston by the Reverend Brother Marrant, Chaplain*—emphasize the name of Prince Hall and indicate his involvement at every stage in the *Sermon*'s production. The text is the product of a collaborative composition by the grandmaster and the minister. It reflects their respective Masonic and ministerial rhetorics, as well as their shared vision of a powerful, transhistorical black community.

The *Sermon* explicitly addresses itself to the challenges of community formation. Marrant opens by announcing his text, Romans 12:10: "Be kindly affectioned one to another, with brotherly love, in honour preferring one another." The scripture recalls Paul's instructions to early Christian converts struggling to forge a united church. Earlier American preachers may have relied on Paul's declaration "We, being many, are one body in Christ, and every one members one of another" (Romans 12:5) to verbally enforce and reinforce homogeneity within their congregations. But Marrant faced a heterogeneous audience of Masons and non-Masons, blacks and whites, insiders and outsiders. Negotiating these social complexities without negating them, Marrant preached to an ambiguous "we." What audience members heard in the "we" depended on their assumptions and inclinations: black and white Masons might hear a fraternal overture; African-Americans a declaration of brotherhood; non-Masonic white auditors might interrogate their implication within the "body" of the address. In each case, Marrant's method underscored his message, that community is the product of conscious affiliation and collective identification.

Marrant prioritized shared consciousness in his definition of community. "First," he charges, "let us learn to pray to God through our Lord Jesus Christ for understanding, *that we may know ourselves*; for without this we can never be fit for the society of man, we must learn to guide ourselves before we can guide others."[31] Here again the ambiguity of the "we" allows Marrant to address the intersecting concerns of Masons and African-Americans. Masons predicated their consociation on shared knowledge of keywords, rituals, and principles. So too were early American black communities actively cultivating shared lexicons, rituals, gestures, religious practices, and political priorities. Out of the profound chaos of colonial race slavery, Africans in America were consciously and creatively establishing a new human community. Marrant invokes this community by referencing an important configuration in early African-American literature—the chain. Joined together in mutual assistance and mutual respect, we "are like so many links of a chain, which when joined together make one complete member of Christ."[32] This chain is not the Great Chain of Being, nor is it a symbol inherited from Masonic tradition. Rather, it demonstrates that the bondage of slavery has been reworked into a bond of community. It is a sign of interlocked interest and conscious affiliation.

The chain metaphor also prefigures the central portion of the *Sermon*: the proof of Masonic anciency, the chain of descent through which Masonic secrets and practices passed from anciency into modernity. Both evidence and common sense indicate that Prince Hall, the more experienced Mason, researched and composed this genealogical narrative. Jeremy Belknap, a prominent white Congregationalist minister, historian, and friend to Prince Hall, annotated a printed copy of the *Sermon*: "Prince Hall claims the whole of this composition as his own except the beginning + the end."[33] Hall's letter book entries for June 1789 contain thirty-five pages of research notes on "Mr. John Edwards compleat History or Summary of the Dispensations and Methods of Religion from the Beginning of the World to the Consummation of All Things" and "The Lives of Some of the Fathers and Learned and Famous Divines in the Christian Church from our Lord and Saviour Jesus Christ."[34] The influence of these and other dispensationalist histories—including works by Samuel Hopkins and Josephus—are indeed sensible within the *Sermon*. What Hall discovered in these earlier texts was the centrality of African places, African peoples, and ostensibly "black" biblical personages to the history of Freemasonry. His reenvisioning of the proof of Masonic anciency establishes black people as the true subjects of this history. It implicitly and explicitly critiques antiblack racism as a violation of the history, spirit, and tenets of Freemasonry. Its design is chiasmatic, both in the formal sense of the term and in the black vernacular tradition of repetition and reversal.[35] With each generation from Adam, the *Sermon* presents an example of true brotherly affection, applies it—sometimes with a radical shift in tone—to the present, and closes the link by returning to his patrilineal framework. Through this chain of signifiers, Hall and Marrant signify on the parallel histories of the Masonic order, the Old Testament patriarchs, and Western civilization. All of these they claim for the African Lodge and for African-Americans in general.

As Marrant tells it, Creation rests on principles of mutuality and respect. God, "the Grand Architect of the Universe," made man "to converse with his fellow creatures that are of his own order, to maintain mutual love and society, and to serve God in comfort."[36] Twice Marrant emphasizes this appointed order. Abruptly, his tone changes:

> Then what can these God-provoking wretches think, who despise their
> fellow men, as tho' they were not of the same species with themselves,
> and would if in their power deprive them of the blessings and comforts
> of this life, which God in his bountiful goodness, hath freely given to all
> his creatures to improve and enjoy? Surely such monsters never came out
> of the hand of God in such a forlorn condition. —Which brings me to
> consider the fall of man.[37]

Ceremony gives way to uncompromising critique as Marrant's focus shifts from history to the present. Calling the "despisers of their fellow men" "monsters," he asserts the deviance of both racism and of the polygenetic view of the human species. This degeneracy belongs not to Creation but to the Fall; those who live above it may inherit not only an ancient wisdom but also their original estate.

The location of Eden invited much speculation from adepts of the eighteenth century. A prevailing view—inherited from ancient authorities like Josephus—mapped its borders at the Ganges, Nile, Tigris, and Euphrates. Marrant concurs, "These [rivers] are the four grand landmarks which the all-wise and gracious God was pleased to draw as the bounds and habitation of all nations which he was about to settle in this world."[38] His choice of words here foreshadows the abolitionist direction of his argument, as he invokes Acts 17:26: God "hath made of one blood all nations of men for to dwell on all the face of the earth, and hath determined the times before appointed, and the bounds of their habitation." Eighteenth-century abolitionists white and black—including Anthony Benezet, Lemuel Haynes, and Quobna Ottobah Cugoano—all used this scripture to assert the injustice of slavery. Going a step further, John Marrant specifies the ancient location of Paradise as "the principal part of African Ethiopia." To specify "African Ethiopia" is to anticipate and prevent the dissociation of North African biblical sites—like Ethiopia and Egypt—from the whole of the continent. This pan-Africanist gesture allows Marrant to situate the African-Americans and the African Lodge of Freemasons as the rightful heirs of Paradise and the chosen people of God. He continues, "If so, what nation or people dare, without highly displeasing and provoking that God to pour down his judgments upon them.—I say, dare to despise or tyrannize over their lives or liberties, or incroach on their lands, or to inslave their bodies?"[39] To colonize, invade, enslave, or abuse the "nations" of this "African Ethiopia," even those scattered across the African diaspora, is to act against the order of Creation.

Marrant centers civilization in Africa and locates racism with its degenerate outcasts. The slave trade, the fall of Lucifer, and the temptation of Adam and Eve prove in parallel examples that "envy and pride are the leading lines to all the miseries that mankind have suffered from the beginning of the world to this present day."[40] Especially potent is his revision of Cain as an oppressor of Africa, and Abel as his oppressed victim:

> Envy at [Adam's] prosperity hath taken the crown of glory from his head, and hath made us his posterity miserable.—What was it but this that made Cain murder his brother, whence is it but from these that our modern Cains call us Africans the sons of Cain? (We admit it if you please) and we will find from him and his sons Masonry began, after the fall of his father.[41]

Some Christians had identified Cain as the "Adam" of racial distinction, claiming that the "mark" with which God punished him was genetically revisited on his descendents as a skin of blackness.[42] Marrant attributes this racist mythology to the envy of a degraded people. "Our modern Cains," he calls them, echoing Phillis Wheatley's disdain for "our modern Egyptians."

Masonic lore gave Marrant another means for reworking Cain's accursed legacy. Masons looked to Cain as a founder of their Craft, as an engineer of weights and measures, and as the builder of the city of Nod. His son Tubal-Cain was credited with the invention of brass and metalworking (Genesis 4:16–22). If "Africans" are "the sons of Cain"—Marrant quips, "we admit it if you please"—learning and authority run in the family:

> Bad as Cain was, yet God took not from him his faculty of studying architecture, arts and sciences—his sons also were endued with the same spirit, and in some convenient place no doubt they met and communed with each other for instruction. It seems that the allwise God put this into the hearts of Cain's family thus to employ themselves, to divert their minds from musing on their father's murder and the woful curse God had pronounced on him, as we don't find any more of Cain's complaints after this.[43]

Marrant uses the example of an educated Cain to shame the Massachusetts politicians, some of them probably seated in his audience, who continued to deny free blacks access to public education. Deprived of education, the so-called "sons of Cain" were cut off from even their mythological legacy.

Masonic legend permitted Marrant to revise not only the legacy of Cain but also the competing racial legend of Ham. Folk belief placed a mark of racial distinction on Noah's son Ham, charging him with the preservation of "blackness" during the time of the Flood. Some claimed his color was punishment for violating Noah's privacy; others suggested that the source of Canaan's color was Ham's spouse, Egypt (Genesis 9:18–27). Marrant remembers Ham as the vessel of a greater legacy: through him the secret wisdom passed on to Cush and Nimrod, to Ethiopia, to Babylon, and across North Africa.

> From Shinar the arts were carried to distant parts of the earth notwithstanding the confusion of languages, which gave rise to Masons faculty and universal practice of conversing without speaking and of *knowing each other by signs and tokens;* they settled the dispersion in case any of them should meet in distant parts of the world who had been before in Shinar.[44]

"Signs and tokens" are manual gestures signifying one's affiliation with and rank within Freemasonry. Only those who could perform these gestures correctly were admitted to a regular lodge meeting. Additionally, "signs and tokens" allowed Freemasons meeting abroad to reliably identify each other or to oblige fraternal bystanders to deliver aid.

Marrant takes an example of this mode of communication from the biblical story of Benhadad and Ahab, leaders of the warring Syrians and Israelites: "[Benhadad] sends a message to Ahab king of Israel to request only his life as a captive; but behold the brotherly love of a Mason! No sooner was the message delivered, but he cries out in rapture—is he alive—he is my brother! Every Mason knows that they were both of the craft, and also the messengers."[45] This story of captivity and rescue closely recalled an incident from recent African Lodge history. On February 27, 1788, Prince Hall and twenty-two lodge members petitioned the Massachusetts legislature on behalf of three free blacks kidnapped from Boston and taken to the West Indies for sale. Captain Solomon Babson lured three men named Wendham, Cato, and Luck onto his ship, the *Ruby*, with false promises of work. Such abductions and sales were not uncommon in the northern states, despite the abolition of slavery by legal decision and legislation.[46] Boston's African-American community lived in fear of such kidnappings, according to the petitioners: "Many of our free Blacks that have entered on board of vessels as seamen, have been sold as slaves. . . . Hence it is, that many of us, who are good seamen, are obliged to stay at home through fear, and one-half of our time loiter about the streets, for want of employ." They also understood that Boston-based ships, traders, and merchants actively engaged in slaving. "Your petitioners have for some time past beheld with grief, ships cleared out of this harbor for Africa, and they either steal our brothers and sisters, fill their shipholds full of unhappy men and women, crowded together, then set out for the best market to sell them there, like sheep for slaughter," the collective testified.[47] On the very day the petition was filed, the Massachusetts legislature responded with the passage of "An Act to prevent the Slave-Trade, and for granting Relief to the Families of such unhappy Persons as may be kidnapped or decoyed away from this Commonwealth."[48] This act provided little relief for the many "unhappy men and women" who were never heard from again. However, thanks to the state of Massachusetts and the power of the Masonic fraternity, the three kidnapping victims who inspired the petition and the act did return to Boston. A letter written by Jeremy Belknap, on April 18, 1788, explains how they negotiated their escape: one of the three was "a Freemason. The merchant to whom they were offered was of this fraternity. They soon became acquainted. The Negro told his story. They were carried before the Governor, with the shipmaster and the supercargo."[49] The key to the captives' release was their ability to engage the attention of their would-be traders and "tell their story." The kidnapped black Freemason probably used special Masonic distress signals to engage the attention of his captor. Perhaps fraternal duty obliged the slave merchant, also a Freemason, to respond to the gestures of the captive, or perhaps his initial inquiry was motivated only by curiosity. Nonetheless, the "signs and tokens" of Freemasonry were powerful enough to open a discursive space which, after significant political persuasion, became an escape route.

Signs and tokens demonstrated both the global character of Masonic fellowship and its anciency as well. In these gestures the ritual core of Masonic affiliation perpetuated itself through time and space. According to Marrant, the sons of Ham carried the order through its crucial years after the scattering of nations at the Tower of Babel: "Thus the earth was again planted and replenished with Masons the second son of Ham carried into Egypt; there he built the city of Heliopolis—Thebes with an hundred gates—they built also the statue of Sphynx . . . the first or earliest of the seven wonders of arts."[50] Ham's brother Shem and his descendents could not be credited with these accomplishments, as they instead "diverted themselves at Ur in mathematical studies, teaching Peleg the father of Rehu, of Sereg, Nachor, and Terah, father of Abram."[51] Abraham came from "a learned race of mathematicians and geometricians," Marrant explains, but his Chaldean education was incomplete without the practical wisdom of Masonry: "The descendents of Abram sojourned in Egypt, as shepherds still lived in tents, practiced very little of the art of architecture till about eighty years before their Exodus, when by the overruling hand of providence they were trained up to the building with stone and brick, in order to make them expert Masons before they possessed the promised land."[52] Apologists had long excused slavery as a means of educating a "heathen" people; dispensationalists like Samuel Hopkins strained to see a Christian purpose in it. Marrant's interpretation of Israelite slavery takes Providence out of the hands of slaveholders and mainline theologians and designates the Kingdom, not a Christian education, as the destiny of the enslaved. It also posits Freemasonry as a stopping place on the way to the "promised land."

As he writes the hand of God into history, Marrant writes so-called "Gentile nations" out of it. It is God who inspires all learned progress and who chooses as his instruments the descendents of Ham—Canaanites, Phoenicians, Sidonians renowned for "their perfect knowledge of what was solid in architecture." These were the nations called on by King Solomon to construct his celebrated temple. Marrant remembers that Solomon sought out the legendary Hiram Abiff, king of Tyre and a key figure in Masonic lore, "for some of his people . . . to cut down and hew cedar trees, as his servants understood it better than his own."[53] In so stating, he signifies on another proslavery myth. To be "hewers of wood and drawers of water" was Joshua's curse on the Gibeonites (Joshua 9: 23–27), a curse some claimed was realized in American slavery. Marrant claims otherwise: "nothing more can redound to [the] honour" of these sons of Ham than their labor on Solomon's temple.[54]

Freemasons viewed Solomon's temple as the apex of achievement and patterned their own lodges after its design. Marrant presents its construction as a template of interracial brotherhood. He recalls that "70,000 men who carried burdens, who were not numbered among Masons," men "of different nations and different colours," worked together on Solomon's temple "strongly cemented in brotherly love and friendship."[55] Even the completion of the temple and the dispersion of the workers across the globe and through the ages did not diminish their loyalty to one another: "These are the laudable bonds that unite Free Masons together in one indissoluble fraternity."[56] Certainly this "laudable" ideal did not accord with the experience of the African Lodge. Many white American Freemasons denied the legitimacy of the lodge and refused to admit black Freemasons to their meetings, preferring skin color over signs and tokens as a means of selection. Responding to this racialist permutation of Masonic practice, Marrant asserts that those who refuse their brothers violate the basic principles of the order:

Let them make parties who will and despise those they would make, if they could, a species below them and as not made of the same clay with themselves; but if you study the holy book of God, you will there find that you stand on the level not only with them, but with the greatest kings on the earth, as Men and as Masons, and these truly great men are not ashamed of the meanest of their brethren.[57]

The Freemasons of history stand with the African Lodge, Marrant claims. The prejudicial views of their contemporaries are an unstudied, unnatural, and temporary aberration.

Marrant counters modern American racism by appealing to history. From early church history, Marrant draws examples of "Africans who were truly good, wise, and learned men, and as eloquent as any other nation whatever," including Tertullian, Cyprian, Origen, and Augustine.[58] History also provides evidence of the temporary quality of slavery and refutes any attempt to naturalize the condition to African peoples: "We shall not find a nation on earth but has at some period or other of their existence been in slavery, from the Jews down to the English nation, under many Emperors, Kings and Princes." On this point, Marrant cites Bede's *Ecclesiastical History of the English People*:

> In the life of Gregory, about the year 580 . . . he passing [through Rome] saw many young boys with white bodies, fair faces, beautiful countenances and lovely hair, set forth for sale; he went to the merchant their owner and asked him from what country he brought them; he answered from Britain. . . . Gregory (sighing) said, alas! for grief that such fair faces should be under the power of the prince of darkness.[59]

"Darkness" is a condition of slaveholders, not slaves—to this the "white bodies" and "fair faces" of young enslaved Britons attest. Perhaps the "fair faces" of America's British colonists demonstrate that masters have not always been masters and that slaves might not always be slaves. Marrant does not say this much. But he does present a view of history in which connections between blackness and slavery or between whiteness and privilege are consistently broken. Neither blackness nor whiteness should be read as symbols, he argues, for "all that is outward, whether opinions, rites, or ceremonies, cannot be of importance in regard to eternal salvation, any further than they have a tendency to produce inward righteousness and goodness" (Romans 2:25–29).[60] Returning to his point of origination in Paul, Marrant exhorts his audience to deny their illusory prejudices and honor "eternal" truths. He concludes, "We shall all, I hope, meet at that great day, when our great Grand Master shall sit at the head of the great and glorious Lodge in heaven."[61] Thus he seals the bonds of brotherhood and the last link of his sermon.

In crafting a consciously African-American genealogy, Hall and Marrant played at a practice of critical revision, or revelation, that would come to be a hallmark of black theology. The Reverend James Cone explains, "Since the biblical story of God's dealings with his people can be told in various ways, the chief concern of the people is not the information the preacher includes in his message but rather *how* he arranges that information into a story and how he relates it all to the daily lives of the people."[62] The constructed quality of this genealogy—its complicated nexus of biblical and historical reference, its playful relationship to those earlier texts, its skillful reversal and revision—defies conventional explication. To look into it is to find not answers but patterns, not systems but similarities and differences. Its references point beyond the meaning of this text, to other texts, to a world of instincts and clues whose value is in their fecundity, not their verification. This is the world of signs and tokens, a world which the African Lodge claimed for themselves and the black community.

Secrecy secured this claim to privileged wisdom and insight. Freemasonry taught that secrets defined the boundaries of community; likewise, the complex textuality of this genealogical narrative served the community's need for self-possession.[63] What Gates says of the protective function of the black vernacular, Cone says also of the story: "Story is not only easy to understand and to remember, it is often deceptive to those who stand outside the community where it was created. White slave masters were no brighter than our contemporary white theologians who can only see in black religion what their axiological presuppositions permit them to see."[64] What audience members actually heard in Marrant's *Sermon* would be determined by their own presuppositions about Marrant, Freemasonry, the African Lodge, African-Americans, African history, and the history of civilization. Some would deny the legitimacy of the genealogy, just as they had denied the legitimacy of black Freemasonry. Others might declare it a clandestine or licentious counterfeit. But none of these detractions could diminish the real power of the *Sermon*: the power that comes with remembering one's primordial place in history.

Still seeking some word from his erstwhile patron, the countess of Huntingdon, John Marrant left Boston for London in February 1790. As his *Journal* relates, "It was a lamentable sight to see the people the last night I preached in Boston, weeping and mourning, but I said the will of the Lord must be done." Marrant died in London in 1791, at the age of thirty-five. "Our late Reverend Brother John Marrant" was remembered by

Prince Hall and the African Lodge when they convened to celebrate St. John the Baptist Day in June 1792. Hall pledged that his remarks on that occasion—later published as *A CHARGE Delivered to the Brethren of the AFRICAN LODGE On the 25th of June, 1792. At the Hall of Brother William Smith, In CHARLESTOWN*—would continue the building project begun with Marrant's 1789 *Sermon*. Upon the "foundation" of anciency there established, he would "raise" one pillar of the "superstructure" of Masonic fraternity: "the duty of a Mason" to "the great Architect of this visible world" who "governs all things below by his almighty power, and his watchful eye is over all works."[65] This "all-seeing eye of God," commemorated most famously on the printed currency of the United States of America, represented to eighteenth-century audiences an omniscient and sovereign Divine. For Prince Hall, God was not the absentee landlord idealized in Deist philosophy, but rather a present power and a constant witness. Moreover, he did not conceive of vision as a neutralizing and clarifying solution, but rather as a force field imbued with the politics of power. As members of a small but distinctive minority population, black Bostonians knew that their phenotypic visibility exposed them to discrimination and mob violence. But Prince Hall imagined that publicity could also be turned to the political advantage of the lodge and the black community. His 1792 *Charge* experiments with the power of visibility as a means to improve the political status of black Bostonians and to expose state-sponsored racism. Additionally, it critiques the reductively racializing tendencies of human sight and recommends a more principled political vision.

If the rhetoric of the American Revolution resounded with the discourse of scientific and philosophical Enlightenment, unseen forces of chaos and conspiracy occupied the American popular imagination in the 1780s and 1790s. Americans turned from the recent memories of their own revolutionary struggle to fear nascent rebellions within the new nation. Secret societies that had served as organizing cells for the American Revolution were newly viewed as potential threats to national stability. The leaders of Shays' Rebellion (1786) were known Freemasons; during the rebellion, Daniel Shays and fellow Regulators Elijah Day and Luke Day attended a Masonic lodge meeting together.[66] It was also rumored that Freemasons masterminded the terrifying turn of the French Revolution; indeed, there were close associations between France's expansive Masonic associations—which numbered five hundred by 1789—and the Jacobin club networks.[67] Consequently, as David Shields observes, Freemasons and other civic-minded secret societies "used publicity to bolster their secrecy, crafting public images which either emphasized their work as learned societies or as clubs of conviviality, to project innocence against suspicions of heresy or sedition."[68] The need to "project innocence" was even more acute for the African Lodge. Hall and his fellows knew that they occupied a unique and influential position as one of Boston's first formally organized African-American associations. Their behavior as a body and as individuals, their public appearances, their ritual processions—all of these would be scrutinized by observers, white and black. Moreover, as Freemasons of color, the members of the lodge sustained a double-weight of suspicion: any gathering of blacks could be seen as insurrectionary, let alone a formally organized secret society. The combination of blackness and Freemasonry was particularly provocative to the conspiracy-minded of the eighteenth-century. For example, the chroniclers of the 1741 New York City slave rebellion pointed to clandestine black Freemasonry as a portent or harbinger of the revolt: they remembered the ominous appearance, in the 1730s, of a group of black men who "assumed the Stile and Title of FREEMASON."[69] Aware of the potential for public suspicion and of the African Lodge's particular vulnerability to state repression, Hall acted quickly to dissociate his Freemasons from insurgency. During Shays' Rebellion, on November 26, 1786, he wrote to Massachusetts governor James Bowdoin to assert the loyalty and to volunteer the "help and support" of the African Lodge. He also explained that Masonry "forbids our having concern in any plot or conspiracies against the state where we dwell."[70]

Hall used the 1792 *Charge* to bolster and promote the reputation of the African Lodge. Indeed, he sent printed copies of the *Charge* to the king of England, the prince of Wales, and to high-ranking officials of the London Grand Masonic Lodge.[71] In the text of the speech, he advises African Lodge members on issues of decorum, reminding them that this day of public procession and celebration will reflect on the character of the black community as a whole: members must show "spectators" that they celebrate St. John the Baptist's Day not as "a feast of Bacchus" but rather as "a refreshment with Masons."[72] Hall also used the publicity of the occasion to reaffirm his loyalty pledge to the state. He declares that the members of the African Lodge "have no hand in any plots or conspiracies or rebellion, or side or assist in them." However, their nonparticipation in open rebellion does not mean a lack of sympathy for either the victims of oppression or those who suffered the consequences of the rebellion. "What heart can be found so hard as not to pity those our distrest brethren, and keep at the greatest distance from them?" he asks. "However just it may be on the side of the opprest, yet it doth not in the least, or rather ought not, abate that love and fellow-feeling which we ought to have for our brother fellow men."[73] Hall refuses to weigh the "justness" of the rebellion against his "pity" for its casualties. Rather than calculate partisan loyalties, Hall appeals to a more principled notion of duty to humanity as a consequence of duty to God: "For if I love a man for the sake of the image of God which is on him, I must love all, for he made all, and upholds all . . . let them be of what colour or nation they may, yea even our very enemies, much more a brother Mason."[74] This careful albeit ambivalent negotiation of early republican politics was calculated to calm the nerves of his conspiracy-vigilant audiences as well as to exculpate the lodge from accusations of insurgency.

Beyond the politics of public image, strategic considerations motivated this declared neutrality. After all, how would a controversy such as Shays' Rebellion profit the black men of Boston? What purchase did the African Lodge have in this argument between propertied white men, rural and urban?[75] Black Bostonians stood in a wholly separate relationship to property: they often feared that they themselves might be appropriated by the captains of the vessels to which they hired themselves as sailors, by kidnappers lurking on the waterfront, by mobs seeking easy targets. At that time, African-Americans in Massachusetts enjoyed nominal voting rights; still, they could not rely on equal protection under the law. The mercy of powerful friends was more dependable than the uneven applications of justice. In the *Charge*, Hall presents to his audience three biblical exemplars of merciful intervention: the Ethiopian eunuch Ebedmelech interceded on behalf of the captive prophet Jeremiah (Jeremiah 38); Elisha preserved the Samarians, though the Israelites, according to Hall, wanted to "kill them out of the way, as not worthy to live on the same earth" (2 Kings 8); and Abraham defused "the storm, or rebellion that was rising between Lot's servants and his" by dividing their land claims (Genesis 13). Each story models nonviolent resolution to disputes over territory, and each asserts humanitarian principles over property rights.

The high visibility afforded the lodge on this occasion also gave Hall an opportunity to expose unprincipled practices of race-based discrimination. Returning to the subject of his October 1787 petition to the Massachusetts legislature, he protested the denial of tax-funded public education to black children. He charged his black audience to aspire to self-improvement despite "the disadvantages you labour under on account of your being deprived of the means of education in your younger days, as you see it is at this day with our children, for we see notwithstanding we are rated for that, and other Town charges, we are deprived of that blessing."[76] Hall also used this public forum to expose white Freemasons who had refused to welcome members of the African Lodge into their fellowship. Taking a page from Masonic history, he reminds his audience that the "Order of St. John" had built temples across northern Africa and then asks:

Query, Whether at that day, when there was an African church, and perhaps the largest Christian church on earth, whether there was no African of that order; or whether, if they were all whites, they would refuse to accept them as their fellow Christians and brother Masons; or whether there were any so weak, or rather so foolish, as to say, because they were Blacks, that would make their lodge or army too common or too cheap?[77]

He does not answer his own question. But he does observe that the labor of black soldiers was welcome in the Revolutionary Army, where blacks and whites "marched shoulder to shoulder, brother soldier and brother soldier, to the field of battle."[78] Many of the leaders of that war, including General George Washington himself, were prominent Freemasons. That the same men should refuse full fellowship to black Freemasons in peace time was, Prince Hall implied, a violation of the duties of their order. Similarly, the race-based denial of public education by Massachusetts state officials—many of whom were Freemasons—was also contrary to the fundamental principles of Masonry. Prejudice against color was a violation of the will of God, the "all-seeing."

Hall recommended a more prophetic vision of the black community. In response to the repressions of mortal governments, he encouraged his brethren to rely on God and to "look forward to a better day." Biblical prophecy confirmed that day would come for black people everywhere; as Prince Hall declares with prophetic zeal, "Hear what the great Architect of the universal world saith: *Aethiopia shall stretch forth her hands unto me.*"[79] Subsequent generations of black political writers and preachers would find a discursive touchstone in Psalms 68:31, "Princes shall come out of Egypt; Ethiopia shall soon stretch out her hands unto God." Scholars generally point to Robert Alexander's *Ethiopian Manifesto* (1829) as the first instance of a fully articulated political "Ethiopianism." Here we see that thirty-five years before the *Manifesto* the prophetic destiny of Ethiopia was a reality to the African Lodge of Freemasons. Whatever injustices the state perpetrated, whatever prejudices white Freemasons promoted, the emancipation and glorification of black peoples was an irrepressible eventuality. The prophetic promises of Psalms 68 did not, according to Prince Hall, exempt African-Americans from progressive action. He charged his audience to act as accomplices in their own liberation:

But in the meantime let us lay by our recreations, and all superfluities, so that we may have that to educate our rising generation, which was spent in those follies. Make you this beginning, and who knows but God may raise up some friend or body of friends, as he did in Philadelphia, to open a School for the blacks here, as that friendly city has done there.[80]

Critics have sometimes maligned black Christianity as fostering an "otherworldly" kind of hope; they claim that prophetic religion defers justice to the afterlife or heaven, thereby fostering quietism on earth.[81] But here we see that from its eighteenth-century beginnings, Ethiopianism has always assumed that African-American activism was critical to the fulfillment of prophecy. Hall called on his audience to undertake self- and mutual improvement efforts, to "make a beginning," and to leave the rest to God.

Prince Hall did not imagine God to be a disinterested observer, but rather an activist witness and judge. His was not a Deist faith in the apparent order of things. On the basis of appearances, black people had been categorically denied basic human rights. If this was the standing order of things—and it was as long as Massachusetts denied the full benefits of citizenship to its black residents—then the African Lodge was not dutybound to uphold it. Hall did not call for open revolt, but he did offer his black audience a different vision of its own destiny. Rational minds might mistake color-coded surveillance for a substantive vision; Hall looked forward to millennial revelation. A postscript poem to the *Charge* so states:

Then shall we hear and see and know,
All we desir'd and wish'd below [. . . .]
Then burst the chains with sweet surprize,
And in our Savior's image rise.[82]

At the end of time, Prince Hall believed, the temporary codes of color would resolve themselves into more significant images. It was the duty of the African Lodge to see through the limitations of racism and to hold to this prophetic vision.

If the African Lodge drew scrutiny and sometimes hostility from whites, it also drew great interest from African-Americans. During the mid-1790s, black community organizations took root in Philadelphia, Providence, and Boston and extended their branches between these cities to create networks. Absalom Jones and Richard Allen founded two independent black churches in Philadelphia—St. Thomas Protestant Episcopal Church and Bethel African Methodist Episcopal Church—in 1794. Peter Mantore, a free black Philadelphian, asked Prince Hall to charter a Masonic lodge there in March 1797. Like his Boston brothers, Mantore was initiated by an Irish-affiliated lodge; six other black Philadelphian Freemasons were initiated in London. Now, Mantore explained, they sought a charter: "The white Masons have refused to grant us a Dispensation, fearing that black men living in Virginia would get to be Masons too. . . . If we are under you, we shall always be ready to assist in the furtherance of Masonry among us."[83] Hall formally organized the lodge on September 22, 1797, appointing Absalom Jones its master and Richard Allen its treasurer. That same year, Hall chartered a third African Lodge in Providence, Rhode Island, for the benefit of members there who had routinely traveled to Boston for meetings. It is likely that Providence's "Hiram No. 3" lodge of Prince Hall Freemasonry was populated by followers of Samuel Hopkins.

Prince Hall's *Charge Delivered to the African Lodge, June 24, 1797, at Menotomy* reflects his growing concern with the work of organizing the black community. It was designed to build on and complete Marrant's 1789 *Sermon* and his own 1792 *Charge*, to add to the "foundation" a second "pillar" of the African Lodge: "our duty to sympathise with our fellow men under their troubles."[84] Julia Stern has characterized two popular modes of early republican sympathy: a consensual, disinterested "republican" fellow-feeling and a compassionately transgressive "proto-liberal" imagination.[85] Hall means to promote neither of these. While he knew the popular proof-texts of sentimentality—Hall refers to the rescue of "the captives of the Algerines," a scenario of white enslavement dramatized in Susanna Rowson's *Slaves in Algiers* (1794), Royall Tyler's *The Algerine Captive* (1797), and numerous Barbary captivity narratives—[86] he did not dedicate his speech to the travails of humanity at large. Rather, he repeatedly called the lodge to the assistance of their "African brethren," in Boston and throughout the world. The 1797 *Charge* breaks from its more cautious precedents as it promotes a bolder Ethiopianist politics.

The *Charge* focuses on the political conditions, collective resources, and particular strengths of African-Americans. Hall first induces his audience to witness the cruelty of enslavement: "Let us see them dragg'd from their native country, by the iron hand of tyranny and oppression, from their dear friends and connections, with weeping eyes and aching hearts, to a strange land and strange people, whose tender mercies are cruel." This sentimental emphasis on the emotional and social traumas of enslavement humanizes the enslaved. It also recalls the language of the African Lodge's 1788 petition to the state of Massachusetts, which demanded an end to the abduction of free black Bostonians for sale in the slave trade: "Your petitioners have for some time past beheld with grief, ships cleared out of this harbor for Africa, and they either steal our brothers and sisters, fill their shipholds full of unhappy men and women, crowded together, then set out for the best market to sell them there, like sheep for slaughter."[87] Even after the Massachusetts General Court declared slavery abolished in 1783, practices such as kidnapping, reenslavement, and mob violence effectively continued a regime of racial domination. Hall describes the abuses suffered by the nominally free black population:

Daily insults you meet with in the streets of Boston; much more on public days of recreation, how are you shamefully abus'd, and that at such a degree, that you may be said to carry your lives in your hands; and the arrows of death are flying about your heads. . . . Helpless old women have their clothes torn off their backs, even to the exposing of their nakedness.[88]

Both here and in his description of enslavement, Hall samples the language of the Old Testament to sacralize the suffering of Africans and African-Americans. Both enslaved and free blacks are subjected to "a strange land and strange people, whose tender mercies are cruel" just as the people of Israel were (Exodus 2:22; Psalms 137:4; Jeremiah 5:19; Proverbs 12:10); like Noah, black Bostonians are stripped of their dignity, "even to the exposing of their nakedness" (Genesis 9:22–23); and they too find the "arrows of death flying about" them (Psalms 91:5). Hall does not annotate this composite of scripture references, nor does he explicitly announce a belief in the chosenness of black people. Rather, he assumed that sympathetic auditors would share both his level of scripture literacy and his Ethiopianist outlook.

Hall viewed the peoples of the African diaspora as the collective heirs of an ancient and ultimately triumphant sacred narrative. In this, he differed from millenarians like Samuel Hopkins who reckoned slavery and African redemption as instruments of a more general plan for the salvation of humanity. Hopkins was undoubtedly known to Hall through mutual acquaintances; indeed, Hall adopts in his 1797 *Charge* some points from Hopkins's *Treatise on the Millennium* (1793), including Hopkins's correlation of the slave trade with the commerce of Babylon described in Revelations 18. But Hall rejected the Rhode Island minister's belief that African colonization would indirectly hasten the return of Christ. Rather, he placed their millennial destiny into the hands of Africans themselves: "And if I mistake it not, it now begins to dawn in some of the West-India islands." From 1791, American presses nervously followed reports of mulatto and slave revolts in the French Caribbean colony of Santo Domingo, or Haiti. When Jacobin, mulatto, and black forces captured the Haitian port city of Cap Francais, in June 1793, refugees flooded American port cities and inflamed domestic fears of slave revolt. Some states attempted to prevent the contagion of revolutionary fervor by barring immigration of free blacks or importation of slaves from the West Indies. But anti-immigrant proscriptions did not prevent African-Americans from learning about the Haitian Revolution. Prince Hall openly celebrated the revolt:

Remember what a dark day it was with our African brethren six years ago, in the French West-Indies. Nothing but the snap of the whip was heard from morning to evening; hanging, broken on the wheel, burning, and all manner of tortures inflicted on those unhappy people . . . but blessed be God, the scene is changed. . . . Thus doth Ethiopia begin to stretch forth her hand, from a sink of slavery to freedom and equality.[89]

Hall situates the Haitian Revolution within the context of the Ethiopianist prophecy in Psalms 68: "Ethiopia shall soon stretch out her hands unto God." He recognized commonalities between black Haitians—whom he calls "our African brethren"—and black Bostonians. Moreover, he viewed Haiti as a starting place for a more general revolution among the peoples of the African diaspora.

Hall did not openly commend the violence of the Haitian revolution to his black audience in Boston. To do so would have been to incite the worst fears and grossest hostilities of already suspicious whites. He did not sacrifice his boldness, however, in claiming that black revolution would be assisted by God:

[Haiti] puts me in mind of a nation (that I have somewhere read of) called Ethiopeans, that cannot change their skin: But God can and will change their conditions, and their hearts too; and let Boston and the world know that He hath no respect of persons; and that that bulwark of envy, pride, scorn, and contempt; which is so visible to be seen in some and felt, shall fall, to rise no more.[90]

Hall equates revolution with redemption, but he takes care to resist and reorganize the conventional color-coding of the latter term. Was racial transmogrification a component of salvation? Many whites suspected, believed, or hoped that it was. Even sympathetic souls like the English poet William Blake imagined in his poem "The Little Black Boy" (1789) that black people would be washed white in the blood of the Lamb. The 1790s also spawned a tremendous fascination with cases of "black albinism," "piebald," and "white Negroes," as reported in popular almanacs and magazines and as epitomized in the exhibition of black Philadelphian Henry Moss in 1796.[91] In June 1797, the physician Benjamin Rush was preparing to announce a new medical theory of blackness as a species of leprosy, communicable but curable. Hall dismissed these prospects and spectacles by invoking Jeremiah 13: 23: "Can the Ethiopian change his skin, or the leopard his spots? then may ye also do good, that are accustomed to do evil." The scripture had been manipulated by white theologians to coindicate blackness with a natural state of sin. But Hall argued that "Ethiopeans" simply could not and should not be expected to "change their skin." If God was "no respecter of persons" (Acts 10:34; Romans 2:11; Colossians 3:25), then God would place no value on race, class, gender, or nation. Correspondingly, redemption did not mean a "change in skin," but rather a revolutionary change in "conditions" and "hearts." The hearts most in need of changing belonged to those enthralled by a racism so virulent as to make itself "visible" in their very countenances. White racism—insightfully characterized as a "bulwark of envy, pride, scorn, and contempt"—would someday "fall, to rise no more." This was to be the complement of Ethiopian ascendance.

Hall elaborates his Ethiopianist views by adding to the lodge's growing catalog of exemplars a number of biblical "Ethiopians." These include Jethro, called by Hall "an Ethiopian" and a Mason, who taught his son-in-law Moses "how to regulate his courts of justice, and what sort of men to choose for the different offices" (Exodus 18:22–24); the Ethiopian eunuch baptized by Philip, a "great monarch" who did not "think it beneath him to take a poor servant of the Lord by the hand, and invite him into his carriage" (Acts 8:27–31); and, most important, the Queen of Sheba, who was led "by the hand" of "our Grand Master, Solomon" "into his court, at the hour of high twelve," to discuss "points of masonry" (2 Chronicles 9).[92] The Queen of Sheba served as a source of legitimation for the African Lodge as well as for the European and American women who asserted their rights to Masonic affiliation. Hannah Mather Crocker, a granddaughter of Cotton Mather, served as the "mistress" of St. Ann's Lodge in Boston in the 1790s; her published writings celebrate the Queen of Sheba as an emblem of the anciency of female education.[93] The fabled relationship between the Queen of Sheba and King Solomon would also come to play a pivotal role in the twentieth-century development of Garveyism and Rastafarianism, establishing modern Ethiopian royalty as descendents of the royal house of David. Hall's 1797 *Charge* demonstrates that African-Americans came to know and honor the Queen of Sheba through a multiplicity of texts and traditions, not only as the "black" and "comely" beloved of the Song of Solomon but also as a woman of political power and learning.

Hall affirms in his fellows a comparable capacity for distinction. He recognizes that African-Americans denied access to public education were developing their own intellectual resources in "thinking, hearing and weighing matters, men, and things in your own mind, and making that judgment of them as you think reasonable to satisfy your minds and give an answer to those who may ask you a question."[94] He also celebrates the literary achievements of the nonliterate, those who "repeat psalms and hymns, and a great part of a sermon, only by hearing it read or preached," and the divinatory skills of black sailors:

> How many of this class of our brethren that follow the seas can foretell a storm some days before it comes; whether it will be a heavy or light, a long or short one; foretell a hurricane, whether it will be destructive or moderate, without any other means than observation and consideration. So in the observation of heavenly bodies, this same class without a telescope or other apparatus have through a smoak'd glass observed the eclipse of the sun: One being ask'd what he saw through his smoaked glass, said, Saw, saw, de clipsey, or de clipseys. And what do you think of it?—Stop, dere be two. Right, and what do they look like?—Look like, why if I tell you, they look like the two ships sailing one bigger than tother; so they sail by one another, and make no noise.[95]

In this passage, one of the earliest representations of the black vernacular by an African-American, Hall lovingly promotes his community's achievements. His exemplary choice of black sailors as naked-eye "observers" and "foretellers" powerfully counters the privilege assigned to technology-assisted vision. Late eighteenth-century portraits of American Enlightenment heroes Benjamin Franklin and Thomas Jefferson prominently featured telescopes and microscopes as indices to the subjects' learning and power, while Hall's depiction of black sailors heralds their use of a "smoaked glass" to view an eclipse. Here was an instance when darkness trumped light, when the technological emblems of enlightenment failed, when divination and older modes of knowing prevailed. The anecdote implies that blackness imparts another lens, a different kind of vision, an enhanced capacity to apprehend change.

Hall encourages his African brethren to recognize their powers of divination as a source of political strength. The unseen world could prove the seat of their resistance. Thus, he exhorts the lodge to keep their secrets, using the example of two successful robbers who betray each other under circumstance of fear:

> if [a man] was truly bold, and void of fear, he would keep the whole plunder to himself: so when either of them is detected and not the other, he may be call'd to oath to keep it secret, but through fear, (and that passion is so strong) he will not confess, till the fatal cord is put on his neck; then death will deliver him from the fear of man, and he will confess the truth when it will not be of any good to himself or the community.[96]

The good of the "community," Hall explains, will not be served by confession, nor by oath-breaking, nor by fear. The secret must be kept within the veil. As to the content of that guarded secret—a formula for resistance? a plan for revolt?—contemporary readers cannot be sure. More powerful than its specific content of the secret, though, is the existence of the secret itself. In a time when free blacks could count on few guarantees of person or property and slaves could count on none, the secret was something the African Lodge could claim as its own. It was a seedling for the concept of self-possession. What was unknown and unseen lodge members could secure for themselves through second sight, a sense educated, according to Hall, "by our *searches and researches* into men and things."[97] The prestige of the visible world would prove, in time, a mere distraction. Hall concludes the *Charge* on this point, with a poem he claims to have "found among some old papers":

> Let blind admirers handsome faces praise,
> And graceful features to great honor raise,
> The glories of the red and white express,
> I know no beauty but in holiness;
> If God of beauty be the uncreate
> Perfect idea, in this lower state,
> The greatest beauties of an human mould,
> Who most resemble him we justly hold;
> Whom we resemble not in flesh and blood,
> But being pure and holy, just and good:
> May such a beauty fall but to my share,
> For curious shape or face I'll never care.[98]

Human "faces" and the "red and white" tokens of nationalism counted only as "curiosities." And for all their seeing, the skeptics and rationalists of the Enlightenment could still never know "the uncreate / Perfect idea in this lower state." The secret of that all-powerful God dwelt in "holiness," revealing itself only to those willing to stand within the veil.

Read as a suite, the 1789 *Sermon* and *Charges* of 1792 and 1797 present a number of suggestive possibilities. They correlate with the three elements of the Masonic motto "Wisdom, Strength, Beauty." Perhaps they were also designed as a series of initiation lectures to prepare members of the African Lodge for the order's three symbolic degrees: Apprentice, Fellow Craft, and Master. Using the governing metaphors of Freemasonry, Prince Hall framed the lectures as steps in a building process. Marrant's 1789 *Sermon* provided a foundation of "anciency," Hall's 1792 *Charge* introduced the pillar of civic duty, and his 1797 *Charge* established a second pillar of sympathy, or racial solidarity. Within the context of Freemasonry, these pillars represent the two columns in the porch at Solomon's Temple. One pillar is named Jachin, meaning strength; the other is Boaz, meaning establishment (1 Kings 7:21, 2 Chronicles 3:17). Together, they refer to the scripture: "In strength shall this house be established." Cabalists and mystics have interpreted them as active and passive principles, the binary and the unitary, the spiritual and the material. Together, they form the portal to the Holy of Holies; between them hangs the veil, which marks the divide between worlds. According to Masonic ritual, the lodge is not just a fraternal gathering place but a model of the universe itself like the temples of Solomon and Ancient Egypt. Entering the temple, under the scrutiny of brother Freemasons, is a ritual enactment of the passage from the prosaic and profane world into the realm of mystery, the Holy of Holies. Perhaps Prince Hall and his fellows saw in this ritual configuration of space and symbol a semblance of their own passage through the profane logic of racial formation into the more sacred realm of community. From outside to inside, from confusion to understanding, from bondage to freedom, from death to life—the initiations and rituals of Freemasonry allowed the African Lodge to sacralize their bond as black people.

Masonic emphasis on history as a source of authority and legitimacy contributed to this sacralization. It sustained the construction of a black identity that was both ancient and modern, primeval and prophetic. Thus, we find in the literature of early Prince Hall Freemasonry a radically heterogeneous, textually based, and politically intended protoblack nationalism. We also find key elements of the anti-imperialist cultural projects described by Frantz Fanon in his essay "On National Cultures": "passionate research" "directed by the secret hope of discovering beyond the misery of today, beyond self-contempt, resignation, and abjuration, some very beautiful and splendid era whose existence rehabilitates us both in regard to ourselves and in regard to others."[99] Following Fanon, Stuart Hall posits two modes of this "research." One "unearth[s] that which the colonial experience buried and overlaid, bringing to light the hidden continuities it suppressed"; another is "the *production* of identity . . . not an identity grounded in the archeology, but in the re-telling of the past."[100] The former revises the content of colonialist history, while the latter contests its privileged association with narrative, continuity, and progress. According to Stuart Hall, radical histories do not invent a fixed, impervious sense of "being" but rather encourage a perpetual and critical process of "becoming."[101] Correspondingly, Prince Hall and John Marrant did not attempt to recover a holistic lost history—be it based in the ancient legends of Egypt, Ethiopia, or Israel. Rather, their speeches reveal how a forcibly displaced population formed a community and forged a common identity through an inspired, unorthodox, and imaginative process of transformation and origination.

To insist that Hall and Marrant played an originary role in the history of black nationalist discourse would be to simplify and overstate the case: their speeches do not articulate the radical separatist tenets of a fully elaborated black nationalism, and there is little evidence that black nationalists of the nineteenth or twentieth centuries recognized Hall and Marrant as progenitors. Still, as organizers and preceptors of the African Lodge, they collected a critical mass of black political and cultural resources. They gathered from biblical, Masonic, and church histories a host of educated, ennobled, and ennobling African exemplars. From hybrid counter-Enlightenment sources, Hall and Marrant fashioned a historical narrative that rehabilitated African-American identities in a space of self-possession. The African lodge established a complementary social and political space that belonged uniquely to black people.[102] The mysticism and privacy of this space marked the limits of and rejected the ideology of the new nation's putatively democratic and enlightened "public sphere." Thus, the lodge was, in Homi Bhabha's words, a "territory of the minority" and an "antagonist supplement of modernity."[103] Premises of secrecy ritualized in Masonic practice safeguarded the sanctity of this space and its potential as a site of political organization. The nineteenth-century membership rosters of Prince Hall Freemasonry evidence a realization of this political potency. Almost every free black male political leader of the nineteenth century—with the notable exception of Frederick Douglass—was also a Prince Hall Freemason: evangelist Lemuel Haynes, African Methodist Episcopal church founders Richard Allen and Absalom Jones, Haitian attorney general Prince Saunders, Alexander Pushkin, Alexander Dumas, Liberian president Joseph Jenkins Roberts, abolitionist James Forten, David Walker, Henry Highland Garnet, William Wells Brown, Josiah Henson, Martin Delaney, Booker T. Washington, and W. E. B. Du Bois.[104]

The literature of nineteenth-century black nationalism is laced with references to and borrowings from Prince Hall Freemasonry. An especially noteworthy instance of this textual mutuality is David Walker's *Appeal to the Colored Citizens of the World* (1829). Walker utilized ritual elements of Freemasonry to convey the conspiratorial nature of the slave power and to engage abolitionist assistance from fellow Masons, black and white. For example, when Walker claims that slaveholders would rather "cut their throats from ear to ear" than liberate their slaves, he is reciting Masonic penalties for incontinence: an initiate agreed that his throat should be cut from ear to ear if he revealed the secrets of the order. The comparison serves to underscore the willful solidarity of slaveholders against the interests of human liberty. Walker does not mean to denigrate Freemasonry. In fact, he criticizes the anti-Masonic fervor of the 1820s as misdirected energy:

> The preachers and people of the United States form societies against Free Masonry and Intemperance, and write against Sabbath breaking, Sabbath mails, Infidelity, &c. &c. But the fountain head [of slavery], compared with which all those other evils are comparatively nothing, and from the bloody and murderous head of which they receive no trifling support, is hardly noticed by the Americans.[105]

According to Walker, the conspiracy most responsible for depredation and evil was not Freemasonry but rather slaveocracy. Walker's Masonic and abolitionist brother Henry Highland Garnet held the slaveholding conspiracy responsible for Walker's demise. Garnet appended to the *Appeal* a prefatory "Sketch" of David Walker's life that implicitly compared Walker to the Masonic martyr Hiram Abiff. According to Masonic lore, conspirators murdered Hiram Abiff, a master builder on Solomon's Temple, for refusing to reveal fraternal secrets. King Solomon's reaction to Abiff's murder—"Is there no hope for the widow's son?"—served as Masons' distress call; Masonic rituals reenacted his resurrection. Garnet describes the death of David Walker as the product of a conspiracy by "a company of Georgia men." Significantly, he describes both Walker and his child as "widow's sons": "His father died a few months before his birth; and it is a remarkable coincidence that the son of the subject of this Memoir was also a posthumous child."[106] For both David Walker and Henry Highland Garnet, the discourse of Freemasonry provided a register of speech commensurate in its heightened intensity and profound implications with the escalating war against slavery.

There is also evidence of a more clandestine, mimetic association between Freemasonry and emancipation in black slave communities. Masonic-style techniques were used to enlist slaves in Gabriel's Revolt, an insurrection led by Gabriel Prosser in Virginia in 1800. A black informant named Ben Woolfolk reported that an insurrectionist recruiter approached him with an invitation to join a "free-mason society"; Woolfolk refused, opining that "all free-masons would go to hell." The recruiter restated his invitation, clarifying that he was inviting Woolfolk to join with "a society to fight the white people for [our] freedom."[107] It seems unlikely that either this recruiter or Ben Woolfolk would use admission to one of Virginia's white Lodges as a satisfactory premise; clearly, both men knew of Prince Hall Freemasonry. In 1843, a Maryland grand jury found black Masonic lodges to be "particularly dangerous" to the system of slavery and thereby to the public interest.[108] Consequently, two Prince Hall Lodges—King David Lodge No. 5 and Lamech Lodge No. 11—were threatened or closed by state officials and their members were arrested or fined. In 1852, whites in Norfolk, Virginia, discovered that local African-Americans had formed a Masonic lodge; the editor of the local paper argued that "times of impudence and insubordination" required that all secret societies among African-Americans be rooted out.[109] Finally, scholars of African-American quilting have recently traced provocative connections between African-American quilt patterns, Masonic symbols, and a code used to direct slaves to the Underground Railroad.[110]

These findings underscore the value of Prince Hall Freemasonry as a social space and a discursive resource. In their speeches and the lodges they chartered, Hall and Marrant institutionalized a crucial lexicon of gestures, keywords, phrases, and concepts, a lexicon revised and reinvigorated with each succeeding generation. They fashioned from mystical, biblical, and Masonic texts an *unnatural* history, a counternarrative to eighteenth-century empiricisms and "natural histories" that classified Africa as a cipher, perpetually primitive and unintelligible.[111] They redrew a veil of blackness around themselves and counted all who stood within it as participants in the unfolding of a mystery, a common consciousness, and a culture.

5

No

Black Identity and Yellow Fever in Philadelphia
Philadelphia, Pennsylvania; August 1793

On August 22, 1793, a select group of black and white Philadelphians celebrated the completion of the African Church building. It was the fulfillment of a dream for Richard Allen (1760–1831), a former slave, a Methodist circuit exhorter, and the future founder of the African Methodist Episcopal church. Allen had come to Philadelphia in February 1786, after converting his owner and purchasing his freedom. When he arrived, amidst an exodus of newly freed blacks to urban centers after the War of Independence, Allen had a striking vision of his people and his new home: "I saw a large field open in seeking and instructing my African brethren, who had been a long forgotten people and few of them attended public worship."[1] His vision was uncannily appropriate to Philadelphia, as it closely resembled the gathered community foretold by Quaker founder George Fox on Pendle Hill almost one hundred and fifty years before. Absalom Jones (1746–1818), a fellow ex-slave and black Philadelphian, who had by his assiduous efforts raised money enough to buy freedom for his wife and then for himself in 1785, soon joined Richard Allen in his visionary endeavors. Allen, Jones, and others founded the Free African Society in April 1787, a mutual assistance and burial society honored by W. E. B. Du Bois as "the first wavering step of a people towards an organized social life."[2] Recognizing their community's need for religious independence as well, Jones and Allen initiated the organization of an "African Church" in 1791, a movement met with criticism and even hostility from white Methodist, Episcopal, and Quaker clergy alike. The controversy crested in the fall of 1792, during Sunday services at St. George's Methodist Church, when white elders instructed black patrons—including Jones and Allen—to abandon their customary seats in the main church hall and remove to a newly constructed, segregated gallery. When the black worshippers refused, white elders disrupted services and attempted to remove them forcibly. Wrote Allen, "We all went out of the church in a body, and they were no more plagued by us in the church."[3] They broke ground for the African Church of Philadelphia a few months later.

The 1780s and 1790s were gathering and building decades for communities of color throughout North America. As previous chapters have shown with the intertribal settlement organized by Samson Occom at Brotherton, New York; the black Loyalist enclave at Birchtown, Nova Scotia; and the African Lodge of Freemasons organized by Prince Hall in Boston, Massachusetts, these communities developed new identities, new fidelities, new histories, new styles of worship, and new modes of discourse. Set into motion by the chaos of the War of Independence, they built on the promises of the revolution and marked its failures to institute equality and freedom for Native and African-Americans. In 1780, Pennsylvania had led the nation with an act for the emancipation of slaves. Although the act provided only for a very limited and gradual emancipation—children born into slavery up until the day the law was implemented would remain slaves for life; children born after March 1, 1780 were destined to twenty-eight years of indentured servitude—it encouraged some slave owners to manumit their slaves or to allow them to purchase their freedom. Hundreds of newly freed slaves migrated to Philadelphia in the next decades, establishing the foundations for the United States' largest free black community and building institutions such as the Free African Society and the African Church.[4] The public emergence of this postslavery society also generated profound racial anxiety among white Philadelphians, exposing in the city—which was then the capital of the United States—the fundamental contradictions of a revolution and a nation that proclaimed democracy, liberty, and equality but truly enfranchised only its white, male, property-holding minority.

The season which saw the completion of Philadelphia's African Church would prove a crucible for race relations in the city and, more fundamentally, for the concept of race itself. In July 1793, more than two thousand refugees—French planters, their families, and their slaves—fled slave revolts in Santo Domingo for Philadelphia. This influx drew great sympathy and support from white Philadelphians, who quickly raised twelve thousand dollars for refugee relief. In a revealing turn of events not unnoticed by Richard Allen and Absalom Jones, many white philanthropists reneged on their pledges to the African Church building fund in order to aid refugee slave owners. Then, in late August, yellow fever descended on Philadelphia, quickly spreading from a few cases in waterfront neighborhoods to epidemic proportions. Between August and November 1793, between four and five thousand Philadelphians died from yellow fever and related ailments; approximately twenty thousand of the city's fifty-five thousand residents fled for the countryside. Among the refugees were United States president George Washington, a majority of his federal officers, and state and local officials. Newspapers folded, merchants failed, and even members of the mayor's civic relief committee left town. Cities from Massachusetts to Georgia imposed quarantines and restrictions on travel and trade with Philadelphia. Not since the Revolutionary War, when British forces occupied the city, had Philadelphia experienced such a large-scale disruption of daily life.

African-Americans would play a critical role in the public health strategy developed by Philadelphia mayor Matthew Clarkson and the city's College of Physicians. From their readings in tropical and colonial medicine—especially John Lining's *A Description of the American Yellow Fever, which Prevailed at Charleston in the Year 1748*—fellows of the college developed the false theory that black people possessed innate immunity to yellow fever. Consequently, they recommended that Afro-Philadelphians be assigned the most odious and hazardous public health capacities. In early September, Benjamin Rush published portions of Lining's arguments for black immunity in the *American Daily Advertiser*. Rush explained:

> The only design of this remark is, to suggest to our citizens the safety and propriety of employing black people to nurse and attend persons infected by this fever; also, to hint to the black people, that a noble opportunity is now put into their hands, of manifesting their gratitude to the inhabitants of that city, which first planned their emancipation from slavery, and who have since afforded them so much protection and support, as to place them, in point of civil and religious privileges, upon a footing equal with themselves.[5]

The declaration of black immunity—compounded by Rush's insinuation that Philadelphia's African-Americans owed their white fellows some "gratitude" for emancipation—colored the whole of the public response to yellow fever. Many African-Americans privately doubted Rush. Nonetheless, the African Society responded to the call for public assistance, with society leaders Richard Allen, Absalom Jones, and William Gray organizing nursing and grave digging corps. Blacks not affiliated with the society were independently contracted or conscripted into nursing or grave digging work, while white residents seized on Rush's declaration to justify their abandonment of ill family members and friends. This division of public health labor enabled massive white flight: historians estimate that one in four white Philadelphians fled the city, while fewer than one in ten blacks did.[6] Soon enough, the black immunity theory was shown to be a falsehood. On September 25, just weeks after his statement in the *Daily Advertiser*, Benjamin Rush wrote to his wife Julia, "The Negroes are everywhere submitting to the disorder. Richd. Allen, who has led their van, is very ill."[7] Allen recovered for three weeks at Bush-hill hospital and then resumed his work, but many others did not. Historians estimate that 198 Afro-Philadelphians died during the epidemic, a death rate of 9 percent. White yellow fever mortalities numbered 3,095, a death rate of 14 percent.[8]

The events of the 1793 Philadelphia fever season and its aftermath generated an unprecedented public discourse about blackness, its significance, its symptomaticity, and its place within the body politic. The stark failure of the black immunity hypothesis challenged an emerging scientific consensus about the nature of immunity and the biological quality of race; it also silenced—for a season—proponents of polygenist views of human variation. Where physicians and scientists had failed, popular writers, public lore, and ministers stepped in to offer interpretations of blackness. So too did the fever season occasion a major development in African-American community formation, political organization, and literary history. This development is documented in *A Narrative of the Proceedings of the Black People, During the Late Awful Calamity in Philadelphia, in the Year 1793: And a Refutation of Some Censures, Thrown upon them in some late Publications* (1794), written by African Society leaders and black church founders Absalom Jones and Richard Allen. The *Narrative* is a principal work in African-American literature. One leading scholar of Afro-Americana calls it "the first account of a free black community in action."[9] Indeed, it is a pioneering black history text, one which establishes covenant theology as an overarching context for African-American experience. Jones and Allen portray the black community's service during the yellow fever epidemic as a spiritual obligation and a trial of faith; their survival was not a consequence of innate immunity but rather the result of divine intervention and protection. Denaturalizing race-based immunity and the biological basis of race itself, the *Narrative* posits a religious and textual conception of resistance and community. The epidemic, its consequence for racialized thinking, and the legacy of the Jones and Allen *Narrative* are the subjects of this chapter.

In its early stages, yellow fever inflicted headaches, high temperatures, chills, body aches, nausea, and vomiting; severe cases brought jaundice, internal hemorrhage, black vomit, liver and kidney failure, coma, and death. Throughout the eighteenth century, Americans living in Atlantic seaboard cities from New York to Charleston faced intermittent yellow fever epidemics; Philadelphia was hit repeatedly, in 1699, 1741, 1762, and, most famously, 1793. Multiple aliases given to the disease—Bronze John, dock fever, stranger's fever, yellow jacket, Barbados distemper, and Palatine fever—mark its association with sea travel, immigration, and foreign trade. British medical, travel, and literary writers specifically coimplicated yellow fever, the Caribbean, and the slave trade, vesting its epidemics with racial implications. For example, in 1799, the English travel writer Robert Renny remembered that he was greeted on his arrival in Jamaica by a number of black women who taunted: "New come buckra, / He get sick, / He tak fever, / He be die, / He be die."[10] Some British abolitionist poets used the contagion of yellow fever as a metaphor for the contaminating effects of slavery. Even the "lank, brown, and lean" body of the protagonist in Samuel Taylor Coleridge's *Rime of the Ancient Mariner* (1798) bore the residuum of the disease. Because it bore these associations with the slave trade and the tropics, the 1793 yellow fever epidemic in Philadelphia challenged residents' privileged conceptions of themselves and their relationship to the wider Atlantic world. Indeed, almost everything about the fever afflicting the federal capital—its invisibility, its mysterious origins, its suspected communicability—suggested other imagined threats to the body politic: sin, aristocracy, Jacobinism, foreign sedition, the Illuminati, and commercial speculation.[11]

The mystery of yellow fever was not fully revealed until 1881, when Cuban physician Carlos Finlay identified mosquito bites as its mode of transmission. Infection by *Aedes aegypti* mosquito was confirmed in 1901 by Walter Reed, a U.S. Surgeon General-commissioned bacteriologist, sent to Cuba following the Spanish American War. But in 1793, long before the advent of germ theory, yellow fever plunged Philadelphia's medical community—including the fellows of the recently founded College of Physicians, America's first medical school—into divisive debate. They knew that yellow fever was by nature "bilious": its symptoms resulted from the hyperproduction and accumulation of bile in the digestive tract. However, its causes and cures were subjects of speculation. The most learned fellows had been educated in principles of nosology, a Linnean-type classificatory system developed by the Scottish doctor William Cullen. According to Cullen, fevers could be categorized by genus, order, and species; yellow fever—*synochus Iteroides*—could not be classed with the more familiar autumnal remitting, scarlet, and camp fevers. Rather, it was of a foreign species. How came this tropical fever to Philadelphia?

Two major schools of thought emerged on this question. The contagionists, headed by William Currie, traced the onset of yellow fever to the recent influx of West Indian slave revolt refugees; these refugees, it was hypothesized, transmitted the fever through a bodily exhalation or effluvia called "contagion." Currie and his fellows prescribed restrictions on immigration and quarantines, as well as purges and tonics for individual patients. Climatists, Benjamin Rush among them, attributed the disease not to the influx of tropical residents but to a season of unusually tropical weather in Philadelphia. Heat and humidity had accelerated Philadelphia's already unhealthful environmental conditions, producing a different species of "contagion" by releasing "vegetable putrefaction" and other putrid "miasmas" into the air. Some climatists even hypothesized—with a nod to the anti-immigrant or importationist medical faction—that the epidemic's epicenter was a rotting coffee cargo disgorged in July by a West Indian sloop onto the streets of Philadelphia's waterside neighborhoods. To remedy this and other travesties of civic hygiene, climatists recommended better sanitation, street-paving, tree-planting, and improved burial practices. In the treatment of individual patients, Rush and his colleagues favored bleeding.

Climatists and contagionists both viewed nativity or nationality as indices of susceptibility to the fever. However, they differed in their understandings of how resistance was constituted. Contagionist William Currie suggested that French West Indians were inured against the fever by virtue of their acclimation to tropical heat. Such heat was thought to accelerate the production and excretion of bile; long exposure, then, could render "the duodenum and biliary ducts insensible to the poison" of bilious fever.[12] Currie continued:

> For it is a singular though a notorious fact, that the disease seldom or ever affect any but strangers or newcomers from a colder or more temperate climate, in the West Indies; as we are informed by almost all the writers on the subject. But we were strangers or newcomers to it to all intents and purposes, with this difference, that it was brought to us instead of our being taken to it; and for that reason were subject to its influence.[13]

Currie's theory bore multiple political implications. Certainly, it might be construed to legitimate an anti-immigrant or xenophobic sentiment. It also suggested that Philadelphians were strangers in their "own" land. Climatists, however, linked acclimation to susceptibility rather than immunity. Doctor David de Isaac Cohen Nassy theorized that Philadelphia natives, "whose organical constitution has great homogeneity with the air of this country," were more disposed "to receive the impressions of the putrid miasmas" than foreigners or immigrants.[14] Nassy, Benjamin Rush, and the French West Indian doctor Jean Deveze criticized contagionists for pathologizing human interaction, provoking anti-immigrant sentiment, and instigating a dissolution of social bonds. Rush in particular accused them of polluting medicine with the "principle of self love": "We find dangerous and loathsome diseases are considered by all nations, as of foreign extraction. Even the yellow fever itself in some parts of the West Indies, is denied to be a native of the Islands. It is said by many of their writers to have been imported from Siam in the East Indies."[15] If contagionists placed the blame for yellow fever abroad, climatists insisted that the real problems were at home.

On one point, on one population, Philadelphia's medical community concurred: they believed black people to be innately immune to yellow fever. The city's two thousand African-American, black West Indian, black Briton, and native African residents shared little by way of common acclimation, whether to Philadelphia or to more tropical climes. But under the broad banner of phenotype, black people appeared to be a group sui generis: domesticated, even American-born, and yet perpetually foreign. This social scientific blind spot cooperated with erroneous published findings in tropical medicine. Most influential among the College of Physicians was John Lining's *A Description of the American Yellow Fever, which Prevailed at Charleston in the Year 1748*. Lining, a contagionist, attributed the Charleston epidemic to an infected carrier from the West Indies. Those most liable to infection included "newcomers," country-dwellers visiting town, "strangers lately arrived from cold climates," "Indians," "Mistees" (an English borrowing from the Spanish *mestizo*, indicating persons of mixed black and Indian ancestry), and "Mulattoes of all ages." Least susceptible were members of Charleston's black population. Wrote Lining, "There is something very singular in the constitution of the Negroes which renders them not liable to this fever; for though many of these were as much exposed as the nurses to the infection, yet I never knew one instance of this fever amongst them, though they are equally subject with the white people to the bilious fever."[16] His observation of unusually low infection rates among African-Americans may have indeed been accurate; his analysis, however, was deeply flawed. Immunity derived not from a racially "singular constitution" but rather from resistance acquired in surviving childhood bouts with the disease. As Winthrop Jordan notes, yellow fever was "endemic" in both West Africa and the West Indies; natives to those regions often "acquired prolonged immunity or relatively high resistance" to the disease.[17] Because it is likely that a large proportion of South Carolina's black population was born in yellow fever endemic regions of Africa or the Caribbean, it is probable that many of Lining's subjects had contracted the fever and developed immunity before arriving in South Carolina. Lining might have discovered the real basis for their immunity, had he been willing to investigate his black subjects' personal and medical histories. Instead, both he and the doctors of Philadelphia privileged their own race-biased observations over a more extensive inquiry.

It is important to note that reductive assumptions about race, innate difference, and immunity had not always governed American medicine. More than eighty years earlier, during an outbreak of smallpox in Boston, Cotton Mather observed that African slaves who tended the sick frequently did not take the disease. As Mather recalled, in a 1716 letter to an English professor of medicine:

> Inquiring of my Negro-man Onesimus, who is a pretty intelligent fellow, whether he ever had the smallpox, he answered, both *yes* and *no*; and then told me that he had undergone an operation which had given him something of the smallpox, and would forever preserve him from it, adding that it was often used among the Garamantese, and whoever had the courage to use it was forever free from the fear of the contagion.[18]

The "operation" Onesimus described was inoculation: the purposeful insertion of smallpox scabs into an incision on the patient's skin. Throughout Africa and the Near East, inoculation was common medical practice; in 1713, Lady Mary Wortley Montague, then stationed in Istanbul, reported on it to the Royal Society. But Mather, ever careful about documenting wonders particular to America, took pains to point out that his conversation with Onesimus predated by "many months" the Royal Society's publication of its findings. It was the Africans, not the English, who brought groundbreaking intelligence about acquired immunity to pox-infected colonial New England.

As inoculation transitioned into the American medical repertoire, its African roots became a point of contention. Cotton Mather aggressively advocated the practice during the Boston smallpox epidemics of 1721–22. His *Account of the Method and Success of Inoculating the Small-pox in Boston in New England* (1722) attempts to answer its critics. To those who claimed "it is not lawful for Christians to learn the Way of the Heathen," Mather replied that Hippocrates himself was a "heathen"; moreover, "our Indians"—also "heathens"—had conveyed to the colonists many "noble Specificks" in medicine.[19] Some charged that Mather invented the conversation with Onesimus to cover for his furtive borrowings from Royal Society publications. Africans were incapable of conceiving such medical advances, insisted Mather's adversary William Douglass in *A Dissertation Concerning Inoculation of the Small-Pox* (1730). To counter Onesimus, Douglass summoned up his own African informant—an unnamed slave—who testified that God gave inoculation "to poor Negroes to save their lives, for they had not knowledge and skill as [Europeans]."[20] This revisionary history cancelled African agency in the development of inoculation: rather than an evidence of African civilization, it was a providential compensation for innate "Negro" deficiency. Similarly, in his *Essay on Inoculation, Occasioned by the Small-Pox being brought into South Carolina in the Year 1738* (1743), South Carolina doctor James Kilpatrick denied that "Women in Turkey, and Negroes in Africa" were capable of conducting a true inoculation, which he expressly reserved to trained medical professionals.[21] It took less than thirty years for Mather's landmark conversation with Onesimus to disappear from American medical literature.

What hastened this "forgetting" was a broader shift in medical and scientific discourse towards professionalization and scientific classification. The watershed publication of Swedish biologist Carolus Linneaus's *Systema Natura* (first edition, 1735) inspired the invention of nosology by William Cullen. Cullenians held that simple empirical diagnosis and treatment was medieval and dangerously amateur; without a systematic, classificatory understanding of diseases, treatment would address only symptoms but not root causes. Systematic nosology established a theoretical basis for the professionalization of medicine. As Cotton Mather's generation of amateur scientists passed away, American medicine became the guarded domain of professionally trained doctors. James Kilpatrick's comments about smallpox inoculation demonstrate that this professionalization was predicated on the delegitimation of traditional practitioners and practice, including midwives, folk and faith healers, barber-surgeons, apothecaries, and root workers. To salvage inoculation—which had proven its worth—doctors like Kilpatrick negated its African history. The move toward a medical science based in systematic observation and Linnean classification also hastened the construction of race as a significant medical category rather than an arbitrary cultural distinction. More sinister was the simultaneous move toward a pathologization of racial difference, based on the alleged inscrutability of blackness. For example, Kilpatrick wrote that black skin hindered the diagnosis of smallpox: "[Blacks] are subject to a greater Number of eruptive Diseases, and cuticular Foulnesses than we are, a slight Pit or two, that look'd like the Small-pox, was less credited."[22] Medical literature of the mid eighteenth century positioned black people as a distinct and problematic class. This formulation was consolidated with the tenth edition of Linnaeus's *Systema Natura* (1758), which included a hierarchical arrangement of the varieties of species *Homo sapiens*: the "black, phlegmatic, indulgent" *afer* ranked below the "white, ruddy, muscular" *europaeus*.

Linnean zoology and Cullenian nosology established systems and suggested principles, but did not posit causes. Consequently, the origins of racial differentiation proved a special problem for eighteenth-century medical science. Polygenists—including Edward Long, author of *The History of Jamaica* (1774); Scottish lawyer Henry Home, Lord Kames, author of *Sketches of the History of Man* (1774); and Thomas Jefferson, author of *Notes on the State of Virginia* (1787)—rejected biblical accounts of the geneses of the human race (in the Garden of Eden) and the human races (in Cain and/or Ham) to argue a strictly "scientific" view of race. They contended that race was a fixed, innate, and perpetual category; different races descended from different genetic origins. The less heretical monogeneticists did not challenge the original unity of the human species, but they did rely on pathology or "degeneration" as an explanation for racial difference. Influential in this regard were George-Louis LeClerc, the comte du Buffon's *A Natural History, General and Particular* (1749–1804) and J. F. Blumenbach's *De Generis Humani Varietate Nativa* (1776). The most famous American advocate of monogeneticism was the Reverend Samuel Stanhope Smith. In February 1787, Smith delivered *An Essay on the Causes of the Variety of Complexion in the Human Species* as a lecture to the American Philosophical Society in Philadelphia. He advanced a climatist view of race centering on bile as a source of human variation:

> The change of climate produces a proportionable alteration in the internal state and structure of the body, and in the quantity of the secretions. In southern climates particularly, the bile, as has been remarked, is always augmented. . . . It appears, that the complexion in any climate will be changed towards black, in proportion to the degree of heat in the atmosphere, and to the quantity of bile in the skin.[23]

Other environmental factors identified by Smith as factors in bilious secretion included "the vapours of stagnant waters with which uncultivated regions abound," "great fatigues and hardships," and "poverty and nastiness."[24] Such conditions were prevalent in regions with large black populations, especially Africa, the Caribbean, and the American South. But evidences of racial drift were also manifesting among the white settler colonists in these regions—in Spanish South America, Portuguese Africa, and the southern and coastal regions of America. According to Smith, "sallowness" was already acutely noticeable among the southern states' "poor and labouring classes," these classes being "always first and most deeply affected by the influence of climate."[25]

When yellow fever beset Philadelphia in 1793, Smith's provocative comments about race, class, bile, and climate were still hanging in the air like a miasma. Their anticipation of yellow fever debates is uncanny; their influence is certain. After all, if one believed that tropical acclimation and bilious hyperproduction caused blackness, then blackness might signify desensitization to the bilious yellow fever. This understanding of blackness—as a category with specific immuno-properties—had seemed common sense to Philadelphia's doctors in August 1793. But by November, when black fever casualties finally mounted to an estimated two hundred, none would assert black immunity without qualification. After the epidemic, medical consensus moved invariably toward environmental rather than innate conceptions of immunity. Among the first to publish a revision was the contagionist William Currie, who observed in his *Treatise on the Synochus Iteroides* (1794) that American-born blacks were susceptible to the fever while African and Caribbean natives and long-term residents of the West Indies were not. Concurring with recent work by the English doctor Robert Jackson, Currie emphasized acclimation: immunity was the result of "the effects produced on the biliary ducts and duodenum, by the frequent and copious secretion of bile, to which the inhabitants of Tropical climates are particularly subject; whereby they are rendered insensible to the contagion of this disease."[26] Benjamin Rush also admitted his error in early 1794, admitting that African-Americans "took the disease in common with the white people, and many of them died with it."[27] His revisionist theory focused on national culture as a basis for immunity. Rush observed that it was "nothing new, for epidemics to affect persons of one nation, and to pass by persons of other nations in the same city or country"—for example, Jews at Modena, and Dutch and Italians in Switzerland—which he attributed to "a difference in diet which is as much a distinguishing mark of nations as dress."[28] Rush and Currie did not abolish but rather modified racialist theories of immunity. They redefined the essence of race not as biology alone but as nativity, climate, or culture. Correspondingly, when yellow fever struck Philadelphia again in 1797, the College of Physicians recommended that only African-born blacks be considered immune to the disease and employed in public health capacities.[29]

More fundamental than the issue of immunity was the challenge yellow fever season death tolls posed to the medical conception of race itself. The revisionary literature on immunity suggested a movement from nature to naturalization, race to nation, constitution to culture. Did not William Currie's climatist revision of immunity strangely mirror Samuel Stanhope Smith's climatist formulation of race? Was the jaundice of yellow fever akin to the "sallowness" Smith observed overtaking the American South? Did the visitation of yellow fever signal that Philadelphia was more tropical, more southerly than it thought? If so, what were the phenotypic implications for the city's white population? Was race itself a fluid and environmentally dependent construct? Philadelphia's medical community did not grapple openly with these racially destabilizing implications. Even an avowed climatist like Benjamin Rush recoiled, his racial theories veering in the years following 1793 toward contagionism. On July 14, 1797, Rush argued before the American Philosophical Society that blackness was a consequence of leprosy, a communicable disease. This new theory reinforced race-based social boundaries: Rush recommended humanity and justice in the treatment of African-Americans but also a maintenance of "existing prejudices against matrimonial connection with them."[30] But most of Rush's American scientific colleagues settled into a stunned silence on the issue. Not until 1808—after a gap of almost fifteen years—was there another major American treatise on race and racial origin.

Yellow fever medicine failed in its assignation of immunity to blackness, but popular fever season stories would supply a new set of values for color. Black people themselves became symptoms of the epidemic's social crisis. The *Federal Gazette* published a morbid-comic dialogue between two farmers about the economic impacts of the fever. "The best news, and that from the Negroes, for they only come to Market now! They told me that 14,200 have already died—29,000 have gone out of town—so that only 1425 people remain," said one. His counterpart replied, "Your account is indeed a black one."[31] "Black accounts" of the epidemic circulated in the popular imagination and the popular presses. An especially virulent rumor had it that African-Americans had poisoned the city's water wells, causing the yellow fever.[32] Others used blackness as an element of Gothic suggestion. For example, a broadside of *A Dream dreamed by one in the year 1757, concerning Philadelphia* (Germantown, 1793) painted a tableau of the yellow fever epidemic in emphatically black hues: human corpses carried by "a multitude of black carts or waggons," "with black horses and drivers," "all very black and dismal as was the sky or upper hemisphere." Similarly, Benjamin Rush conveyed the gravity of the epidemic in a letter dated September 18, 1793, to his wife Julia: "In every room you enter you see no person but a solitary black man or woman near the sick."[33]

Ephemeral as these popular legends were, they nonetheless indicated that blackness was taking on a new value in the postemancipation era. Black skin was an increasingly unreliable indicator of an individual's legal status, slave or free; nor did it represent innate physiological difference, as the failure of the yellow fever immunity hypothesis had shown. What it would mean—how white people would react and relate to the ascendant free black community—was yet to be determined, and the yellow fever epidemic played a critical role in its determination. It was not that yellow fever ushered blacks and whites into unprecedented intimacy. Before the fever, the majority of Philadelphia's black population lived and worked in white households, with access to and responsibilities for the care of persons and property. Many white families were accustomed to the presence of black domestics in "private" spaces and their provision of intimate services. This considered, the ascription of African-Americans into the fever care-giving corps constituted no major change to the status quo. What did change, however, was the conduct of the white population, thousands of whom abandoned sick friends and family to flee the city. This white flight left African-Americans to continue their work unsupervised. More important, it removed white refugees from firsthand observation and left the state of the city to their own imaginations. White Philadelphians imagined blackness as a sign of disorder, even danger. Indeed, the gothic fantasy of blacks poisoning white wells merely recycled a dominant trope from slave revolt lore. If yellow was the color of the plague, then black was the color of its social consequences: a world turned upside down, the demise of white society.

For information about the yellow fever epidemic, most Philadelphians relied on Irish émigré and publisher Mathew Carey's *A short account of the malignant fever, lately prevalent in Philadelphia: with a statement of the proceedings that took place on the subject in different parts of the United States.* Appointed by Mayor Clarkson to serve on the civic relief committee, Carey hardly distinguished himself in service or philanthropy. Just days after his appointment, he fled Philadelphia for three critical weeks of the epidemic—from September 16 to October 8; whereas the average committee member expended $2,000 of his own funds on relief, Carey spent only $66.46.[34] His distinctive contribution to Philadelphia's recovery from yellow fever was to be a literary one: when he returned to the city, he accomplished his civic duty in composing and publishing the history of the epidemic. From committee minutes, popular legends, and newspaper accounts, Carey compiled the details of its portents, onset, transmission, and outcomes; appendices to the *Account* listed the names of the dead. Demand for this comprehensive information ran high, especially among those who had fled and were returning to the city. Indeed, Carey timed his publishing efforts to coincide with the season of the return: four English-language editions of the *Account* appeared in Philadelphia between November 14, 1793 and January 16, 1794. One of these editions was printed expressly for export, to satisfy the inquiries of European creditors.[35] French- and German-language editions followed in January 1794, for Pennsylvania's immigrant communities; a foreign edition was published in London in 1794. Altogether, Carey's *Accounts* sold more than ten thousand copies.

The *Account* portrayed Philadelphia under siege by pestilence. Only heroic action by the mayor's select committee saved the city from social, commercial, and vital ruin. Carey set the heroism of these white male citizens in sharp relief, against a darker background of petty criminality, gross incompetence, and failed virtue. To achieve this effect, he capitalized on and perpetuated white prejudices against and negative perceptions of black people. It was a point of horror, in the *Account*, that the city's "respectable" and "affluent" citizens were abandoned to and buried by black care givers.[36] Carey knew quite well that the racial composition of the service corps was a consequence of the black immunity hypothesis. By the time the *Account* was published, he also knew that the hypothesis had proven false. He himself had reviewed, albeit "very cursorily," the records of Philadelphia's Bush-hill hospital, which placed black mortality rates at 75 percent.[37] The mortality lists appended to his *Account* also identify black victims by name and race: "John Brown, a Negro," "Qua, a Negro," "Elsy, a black," "Juda, a black woman." Still, neither the overt failing of the medical community in its treatment of black people, nor the casualties sustained by the black community incurred Carey's sympathies. He portrayed the faulty theory of black immunity as a providence and the service of black caregivers as an affliction:

> The error that prevailed on this subject had a very salutary effect; for at an early period of the disorder, hardly any white nurses could be procured; and had the negroes been equally terrified, the sufferings of the sick, great as they actually were, would have been exceedingly aggravated. At the period alluded to, the elders of the African church met, and offered their services to the mayor, to procure nurses for the sick, and to assist in burying the dead. Their offers were accepted; and Absalom Jones and Richard Allen undertook the former department, that of furnishing nurses, and William Gray, the latter—the interment of the dead. The great demand for nurses afforded an opportunity for imposition, which was eagerly seized by some of the vilest of the blacks. They extorted two, three, four, and even five dollars a night for attendance, which would have been well paid by a single dollar. Some of them were even detected in plundering the houses of the sick.[38]

Nowhere does Carey acknowledge the danger faced by black nurses and gravediggers, who "offered their services" despite evidence of their own susceptibility to yellow fever. Nor is it suggested that white doctors and politicians bear any accountability for putting the black community in this dangerous position. He does modulate his racial characterizations in a postscript to the passage: "It is wrong to cast a censure on the whole for this sort of conduct, as many people have done. The services of Jones, Allen, and Gray, and others of their colour, have been very great, and demand public gratitude."[39] A terse new footnote appeared in the fourth edition of the *Account*: "The extortion here mentioned, was very far from being confined to the negroes: many of the white nurses behaved with equal capacity."[40] But neither the meritocratic celebration of virtuous black individuals nor the qualifying footnote modify the deep racial politics of the passage. Carey establishes an inverted, opponential relationship between the well-being of Philadelphia's white and black communities: the medical error that endangers the black community is "salutary" for whites; the fever which endangers the white community benefits black criminal "opportunism": the fever seized upon whites, and blacks seized upon the fever. Black care givers become but another element of the epidemic assault on the white population.

Blackness recurs as an element of gothic suggestion in the final chapters of the *Account*. Chapters 16 and 17 offered "Desultory facts and reflections—A collection of scraps," or a loosely assembled, sensationalistic series of anecdotes from the epidemic. Some feature black nurses and gravediggers. One Philadelphia refugee fell ill on the road, laying there for two days without assistance before dying; he was not buried until locals hired "two black butchers," who dragged his putrefacted body into a pit with a rope and pitchfork.[41] There were no marriages recorded in Philadelphia during the fever season, until November 5, when two nurses—a "Portuguese mulatto" named Nassy and Hannah Smith, "a bouncing German girl"—were wed. Other anecdotes return to the theme of black criminality, as Carey reported that "a hardened villain from another state" had organized "a large partnership" with blacks in Philadelphia to "plunder houses."[42] Blackness itself overtakes white individuals in a few instances. One Philadelphia refugee was tarred and feathered by residents of a Maryland country town.[43] A boy wore "a tarred rope" around his neck day and night—tar being a popular prophylactic—until he "woke in the night half strangled and black in the face."[44] In the chaos of yellow fever, black thieves violate homes, black men marry white women, and black tar stains white complexions. Taken together, these anecdotes force a connection between blackness and white victimization. Blackness indicates the vulnerability and weakness of white corporate identity.

Some historians have suggested that Carey was motivated by antiblack racism, which itself derived from tensions between Irish immigrants and free blacks. His public stance on race relations tended toward colonizationism: in the first edition of his *Columbian Magazine* (October 1786), he promoted the resettlement of blacks in Africa, fantasizing that by 1850 "very few" might remain in America.[45] But the criminalization of African-Americans and the gothic invocation of blackness in the *Account* must not be written off as one man's racist fantasy. Rather, it reflects postemancipation anxieties about the meaning of race. The failure of race-based science in the context of the epidemic certainly provoked such anxieties, as did the frailty of white fellow-feeling revealed in the abandonment of the sick. Even the symptomology of the fever suggested a threat to phenotypic whiteness. After all, Samuel Stanhope Smith and Benjamin Rush had theorized that blackness was a condition induced by the hyperproduction of bile and bilious fevers. Doctors' catalogues of symptoms suggested as much: white victims turned "tawny"-skinned, "face and breast became spotted, as if sprinkled with ink," "a deep dusky yellow and purple colour, resembling blood settled in a bruised part, pervaded the whole surface of the body;" mortal symptoms included black tongue and black vomit.[46] Mercury purges left even the survivors with black teeth.[47] Inasmuch as the *Account* played to existing racial anxieties, it also promoted a new scheme for understanding and managing racial difference. Salvaging from bad science the idea of innate race-based difference, it transformed blackness from a physiological classification into a sociological characterization that indexed criminality, incompetence, and opportunism.

Philadelphia's black community felt the racial panic of the fever season as an "unprovoked attempt" "to make us blacker than we are"—so wrote Absalom Jones and Richard Allen in *A Narrative of the Proceedings of the Black People, During the Late Awful Calamity in Philadelphia.* The twenty-four page *Narrative*, published in January 1794, reclaimed blackness from feverish overdetermination. It responded both to Mathew Carey's scandalous misrepresentations of black nurses and gravediggers and to a more general failure to account for black experience in other official fever season publications. Even the published minutes of Mayor Clarkson's civic relief committee made no mention of the contributions of black men and women to public welfare, and Carey himself admitted that his accounting of black deaths was conducted but "very cursorily."[48] Jones and Allen responded by contesting accusations of black criminality, critiquing medical racial profiling, reporting black mortality rates, and reminding white Philadelphia of its own failures of humanity during the late fever season. They also reprinted an accounting of African Society funds expended and received during the epidemic and a note of commendation from Philadelphia mayor Matthew Clarkson. Beyond this "refutation," as the title of the work indicated, Jones and Allen offered a "narrative of the proceedings of the black people": the first published story to center on African-Americans as a corporate subject. As a document of conscious community formation, the *Narrative* marks a constituting moment in black political, cultural, and textual history.

Jones and Allen were uniquely positioned to articulate the emergent consciousness of America's largest free black community. In the decade before the yellow fever epidemic, together they had presided over a remarkable phase of community mobilization, which saw the organization of separate and independent black churches and community organizations. This black corporate consciousness shapes their *Narrative*. Throughout, the authors use the first person plural pronoun, "we." Dual authorship merges strategically into collective authority; individual identities recede. Even on the frontispiece to the work the authors are identified only by their initials, "A.J. & R.A." Among early national republicans, this near-anonymity or pseudonymity was a literary formula for establishing an author's disinterested virtue and dedication to the common good. But republican assumptions about individual virtues and public goods did not extend to early African-America. As long as color mediated estimations of character and organized public policy, there was no such thing as a black individual, nor a meritocracy. Jones and Allen indicted Carey's "partial representation" of their community: "The bad consequences many of our colour apprehend from a partial relation of our conduct are, that it will prejudice the minds of the people in general against us—because it is impossible that one individual can have knowledge of all."[49]

At particular issue was Mathew Carey's racialized representation of criminality during the epidemic. The *Accounts* emphasized petty thefts and opportunism by black nurses; white thieves and opportunists were not racially characterized. Additionally, this narrow construction of criminality ignored broader conditions that initiated wage inflation during the epidemic. A shortage of willing nurses, abandonment by friends and family, willingness to pay—did not some responsibility fall to those who fled the city? And did not economic inequality, predating and outliving the epidemic, contribute to these circumstances? Jones and Allen observe that "it was natural for people in low circumstance to accept a voluntary, bounteous reward."[50] Should not the dangerous, even "loathsome" nature of the work rather than the color or class status of the nurses determine appropriate wages? They ask, "Had Mr. Carey been solicited to such an undertaking, for hire, *Query*, what would *he* have demanded?" Carey, who abandoned his appointed duties and fled the city, returning to undertake his publishing endeavor, might also be indicted by a broader definition of opportunism:

> He was wrong in giving so partial and injurious an account of the black nurses; if they have taken advantage of the public distress, is it any more than he hath done of its desire for information? We believe he has made

more money by the sale of his 'scraps' than a dozen of the greatest extortioners among the black nurses. . . . Is it a greater crime for a black to pilfer, than for a white to privateer?[51]

In addition to this critique of classism, Jones and Allen attempt to rebalance Carey's racial profiling by contrasting the "poor blacks'" "humanity" and "sensibility" with the behavior of "the poor whites," who "hid themselves"—like Adam and Eve after the fall (Genesis 3:8)—rather than offer their services.[52] "Had Mr. Carey said, a number of white and black Wretches eagerly seized on the opportunity to extort from the distressed, and some few of both were detected in plundering the sick," the authors charged, "it might extenuate, in a great degree, the having made mention of the blacks."[53] Importantly, Jones and Allen refuse the praise Carey extended to them individually. Honoring a few distinguished black citizens (as Carey had) aggravated rather than mitigated racial profiling, for it left all other African-Americans in "the hazardous state of being classed with those who are called the 'vilest.'"[54] In the corporate subject of the *Narrative*, Jones and Allen defuse this false meritocracy and merge themselves with the broader black community.

Additionally, by designating a black corporate subject, Jones and Allen establish their yellow fever account within a distinctive context of black experience and belief. Black experience and white discourse diverge almost immediately. "Early in September," write Jones and Allen, "a solicitation appeared in the public papers, to the people of colour to come forward and assist the distressed, perishing, and neglected sick; with a kind of assurance, that people of our colour were not liable to take the infection."[55] Jones and Allen indicate—if subtly—their original suspicion of black immunity theories, which provided only "a *kind* of assurance." Disbelief in racialist science predicates the community's faith-based response to the epidemic. They continue, "We found a freedom to go forth, confiding in him who can preserve in the midst of a burning fiery furnace, sensible that it was our duty to do all the good we could to our suffering fellow mortals."[56] The phrase "burning fiery furnace" is not a rhetorical flourish; rather it is a point of reference to the Bible. The words "burning fiery furnace" appears eight times in Daniel 3 and nowhere else in the Bible; with this unannotated phrase, Jones and Allen quietly and powerfully connect the black community's yellow fever predicament to the story of Shadrach, Meshach, and Abednego. That story, briefly, is as follows: Babylonian Jews Shadrach, Meshach, and Abednego refused to worship a "golden image" fashioned by King Nebuchadnezzar, who consequently "cast [them] into the midst of a burning fiery furnace" (Daniel 3:1, 6); by divine intervention, the men emerged from the flames unharmed, causing Nebuchadnezzar to acclaim the God who "delivered his servants," "changed the king's word," and "yielded their bodies, that they might not serve nor worship any god, except their own God" and to issue a decree prohibiting slander against the three men (Daniel 3:28). Jones and Allen paratextually index the chosenness of the black community, its divinely intended survival of lethal situations, and, importantly, its refusal to worship the golden images of Babylon.

Or, its recusal from Philadelphia's commercial society. Financial speculation, commercial credit schemes, and conspicuous consumption appear in several yellow fever narratives—including Mathew Carey's—as portents or factors of the epidemic. What preserves the humanity and health of black nurses, according to Jones and Allen, is their decision not to set a price for their own services. Several anecdotes embedded within the *Narrative* testify to this principle: black nurses who demanded payment died; those who did not were spared. "Sampson" "went house to house," providing "no assistance without fee or reward; he was smote with the disorder and died, after death his family were neglected by those he had served."[57] "One young black woman," solicited as a nurse, said, "I will not go for money, if I go for money God will see it, and may be make me take the disorder and die, but if I go, and take no money, he may spare my life"; she lived.[58] Free African Society cofounder Caesar Cranchal offered his services but insisted, "I will not take your money, I will not sell my life for money;" he died, but from influenza and not the yellow fever.[59] This refrain—"I will not sell my life for money"—echoes the story of Jacob and Esau and conjures up ghosts of slavery. It testifies that the struggle against slavery continued in the nominally postemancipation years as a struggle against the dehumanizing and dangerous effects of white racism and commercialism. According to Jones and Allen, the yellow fever epidemic was a crucible of black identity and an intensive test of black commitment to freedom. Whatever immunity they enjoyed came by their obedience to the terms of their covenant with God.

The narrative further denaturalizes black immunity by directly critiquing medical science. Recalling that the theory was derived from observations of black resistance to the fever in "the West-Indies and other places where this terrible malady had been," Jones and Allen write, "Happy would it have been for you, and much more so for us, if this observation had been verified by our experience."[60] Moreover, the authors allege, even after evident black fever casualties, white doctors and politicians conspired to deny the infectious risk of yellow fever: "We were imposed upon and told it was not with the prevailing sickness, until it became too notorious to be denied, then we were told some few died but not many."[61] Misinformation is supplanted with black observation and experience. The authors report that African-Americans did indeed contract and die from the disease: "We can assure the public we have taken four and five black people a day to be buried."[62] Additional corroboration comes in data from the published bill of mortality, which demonstrates black death rates proportionate to the white population's. These deaths— which represented a "more than fourfold" annual increase, from 67 in 1792 to 305 in 1793—Jones and Allen firmly connect to care-giving responsibilities undertaken by "the unjustly vilified black people."[63] Additionally, by virtue of these care-giving labors, the collective "we" of the Narrative assumes medical authority. After all, black nurses had served at the front-lines of the epidemic, often working independently of Philadelphia's overloaded doctors. Jones and Allen reproduced and distributed Benjamin Rush's directions for bleeding the sick; Rush credited them with nursing back to health two to three hundred working-class fever sufferers, while more recently historian Gary Nash has revised that figure upward to eight hundred.[64] Jones and Allen also made careful notes on many of their patients. The Narrative represents this firsthand medical knowledge, bolstering the authors' charge that African-Americans were capable of recognizing yellow fever when it struck them. Initial symptoms included "a chill, a headache, a sick stomach, with pains in their limbs and back." Jones and Allen carefully point out that not all patients manifested the same set of symptoms, but "what confirmed us in the opinion of a person being smitten was the colour of their eyes."[65] Deftly, the authors address the intersection of racial difference and symptomology. In white patients, yellow skin had served as proof of yellow fever; the alleged illegibility of black skin—or, rather, inability to see yellowness manifest there—was one of the roots of the black immunity hypothesis. Jones and Allen establish a superior criterion applicable to a phenotypically diverse sample population: "the colour of the eyes" was a reliable indicator of jaundice.

Their firsthand observations as nurses also vested the black community with a certain moral authority. Some doctors connected all illness to the condition of the nervous system; a popular variation on this idea held that fear or panic aggravated disease, while self-composure and good character relieved it.[66] A patient's conduct both revealed the quality of his or her soul and determined the course of the illness. What black nurses witnessed in their white patients was revelatory indeed. The worst cases were "raging and frightful to behold," "made attempts to jump out of a window," and required restraints "to prevent them from running away, or breaking their necks."[67] Jones and Allen continued:

> Some lost their reason, and raged with all the fury madness could produce, and died in strong convulsions. Others retained their reason to the

last, and seemed rather to fall asleep than die. We could not help remarking that the former were of strong passions, and the latter of a mild temper. Numbers died in a kind of dejection, they concluded they must go, (so the phrase for dying was) and therefore in a kind of fixed determined state of mind went off.[68]

In addition to these qualities of character, the conduct of white patients revealed a failure of will or self-determination. White men and women in full health sought out black care givers to make advance funeral arrangements. "It struck our minds with awe," wrote Jones and Allen, that "some have lain on the floor, to be measured for their coffin and grave."[69] These moral and spiritual failures took an emotional toll on black nurses: "White people, that ought to be patterns for us to follow after, have acted in a manner that would make humanity shudder."[70] Widows mistreated or abandoned, aid to the dying refused, sick black nurses turned out of homes; "We even know of one who died in a stable," Jones and Allen report.[71] When black nurses discovered young white children playing around their parents' corpses, it was left to them to explain the deaths and find homes for the orphans. "A white man threatened to shoot us if we passed by his house with a corpse," write Jones and Allen. "We buried him three days after."[72] This collection of anecdotes strongly implies that the survival of the black community was a matter of spiritual determination.

The concluding pages of the *Narrative* resound a theme of spiritually covenanted survival. During the epidemic, Jones and Allen remember, "through mercy, we were enabled to go on"; "we have been so wounded and our feelings so hurt, that we almost concluded to withdraw from our undertaking, but seeing others so backwards, we still went on."[73] Survival and transcendence are formulated as forward movement, connecting this specific yellow fever narrative to a larger story of the black community as a chosen people in exodus. Redemption from bondage—whether the social death of slavery, the physical threat of yellow fever, or the spiritual tolls of racism—comes by spiritual dispensation and a conscious rejection of human depravity. In brief essays appended to the body of the *Narrative*, Jones and Allen apply these principles more broadly. "An Address to those who keep Slaves, and approve the practice" asserts the chosenness of the black community: "That God who knows the hearts of all men, and the propensity of a slave to hate his oppressor, hath strictly forbidden it to his chosen people, 'thou shalt not abhor an Egyptian, because thou wast a stranger in his land. Deut. Xxiii. 7.'"[74] In comments addressed "To the People of Colour," Jones and Allen recall both the "impatient" and "patient waiting" with which they had endured slavery. Banish fear and vengeance from your souls, they counsel. This alone will preserve you in the burning fiery furnace.

Jones and Allen's narrative functions as an immune system for Philadelphia's black community: it absorbs, denaturalizes, negates, redirects, and reinterprets racism and its science fictions. To faulty hypotheses of innate biological difference, to popular imaginings of blackness as a condition of character, they counterpose a spiritual conception of their community. Michelle Wallace has observed that modern black culture "reincorporates the 'negative' or 'racist' imagery of the dominant culture."[75] Similarly, in their study of "minor literatures," Abdul JanMohammed and David Lloyd assert that "the minority's attempt to negate the prior hegemonic negation of itself is one of its most fundamental forms of affirmation."[76] Jones and Allen represent a pioneering instance of this dynamic. This is the first moment in African-American literature when writing assumes both a collective subject and a specific cultural function: here, text becomes the means by which the community inoculates itself against racism, developing a corporate story, a shared resistance, a coimmunity, a vital community.

A noteworthy though easily overlooked element of the publication bolsters the incorporative function of Jones and Allen's text. On the second page of the *Narrative*—a spot usually reserved for an amanuensical preface, a subscription list, or a patron dedication—stands this notice:

> Be it remembered, That on the twenty-third day of January, in the eighteenth year of the Independence of the United States of America, Absalom Jones and Richard Allen, both of the said District, have deposited in this office, the title of a book, the right whereof they claim as authors and proprietors, in the words following, to wit: *"A Narrative of the Proceedings of the Black People, during the late and awful Calamity in Philadelphia, in the year 1793: and a Refutation of some Censures thrown upon them in some late Publications. By A.J. & R.A."* In conformity to the act of the Congress of the United States, intitled, "an Act for the encouragement of learning, by securing the copies of maps, charts, and books, to the authors and proprietors of such copies, during the times therein mentioned."

Absalom Jones and Richard Allen may have been the first African-American authors to avail themselves of federal copyright.[77] In 1790, Congress passed "An Act for the encouragement of learning, by securing the copies of maps, charts, and books, the authors and proprietors of such copies, during the times therein mentioned" (ch. 15, § 1, 1 Stat. 124), which secured to "authors"—either United States "citizens" or "residents"—"the sole right and liberty of printing, reprinting, publishing and vending" their works for a fourteen-year term, with an optional fourteen-year renewal (Section 1). The act stipulated a multistep process for gaining copyright, including registration with the district court and publication of copyright notice. It appears that Jones and Allen took every step necessary to securing their rights as authors of the *Narrative*.

Their motive was not profit. Pamphlets were known to be an unprofitable print genre, and the *Narrative* was republished only once, in London, beyond the domain of federal law.[78] Rather, the authors' primary concern was retention of rights to their story, a concern necessitated by a fever season epidemic of opportunistic and even predatory literary practices. Mathew Carey himself observed that one symptom of the epidemic was "a proneness to terrific narration."[79] There was also a proneness to prolific publication, as intense public demand for yellow fever information, analysis, and anecdote created a seasonal market. Yellow fever literature ran the gamut, from poems, broadsides, and sermons to learned medical treatises. Many informational histories of the fever—like Mathew Carey's—were not original works but rather composites of other texts. This hodgepodge, piecemeal style of composition was standard fare for most early republican presses. Carey did much of his business in reprints, authorized and unauthorized: his periodical *American Museum, or Repository of Ancient and Modern Fugitive Pieces, etc, Prose and Poetical* (1787–92) republished selections from a broad range of printed sources. During the epidemic, he used the technology of copyright to privatize public information about the fever; his copyrighted *Short Accounts* rely heavily on the public minutes of the civic relief committee on which he served. Carey, an avowed importationist, even used the press to embarrass his opponents in yellow fever medical debate, particularly Benjamin Rush. In December 1793, he republished correspondence from Benjamin Rush to John Redman, president of Philadelphia's College of Physicians; soon after, Carey issued his own refutation of Rush's stated views. These opportunistic practices drew substantial criticism and untold antipathy. Jones and Allen charged him with "privateering." Another of Carey's adversaries, who adopted the penname "Argus," initiated a campaign to prevent the city of Philadelphia from commending Mathew Carey's service during the epidemic. Wrote "Argus":

Had this man been actuated by that generous temper and enthusiasm, which filled other members of the committee, why did he not bestow, a least, A SMALL, A VERY SMALL part of the profits of the sale of his history of the fever, on some of those forlorn beings who have become victims to its power?—He is the only member of the committee, who has replenished his purse in consequence of the city's sufferings.[80]

Carey defended himself in an April 1794 *Address to the Public*, arguing that he acted not out of self-interest but in the interest of documented history: "My intention was to prevent such an utter deficiency of records on the subject of our late scourge, as has been often regretted, respecting the former instances of this kind."[81] Still, it is clear that he manipulated privileged access both to information and to the press in order to privatize and profit from fever season discourse.

Jones and Allen sought copyright to protect their *Narrative* within this aggressive print market and against a notoriously predatory opponent in Mathew Carey. Olaudah Equiano had wisely secured English copyright protection for his *Interesting Narrative* in 1789; Jones and Allen were the first African-American authors to avail themselves of American copyright laws. African-American writers before them had struggled for creative, editorial, and financial control over their publications. Slave masters, amanuenses, patrons, and subscribers mediated access to print media and consequently mediated the shape and content of black authors' publications. Enslaved black writers like Briton Hammon and Jupiter Hammon had no actionable legal right to property at all. After her manumission, Phillis Wheatley issued careful directives to printers and vendors of her *Poems*, as book sales were her sole financial support. John Marrant, a free black, had struggled to regulate dozens of unauthorized editions of his life *Narrative* (1785); only one edition was printed expressly "for the benefit of the author." Marrant's case clearly demonstrates how appropriation impacted the literary integrity of these works: his authorized fourth edition offers expanded, explicit abolitionist content not available in the others. Moreover, John Marrant's life shows the grave financial consequences of appropriation, as he starved his way through a mission in Nova Scotia while his life story was a minor hit back in London. American copyright laws—at least as they were initially conceived in 1790—promised authors some leverage against printers' technological and entrepreneurial advantages in the proprietorship of text.

Copyright also helped establish authoritative information about the black community. Yellow fever discourse about black immunity and especially black criminality was specious, shadowy rumor; it was text without author, authority, or accountability. These rumors functioned to perpetuate beliefs about the inassimilability and alienness of black people. Rumor was the communicable substance, the contagious matter, the miasma of white racism. Its unauthorized status only bolstered its power to dehumanize both the subjects and the objects of the discourse, to advance the mutual dehumanization that is the outcome of racism. Copyright was a legal, if technical, means to rehumanizing the discourse and to reclaiming subjective authority in matters concerning blackness.[82] Copyright vested the "official" story with a bounded corporeality. It was an authoritative legal and textual means to self-determination and self-reappropriation. The black text, therefore, was a property that conveyed belonging on its subjects.

It is striking that under copyright black texts enjoyed a more secure public presence than black persons did. This was especially true for the emerging urban American free black communities of the late eighteenth and early nineteenth centuries, whose members experienced aggravated levels of street violence and mob-rule racism. Prince Hall, the founder and grandmaster of Boston's African Lodge of Freemasons spoke to his membership: "Daily insults you meet with in the streets of Boston; much more on public days of recreation, how are you shamefully abus'd, and that at such a degree, that you may be said to carry your lives in your hands; and the arrows of death are flying about your heads."[83] John Marrant was assaulted by mobs when he visited Hall and the Boston Lodge. Free northern blacks, including African Lodge members, were also subject to kidnapping, transport to southern states, and reenslavement. A regime of white-on-black violence supplanted legal slavery in the post-emancipation northern states. As historian Joanne Pope Melish explains, whites "tranfer[red] a language and a set of practices shaped in the context of slavery to their relations with a slowly emerging population of free people of color."[84] Public gatherings of black people—in black churches and Masonic lodges especially—were favored targets for mob violence.[85]

The publication of Jones and Allen's *Narrative* preceded the formal incorporation of Philadelphia's black churches and Masonic lodges. As a protected black public presence, it served as a textual template for the formal incorporation of black community associations. It demonstrated the value of boundaries—here, the copyright—as a tool in the formation of a self-determining community. This was an important lesson for Philadelphia's fledgling black organizations, which had struggled to balance their own values against those of white patrons. Subsequent developments in black community life followed this incorporative model. In October 1796, Richard Allen and his associates filed "Articles of Association for the African Methodist Episcopal or 'Bethel' Church" with Pennsylvania's attorney general Jared Ingersoll, in a process of legal registration that shadowed that of copyright. Furthermore, these *Articles* were published in 1799. They enshrined in AME ecclesiastical polity a mechanism for resisting white appropriation, infiltration, or influence: article 2 reserved church offices and properties to "our African brethren, and the descendents of the African race"; article 6 declared that "none but coloured persons shall be chosen as trustees of the said African Episcopal Bethell Church"; and article 10 stipulated that "local preachers, exhorters, and class leaders, shall be of the African race."[86] Significantly, Richard Allen chose to publish the 1793 *Narrative of the Proceedings of the Black People* and the 1799 *Articles of Incorporation* as twin appendices to his published *Life Account* (1833). Both the *Narrative* and the *Articles* have survived in ten editions of Allen's *Life*, dual testaments to the incorporative legacy of the early black text.

White authors from Mathew Carey forward formulated a racially specific response to the 1793 yellow fever epidemic, which reinscribed yellow fever as a threat to white bodies personal and politic. The first full-blown American gothic novels followed Carey's protogothic "scraps." Charles Brockden Brown chose the yellow fever epidemic as the setting for *Arthur Mervyn* (1798–99) and *Ormond* (1799). Brown himself had endured a bout of yellow fever and buried some of his closest friends and associates—notably, fellow Friendly Club member Elihu Hubbard Smith—during the 1795 New York City epidemic. Surviving Friendly Club members dedicated themselves to the propagation of moral, political, and scientific knowledge about this public health threat. In his preface to *Arthur Mervyn*, Brown parlayed the historical and social magnitude of the epidemic into a suitable basis for novelistic commemoration:

> The evils of pestilence by which this city has lately been afflicted will probably form an aera in its history. The schemes of reformation and improvement to which they will give birth, or, if no efforts of human wisdom can avail to avert the periodical visitations of this calamity, the change in manners and population which they will produce will be, in the highest degree, memorable.[87]

Brown clearly hoped that his novel could contribute to the causes of moral "improvement" or social "reformation." But he does not specify precisely what "change in manners and populations" he feared as the unimproved consequence of yellow fever.

Early American novels have won a reputation as literary devices of nationalist formation that educated readers in modes of sentiment and deportment appropriate to citizenship. This education highlighted internal and external dangers to public interest and virtue that had been unleashed as a result of the radicalizing effects of the American Revolution on class boundaries and gender relations. The best-selling novels *Charlotte Temple* and the *Coquette* portrayed the nation as an American "Eve," endangered by the seductive advances of libertinistic Frenchmen, by her uneducated independence, her filial impiety, and her own constitutional weakness. Yellow fever offered Brown a masculinist counterpart to the creeping, conspiratorial danger of seduction: the American "Adam" of *Arthur Mervyn* is endangered by foreign criminals, yellow fever, his own country innocence, and misplaced charity. His medical apprenticeship, his professionalization, his emerging narrative control, and his patriarchal ascendance secure Mervyn against the social destabilization and urban decimation yellow fever represents.

Few of these early American novels, with the exception of Brown's Indian-obsessed *Edgar Huntly* (1799), explicitly configure racial difference as a threat to national citizenship. African-Americans play minor but deeply implicative roles in Brown's yellow fever novels. It is noteworthy that Brown does not perpetuate myths of black immunity—which had been roundly disproved by the late 1790s—but neither does he address the horrific situation of black servitude these theories incurred. Both *Arthur Mervyn* and *Ormond* assume the necessary presence of willing black fever functionaries; in both novels, this immune blackness returns as an index to white susceptibility. In *Ormond*, the benevolent, familiar black wood-carter who relieves Constantia Dudley of handling pestilent corpses finds a Gothic double in Ormond's black-faced imposture as a chimney sweep. Racial segregation and racialized division of labor permit black folks a certain access to the white private sphere, which black-faced villains then use to ill purpose. *Arthur Mervyn* offers a similarly gothic double-vision of racial identity and racialist science. On his ride to Baltimore, Mervyn scans the features of his fellow travelers, a "sallow Frenchman from Saint Domingo," "two female blacks," and "an ape," observing similarity and difference, interrogating and appreciating, this chain of being.[88] Joan Dayan has observed the recurring presence of monkeys throughout the American gothic, and particularly in Poe;[89] here in *Arthur Mervyn* we see the first instance of this great chain of monkeys. Monkeys simultaneously reinforce and undermine racial classification: they emphasize a gradationist or continuum concept of racial difference; for example, in the observational sequencing of Anglo-American, "sallow" Creole, female Africans, and "ape." The permeability of these racial categories overtakes Arthur Mervyn in his mirror-vision of a feverish visage:

One eye, a scar upon his cheek, a tawny skin, a form grotesquely misproportioned, brawny, as Hercules, and habited in livery, composed, as it were, the parts of one view. To perceive, to fear, and to confront this apparition were blended into one sentiment. I turned towards him with the swiftness of lightning, but my speed was useless to my safety. A Blow upon my temple was succeeded by an utter oblivion of thought and of feeling. I sunk upon the floor prostrate and senseless. My insensibility might be mistaken by observers for death, yet some part of this interval was haunted by a fearful dream. I conceived myself lying on the brink of a pit whose bottom the eye could not reach. My hands and legs were fettered, so as to disable me from resisting two grim and gigantic figures, who stooped to lift me from the earth. Their purpose methought was to cast me into this abyss. My terrors were unspeakable, and I struggled with such force, that my bonds snapt and I found myself at liberty. At this moment my senses returned and I opened my eyes.[90]

Is the specter a criminal black servant, a jaundiced and delirious white fever victim, or Mervyn's misrecognition of his own sallowed image? Just as bilious fever overtakes its victims with bile-permeated complexions, it induces Mervyn to imagine himself a victim of enslavement and social death. Blackness haunts as it exposes the permeability of racial categories and schemes, social, political, scientific. The gothic infects readers with a haunted sense of their fragile, false embodiment and a renewed appreciation for the apparently safe fiction of whiteness.

The literary products of the 1793 yellow fever epidemic reveal racially divergent modes of textual response to social crisis. While white authors imagined America as an impervious Adam or an unsteady Eve, black authors adopted the persona of an American Lazarus. As I have argued in earlier chapters, this Lazarus embodied the travail of early American communities of color: their survival of deadly circumstances, their ongoing process of incorporation, and their inspired resistance to reductive and even deadly schemes of racial classification and segregation. Black authors like Jones and Allen create narratives of oppositional, inspired incorporation; white authors like Carey and Brown create narratives haunted by the specter of racial destabilization and physical decomposition. White narratives infect readers with a sense of their susceptibility and powerlessness, while black narratives inoculate the community against racist pathogens. Brockden Brown's fever narratives track individual fortunes in the emergent bourgeois public sphere, while the black literary response reclaims African-American bodies from that commerce. Michael Warner argues in *The Letters of the Republic* that the yellow fever gothic novel fantasized scenes of "disclosure," which constituted the subject in the perpetual unraveling of mysteries.[91] Black writers pursue a different end in their writings: not disclosure, or compulsory exposure of the individual, but revelation: narrative delimitation that establishes blackness as a bounded, covenant, corporate body. Early African-American communities did not desire from their literature horror for horror's sake. Instead, in writing, they effected a spiritual and supernatural transcendence of mortal circumstances.

No

Conclusion

Lazarus Lives

The first generation of African- and Native American authors set into motion processes that forever changed the course of American literature, religion, and culture. In addition to setting powerful precedents for future authors of color, they established a defining trajectory for the development of American literature in the next century. The end of the eighteenth century found white American writers striving toward the privatization, professionalization, and domestication of literary enterprise and the presentation of literary products as ornaments of entertainment and refinement. Meanwhile, African- and Native American writers defined authorship as the public exercise of creative, intellectual, and political agency. They created literature not for individual consumption but rather in connection with their respective communities. Black churches, conventions, and fraternal organizations sustained the careers of Maria Stewart, David Walker, Jarena Lee, Zilpha Elaw, Henry Highland Garnet, Francis Ellen Watkins Harper, Frederick Douglass, and Harriet Jacobs. Meanwhile, a firebrand Pequot Methodist named William Apess used his ministerial office to defend his tribal community and to challenge white supremacy. In *An Indian's Looking Glass for the White Man* (1833), Apess argued that Jesus Christ was not a white man, but rather a man of color. His bold and altogether correct statement cancels the assumption of godly assent and Christic solidarity so critical to American white supremacy. It also exemplifies how American communities of color used religious discourse to negate the racist presumptions directed against them and how literature served as a space for the construction of newly resistant identities and communities.

Apess's resignification of Jesus as a man of color also emblematizes broader processes of cultural revitalization set into motion by pioneering black and Indian authors. As evangelists and community leaders, they asserted the sacred significance of black and Indian experience. They also established separate and independent religious bodies. Out of these movements and churches emerged new modes of American Christianity that honored the histories, customs, values, desires, and pleasures of black and Indian communities. In this momentous cultural emergence, literature played an instrumental role. Hymns were not just published, but breathed, memorized, harmonized, sung privately, sung in common; sermons were not just printed, but preached, heard, contested, and applauded. Early African- and Native American writings thus demonstrate the value of literature as liturgy: as a textual anchor for performed expressions of faith, despair, and hope; as a register of the community's shared consciousness. These texts survived the dusty terminus of their original imprints to be reincorporated within the living bodies of black and Indian cultures.

One of the most remarkable aspects of this body of early American literature is its connection to lasting and influential cultural forms. Christian Indian churches remain important venues for Native cultural and political identification—from the recently renovated Mohegan Congregational Church in Samson Occom's hometown of Uncasville, Connecticut, to the Christian-peyotist peregrinations of Native American church roadmen throughout Indian country today. So too has Christian Indian hymnody outlived Samson Occom as a vital mode of expression. The Brotherton Indians maintained their hymnody, even after the community's forced removal to Wisconsin in the 1820s; Thomas Commuck, a Narragansett Indian who joined this second Brotherton exodus, composed and published 120 hymn tunes—one of them dedicated to Occom—in a collection entitled *Indian Melodies* (1845). Among the contemporary Wisconsin Brothertown Indians, the Oneida, the Cree, the Seneca, and other tribal communities, hymn singing is the oldest continuously practiced tribal song tradition; hymn-singing societies contribute to indigenous language revitalization efforts and to rituals of worship and mourning. Hymnody has also been an important force in uniting urban Indian communities, from the hymn-singing wakes of Ojibwa in Minneapolis to the "Fifth Sunday Sings" of pantribal Los Angeles.[1] Black churches and fraternal organizations have been equally instrumental in the formation of black community life, consciousness, and culture. Richard Allen and Absalom Jones are remembered in the mighty influence of the African Methodist Episcopal and AME Zion churches, which now claim more than 3.5 million members worldwide. So too has Prince Hall Freemasonry conducted generations of black men through its defining rituals of death, rebirth, and community regeneration. These rituals united black abolitionists and authors in the nineteenth century and contributed an important mystical and symbolic dimension to Harlem Renaissance–era constructions of blackness. Today, there are an estimated 450,000 Prince Hall Freemasons in North America and the Caribbean, with thousands more black women participating in the Eastern Star auxiliary.[2]

Finally, then, the most revolutionary aspect of early African- and Native American literatures is their revelation of deep continuities between the past and the present. If the contemporary restoration of these forgotten texts demands a new accounting of American literary and cultural history, it also demands a new understanding of our relationship to that history. The historian Walter Benjamin characterized that relationship as a covenant of mutual redemption: only in the full revelation of the past is the present complete. Following Benjamin, it would be a mistake to imagine ourselves accomplished as scholars in the mere retrieval of these early American writings from their archival tombs. We do not reveal the past to itself; rather, the past reveals itself to us and it transforms us in the process. This restored body of improbable and oft- forgotten literature revives in its contemporary readers a more humble appreciation of the longevity of resistance in American communities of color, a more vigilant faith in the meaningfulness of American literature, and a more expectant sense of the possibilities of cultural regeneration.

Appendix 1

Samson Occom's *Collection of Divine Hymns and Spiritual Songs* (1774)

Indexed by Author

Although Occom does not name the authors of the 109 hymns compiled in his *Collection*, a majority can be identified with the assistance of dictionaries of hymnology: John Julian, ed., *A Dictionary of Hymnology* (New York: Dover Publications, 1957) and the Hymn Society of America, *Dictionary of American Hymnology: First Line Index*, ed. Leonard Ellinwood (179 microfilm reels; New York: University Music Editions, 1984).

Isaac Watts

1. Terrible God, That Reigns on High
5. Sing to the Lord, Ye Heav'nly Hosts
6. My Thoughts on Awful Subjects Roll
7. With Holy Fear, and Humble Song
8. O the Immense! th'Amazing Height
13. Come Hither, All Ye Weary Souls
19. From All Who Dwell below the Skies
20. Behold the Wretch Whose Lust and Wine
21. Alas! and Did My Saviour Bleed?
30. Descend from Heaven Immortal Dove
31. My God the Spring of All My Joys
32. We are a Garden Wall'd Around
33. When I Can Read My Title clear
34. There is a Land of Pure Delight
35. Oh! the Delights, the Heavenly Joys!
36. Lord What a Wretched Land is This
41. Saints, at Your Heav'nly Father's Word
47. Join All the Gracious Names
60. The King of Glory Sends His Son
69. He Dies! the Friend of Sinners Dies!
79. Christ Our Lord is Ris'n Today
97. What Heav'nly Man, or Lovely God

99. Arise, My Soul, with Wonder See
102. 'Twas on that Dark, that Doleful Night
103. How Sweet and Awful is the Place
107. When the Fierce North Wind with his Airy Forces
108. Thee We Adore, Eternal Name
109. My Soul, Come meditate the Day

Charles and John Wesley

11. Weary of Struggling with My Pain
12. Jesus, the Sinner's Friend, to Thee
14. Ho! Every One That Thirsts Draw Nigh
15. Sinners, Obey the Gospel Word
16. Come Sinners, to the Gospel Feast
23. Oh That My Load of Sin Were Gone
26. Wretched, Helpless, and Distrest
27. Where Shall My Wond'ring Soul Begin?
42. O For a Thousand Tongues to Sing
43. Meet and Right it is to Sing
44. Hail Holy, Holy, Holy Lord!
55. Hosanna to Jesus on High!
56. Shall I for Fear of Feeble Man
62. Hark! the Herald, Angels Sing
63. O Love Divine, What Hast Thou Done?
65. Hail, the Day, that Sees Him Rise
66. God of My Salvation Hear
67. Blow Ye the Trumpet, Blow
74. He Comes! He Comes! the Saviour Dear (variant, "He Comes!
He Comes! the Judge Severe")
76. Rejoice, the Lord is King
85. Jesus, Friend of Sinners Hear
86. Son of God, if thy Free Grace

Samuel Hall, *Hymns and Spiritual Songs* (1766)

4. Hail! Happy Pilgrims, Whence Came Ye
18. Now See the Publican Opprest
78. Lo! th'Almighty King of Glory
87. I Am that I Am
88. Well Met, Dear Friends, in Jesus' Name
89. Lord, when Together Here We Meet

John Mason

2. Alas! For I Have Seen the Lord
3. Ah Lord! Ah Lord! What Have I Done
9. So Foolish, So Absurd Am I

24. My Soul Doth Magnify the Lord
28. I Sojourn in a Vale of Tears
29. My God, My Reconciled God

John Cennick

37. Children of the Heavenly King
73. Lo! He Cometh! Countless Trumpets
83. Lo! He Comes with Clouds Descending
93. Tell Us O Women We Would know

Samuel Crossman

45. Farewell Vain World, I Must Be Gone
54. My Life's a Shade, My Days Apace Decline
95. Farewell Vain World, I Must Be Gone (same as 45)

George Herbert

25. Awake Sad Heart, Whom Sorrows Drown
75. Come to Judgment, Come Away

Others

57. Rise, My Soul, and Stretch thy Wing, Robert Seagrave
61. Hark the Clad Sound! the Saviour Comes, Phillip Dodderidge
70. Come, Ye Sinners, Poor and Wretched, Joseph Hart
71. Come, Ye sinners, Come to Jesus, John Newton
77. Throughout the Saviour's Life We Trace, Samson Occom
80. Who Can Have Greater Cause to Sing, George Whitefield's *Collection*
91. Vital Spark of Heav'nly Flame!, Alexander Pope
105. While Shepherds Watched their Flocks by Night, Nahum Tate

APPENDIX 2

Author-Unknown Hymns Original
to Occom's *Collection*

Occom's *Collection* includes twenty-nine hymns of unknown authorship and origin, which are indexed here by number and first line. Biographer William deLoss Love suggested that eighteen hymns (marked below with an "*") were written by Samson Occom himself; dictionaries of hymnology, the papers of Samson Occom, and the papers of Occom's mentor Eleazar Wheelock contain nothing to prove or disprove this claim. Thus, it is indeed possible that these twenty-nine hymn texts belong to Samson Occom. It is also possible that some were composed by Occom's Native colleagues Joseph Johnson, David Fowler, and Jacob Fowler, each of whom also taught hymnody in New England and Long Island Indian communities and demonstrated an aptitude for hymnodic writing in their letters and journals.

10. Lord I Confess My Sin is Great *
17. The Prodigal's Return'd *
22. Laden with Guilt, Sinners Arise *
38. Christ Jesus is the Greatest Good
39. Tell Us, o Women Travelers
40. Lo! We are Journeying Home to God
46. What Poor Despised Company
48. Ah Me, I'm Never Well but When
49. Now Has the Ever Rolling Year
50. Behold that Splendor Hear the Shout *
51. Most Gracious God of Boundless Might *
52. The Eternal Speaks, All Heaven Attends
53. O Sight of Anguish, View It Near *
58. I Bless the Lord *
59. Come My Father's Family
64. Ye that Seek the Lord, Who Dy'd *
68. Welcome, Welcome Blessed Servant *
72. Behold Jesus Christ in the Clouds *
80. Hail thou Happy Morn so Glorious *

Appendix 3

Original Hymns by Samson Occom

"The Sufferings of Christ," or,
"Throughout the Saviour's Life We Trace"

1 Throughout the Saviour's Life we trace
   Nothing but Shame and deep Disgrace
       No period else is seen;
   Till he a spotless Victim fell,
   Tasting in Soul a painful Hell,
       Caus'd by the Creature's Sin.
2 On the cold Ground methinks I see
   My Jesus kneel, and pray for me;
       For this I him adore;
   Siez'd with a chilly sweat throughout,
   Blood-drops did force their Passage out
       Through ev'ry open'd Pore.
3 A pricking Thorn his Temples bore
   His Back with Lashes all was tore,
       Till one the Bones might see;
   Mocking, they push'd him here and there,
   Marking his Way with Blood and Tear,
       Press'd by the heavy Tree.
4 Thus up the Hill he painful came,
   Round him they mock, and make their Game,
       At length his Cross they rear;
   And can you see the mighty God,
   Cry out beneath sin's heavy Load,
       Without one thankful Tear?
5 Thus vailed in Humanity,
   He dies in Anguish on the Tree;
       What Tongue his Grief can tell?
   The shudd'ring Rocks their Heads recline,

The mourning Sun refuse to shine,
    When the Creator fell.
6   Shout, Brethren, shout in songs divine,
    He drank the Gall, to give us Wine,
        To quench our parching Thirst;
    Seraphs advance your Voices higher;
    Bride of the Lamb, unite the Choir,
        And Laud thy precious Christ.

"The Slow Traveller," or, "O Happy Souls How Fast You Go"

1   O happy souls how fast you go,
    And leave me here behind,
    Don't stop for me for now See,
    The Lord is just and kind.
2   Go on, go on, my soul says go,
    And I'll Come after you,
    Tho' I'm behind, yet I can find,
    I'll Sing Hosanna too.
3   Lord give you strength, that you may run,
    And keep your footsteps right,
    Tho' fast you go, and I go slow,
    You are not out of Sight.
4   When you get to the Worlds above,
    And all his Glory See,
    When you get home, Your Journey's done,
    Then look you out for me.
5   For I will come fast as I Can,
    A long that way I fear
    Lord give me Strength, I shall at length
    Be one amongst you there.

[CHORUS]
    There all together we shall be,
    Together we will Sing,
    Together we will praise our god,
    And everlasting King.

"A Morning Hymn," or, "Now the Shades of Night are Gone"

1   Now the shades of night are gone,
    Now the morning light is come;
    Lord, we would be thine to-day;
    Drive the shades of sin away.
2   Make our souls as noon-day clear,
    Banish every doubt and fear,

In thy vineyard Lord, today,
We would labor, we would pray.
3 Keep our haughty passions bound;
Rising up and sitting down;
Going out and coming in,
Keep us safe from every sin.
4 When our work of life is past,
O receive us then at last;
Labor then will all be o'er,
Night of sin will be no more.

"A Son's Farewell," or, "I Hear the Gospel's Joyful Sound"

1 I hear the gospel's joyful sound,
An organ I shall be,
For to sound forth redeeming love,
And sinner's misery.
2 Honor'd parents fare you well,
My Jesus doth me call,
I leave you here with God until
I meet you once for all.
3 My due affections I'll forsake,
My parents and their house,
And to the wilderness betake,
To pay the Lord my vows.
4 Then I'll forsake my chiefest mates,
That nature could afford,
And wear the shield into the field,
To wait upon the Lord.
5 Then thro' the wilderness I'll run,
Preaching the gospel free;
O be not anxious for your son,
The Lord will comfort me.
6 And if thro' preaching I shall gain
True subjects to my Lord,
'Twill more than recompence my pain,
To see them love the Lord.
7 My soul doth wish mount Zion well,
Whate'er becomes of me;
There my best friends and kindred dwell,
And there I long to be.

"Conversion Song," or, "Wak'd by the Gospel's Pow'rful Sound"

1 Wak'd by the gospel's pow'rful sound
My soul in sin and thrall I found,

Expos'd to endless woe;
Eternal truth did loud proclaim,
The sinner must be born again,
    Or down to ruin go.

2 Surpriz'd indeed, I could not tell,
Which way to shun the gates of hell,
    To which I's drawing near;
I strove alas! but all in vain,
The sinner must be born again,
    Still sounded in mine ears.

3 Into the law then run for help,
But still I felt the weight of guilt,
    And no relief I found;
While sin my burden'd soul did pain,
The sinner must be born again,
    Did loud as thunder sound.

4 God's justice now I did behold,
And guilt lay dreadful on my soul,
    It was a heavy load:
I read my bible, it was plain,
The sinner must be born again,
    Or feel the wrath of God.

5 I heard some speak how Christ did give
His life, to let the sinner live,
    But him I could not see;
This solemn truth did still remain,
The sinner must be born again,
    Or dwell in misery.

6 But as my soul with dying breath,
Was gasping in eternal death,
    Christ Jesus I did see:
Free grace and pardon he proclaim'd,
I trust I then was born again,
    In gospel liberty.

7 Not angels in the world above,
Nor saints could glow with greater love
    Than what my soul enjoy'd;
My soul did mount on faith its wing,
And glory, glory, I did sing
    To Jesus my dear Lord.

8 Now with the saints I'll sing and tell,
How Jesus sav'd my soul from hell,
    And praise redeeming love:
Ascribe the glory to the Lamb;
The sinner now is born again,
    To dwell with Christ above.

"Come all my Young Companions, Come"

1 Come all my Young Companions Come,
   And hear me boldly tell,
   The wonders of Redeeming Love,
   That Sav'd my Soul from Hell.

2 It was but a few Days ago,
   I Saw my awful Case,
   Nothing but hell and dark Disgrace
   Lay plain before my face.

3 O then I view[']d the damned Crew,
   Of all the numerous race,
   And I of all that went to hell
   Deserv'd the lowest place.

4 Justice of God so on me lay,
   I Could no Comfort find
   Till I was willing to forsake,
   And leave all my sins behind.

5 The Lord was Strong he bow'd my Will,
   And made me this to be,
   Nothing but Jesus Crucified,
   Could save a wretch like me.

6 O then I view[']d mount Calvary,
   With gods eternal son,
   Who on the Cursed Tree did Die,
   For Sins that I had done

7 O how Rejoic'd I was to think,
   A Saviour I had found,
   It turn[']d my Sorrows into Joy,
   To hear the Blessed Sound.

8 Salvation from my God on high,
   So pleasantly did Ring,
   It set my Soul at Liberty,
   To praise my heavenly King.

9 And while I dwell on Earth below
   I'll praise my Jesus here,
   And then go to yonder World
   And praise my Jesus there.

10 And there thro' all Eternity,
   In the Sweet Realms above
   There I shall Sing that blessed Song
   Free grace and Dying Love

"Wak'd by the Gospel's Pow'rful Sound"

1 Wak'd by the gospel's pow'rful sound
   My soul in sin and thrall I found,

Expos'd to endless woe;
Eternal truth did loud proclaim,
The sinner must be born again,
    Or down to ruin go.

2 Surpriz'd indeed, I could not tell,
Which way to shun the gates of hell,
    To which I's drawing near;
I strove alas! but all in vain,
The sinner must be born again,
    Still sounded in mine ears.

3 Into the law then run for help,
But still I felt the weight of guilt,
    And no relief I found;
While sin my burden'd soul did pain,
The sinner must be born again,
    Did loud as thunder sound.

4 God's justice now I did behold,
And guilt lay dreadful on my soul,
    It was a heavy load:
I read my bible, it was plain,
The sinner must be born again,
    Or feel the wrath of God.

5 I heard some speak how Christ did give
His life, to let the sinner live,
    But him I could not see;
This solemn truth did still remain,
The sinner must be born again,
    Or dwell in misery.

6 But as my soul with dying breath,
Was gasping in eternal death,
    Christ Jesus I did see:
Free grace and pardon he proclaim'd,
I trust I then was born again,
    In gospel liberty.

7 Not angels in the world above,
Nor saints could glow with greater love
    Than what my soul enjoy'd;
My soul did mount on faith its wing,
And glory, glory, I did sing
    To Jesus my dear Lord.

8 Now with the saints I'll sing and tell,
How Jesus sav'd my soul from hell,
    And praise redeeming love:
Ascribe the glory to the Lamb;
The sinner now is born again,
    To dwell with Christ above.

Notes

Introduction

1. Thomas Jefferson, *Notes on the State of Virginia.*, ed. William Peden (1787; reprint, New York: Norton, 1982), 140; Thomas Clarkson, *Essay on the Slavery and Commerce of the Human Species, Particularly the African* (London: J. Phillips, 1786), 171–175; Richard Nisbet, *The Capacity of Negroes for Religious and Moral Improvement Considered* (London: J. Phillips, 1789), 31; Gilbert Imlay, *Topographical Description of the Western Territory of North America*, 3d ed. (London: J. Debrett, 1797), 229–230.

2. Russell Thornton, *American Indian Holocaust and Survival: A Population History Since 1492* (Norman: University of Oklahoma Press, 1987), 42–59.

3. Jefferson, *Notes*, 163.

4. Frank Shuffleton provides another account of Jefferson on race in "Thomas Jefferson: Race, Culture, and the Failure of Anthropological Method," in *A Mixed Race: Ethnicity in Early America*, ed. Frank Shuffleton (New York: Oxford University Press, 1993), 257–277.

5. Lucy Terry also deserves acknowledgment as a groundbreaking black poet. Although her composition "Bars Fight" was first performed in 1746, the date of its initial publication in 1855 places it outside the parameters of my study.

6. The groundbreaking first edition of the *Heath Anthology of American Literature* (Lexington, Mass.: D. C. Heath, 1990)—a landmark work in the diversification of the American literary canon—has been succeeded by similar efforts specific to early American literature: Myra Jehlen and Michael Warner, eds., *The English Literatures of America, 1500–1800* (New York: Routledge, 1997); Carla Mulford, Angela Vietto, and Amy Winans, eds., *Early American Writings* (New York: Oxford, 2001); and Ivy Schweitzer and Susan Castilo, eds., *The Literatures of Colonial America* (Malden, Mass.: Blackwell Publishers, 2001). Recently published (or reissued) anthologies focusing on early black writers include Adam Potkay and Sandra Burr, eds., *Black Writers of the Eighteenth Century: Living the New Exodus in England and the Americas* (New York: St. Mar-

tin's, 1995); Dorothy Porter, ed., *Early Negro Writing, 1760–1837* (1971; reprint, Baltimore: Black Classic Press, 1995); Vincent Carretta, ed., *Unchained Voices: An Anthology of Black Authors in the English-Speaking World of the 18th Century* (Lexington: University of Kentucky Press, 1996); Richard Newman, Patrick Rael, and Philip Lapsansky, eds., *Pamphlets of Protest: An Anthology of Early African-American Protest Literature, 1790–1860* (New York: Routledge, 2000); John Edgar Wideman, ed., *My Soul Has Grown Deep: Classics of Early African-American Literature* (Philadelphia: Running Press, 2001); and Joanna Brooks and John Saillant, eds., *Face Zion Forward: First Writers of the Black Atlantic, 1785–1798* (Boston: Northeastern University Press, 2002). Among the new single-author editions are Laura Murray, ed., *To Do Good to My Indian Brethren: The Writings of Joseph Johnson, 1751–1776* (Amherst: University of Massachusetts Press, 1998) and Vincent Carretta, ed., *Complete Writings of Phillis Wheatley* (New York: Penguin, 2001). It is important to note that the publishing efforts of the last decade do not constitute an original impulse but rather another wave in the ongoing effort to remember early black and Indian literary history. Three decades ago, these efforts were shouldered by faculty and archivists at Howard University: William Robinson, ed., *Early Black American Poets* (Dubuque, Iowa: William Brown Publishers, 1969) and Dorothy Porter, ed., *Early Negro Writing, 1760–1837* (Boston: Beacon Press, 1971).

7. R. W. B. Lewis, *The American Adam: Innocence, Tragedy, and Tradition in the Nineteenth Century* (Chicago: University of Chicago Press, 1955), 5.

8. Joseph Roach, *Cities of the Dead: Circum-Atlantic Performance* (New York: Columbia University Press, 1996), 4.

9. Sharon Patricia Holland, *Raising the Dead: Readings of Death and (Black) Subjectivity* (Durham, N.C.: Duke University Press, 2000), 40.

10. Abdul JanMohamed and David Lloyd, "Toward a Theory of Minority Discourse: What Is to Be Done?" in *The Nature and Context of Minority Discourse*, ed. Abdul JanMohamed and David Lloyd (New York: Oxford University Press, 1990), 6.

11. Ibid., "Toward a Theory of Minority Discourse," 8.

12. My observation here parallels Benedict Anderson's famous arguments about the affinity of "nationalist" and "religious" thought and the instrumentality of print and the vernacular in the "imagination" of modern nations. See *Imagined Communities: Reflections on the Origin and Spread of Nationalism* (1983; reprint, London: Verso, 1991), 10, 14.

13. Anthony Marx, *Making Race and Nation: A Comparison of South Africa, the United States and Brazil* (Cambridge: Cambridge University Press, 1998), 191–193; Michael Omi and Howard Winant, *Racial Formation in the United States: From the 1960s to the 1990s* (New York: Routledge, 1994), 99. See also Eddie Glaude, Jr., who writes in *Exodus! Religion, Race, and Nation in Early Nineteenth-Century Black America* (Chicago: University of Chicago Press, 2000) that "black religious institutions, through their ability to sustain numerous newspapers and other activities as well as their ability to render black experiences in the dramatic terms of the Bible, *rearticulated* the racial practices of the U.S. racial state and helped construct a collective identity" (emphasis added; 21).

14. In his groundbreaking study of early Afro-British writers, *Measuring the Moment: Strategies of Protest in Eighteenth-Century Afro-English Writing* (London: Associated University Presses, 1988), Keith Sandiford demonstrates how Ignatius Sancho, Ottobah Cugoano, and Olaudah Equiano helped build anti-slavery sentiment among white Britons through persuasive autobiographical writings. David Murray's *Forked Tongues: Speech, Writing, and Representation in North American Indian Texts* (Bloomington: Indiana University Press, 1991), investigates tensions between assertions of subjectivity and processes of subjection, between authentic "self-expression" or "voice" and Euro-American discursive "conventions," in the autobiographical writings of Samson Occom and William Apess. Dwight McBride observes the shaping force of abolitionist rhetorical conventions in the writings of Phillis Wheatley, Olaudah Equiano, and their nineteenth-century literary descendents in his *Impossible Witnesses: Truth, Abolitionism, and Slave Testimony* (New York: New York University Press, 2001). Similarly, in *Eloquence Is Power: Oratory and Performance in Early America* (Chapel Hill, N.C.: Omohundro Institute of Early American History and Culture, University of North Carolina Press, 2000), Sandra Gustafson argues that Samson Occom and John Marrant appealed to white evangelical expectations and desires in performing the "refiguration of the 'savage' speaker" into a "hybridized, evangelical savage persona, whose liminal position between cultures permitted a range of identifications across culture" (78, 91).

15. See Jace Weaver, "From I-Hermeneutics to We-Hermeneutics: Native Americans and the Post-Colonial," in *Native American Religious Identity: Unforgotten Gods*, ed. Jace Weaver (Maryknoll, N.Y.: Orbis Books, 1998), 1–25.

16. Jace Weaver, *Other Words: American Indian, Law, and Culture* (Norman, Okla.: University of Oklahoma Press, 2001), 51; Weaver, *That the People Might Live: Native American Literatures and Native American Community* (New York: Oxford University Press, 1997), 44–45.

17. My method here diverges from that advanced by Arnold Krupat in *The Voice in the Margin* (Berkeley: University of California Press, 1988), where he repositions American literature, critical theory, and Native American literature as elements of a liberal "secular heterodoxy" (52–53), and in *The Turn to the Native* (Lincoln: University of Nebraska Press, 1996), where he suggests that all Native American literature is written for white audiences (22).

18. I find a parallel call for the recognition of black intellectual self-determination in Houston Baker's *The Journey Back: Issues in Black Literature and Criticism* (Chicago: University of Chicago Press, 1980), wherein he claims for early black literature an intellectual sovereignty founded in conscientious differentiation. Even early writers like Jupiter Hammon and Phillis Wheatley, he argues, "insisted on the privileged status of their own semantic fields, those abstract domains in which certain basic units"—such as Africa and Christianity—"had properties quite different from those that the large culture tried to encode" (19). Just as Native literary critics challenge white readers to recognize the distinctive intellectual and cultural traditions and political status of Native peoples, Baker charges white readers to recognize an equally powerful difference in black texts: "If Blacks 'entered' the English language with values

and concepts antithetical to those of the white externality surrounding them, then their vocabulary is less important than the underlying codes, or semantic fields, that governed meaning. What I am suggesting is the possibility that whites—moving exclusively within the boundaries of their own semantic categories—have taken the words of the black work of verbal art at face value, or worse, at a value assigned by their own limiting attitudes and patterns of judgment" (157).

19. See Philip Gould and Vincent Carretta, eds., *Genius in Bondage: Early Black Atlantic Literature* (Lexington: University of Kentucky Press, 2002), 4, 11.

20. See Paul Gilroy, *The Black Atlantic: Modernity and Double-Consciousness* (Cambridge: Harvard University Press, 1993), 1–40. One of the editors of *Genius in Bondage* explicitly rejects the "countercultural" aspect of Gilroy's black Atlantic. In his collected essay on John Marrant, Philip Gould argues that the radical challenge of the early black Atlantic has been overstated, and that early black autobiographers like Marrant were instead more indebted to notions of "liberty" derived from Enlightenment "liberal ideology" and the American Revolution. Even the facts of Marrant's biography do not sustain Gould's argument. Throughout his career as a Calvinist Huntingdonian preacher, black Loyalist exile, resident minister to black separatist communities in Nova Scotia, and chaplain to Boston's African Lodge of Freemasons, Marrant conscientiously associated with black Atlantic communities founded in tension with if not in outright rejection of the liberal Enlightenment and American nationalism. See Philip Gould, "'Remarkable Liberty': Language and Identity in Eighteenth-Century Black Autobiography," in Carretta and Gould, *Genius in Bondage*, 116–129.

21. On the inconsistency of racial theorization and imagination in Europe, see Roxann Wheeler, *The Complexion of Race: Categories of Difference in Eighteenth-Century British Culture* (Philadelphia: University of Pennsylvania, 2000). I will review the history of racialization in America in chapter 1.

22. On the history of "hybridity," see Robert J. C. Young, *Colonial Desire: Hybridity in Theory, Culture, and Race* (New York: Routledge, 1995), 1–28; Bart Moore-Gilbert, *Postcolonial Theory: Contexts, Practices, Politics* (London: Verso, 1997), 181–183, 192–195.

23. For example, Arnold Krupat writes in *The Turn to the Native*, "In varying degrees, all verbal performances studied as 'Native American literature,' whether oral, textualized, or written, are mixed, hybrid; none are 'pure' or strictly speaking, 'autonomous'" (21). Note his use of "hybridity" as a marker of modern Native culture against the "autonomy" or political status of Native peoples.

24. Katherine Clay Bassard, *Spiritual Interrogations: Culture, Gender, and Community in Early African American Women's Writing* (Princeton, N.J.: Princeton University Press, 1999), 140–141.

25. Jacques Derrida and Gianni Vattimo, eds., *Religion* (Palo Alto, Calif.: Stanford University Press, 1998), 36–37.

26. Walter Benjamin, *Illuminations* (New York: Harcourt, Brace and World, 1968), 254.

Chapter 1

1. "A True and Genuine Account of a Wonderful Wandering Spirit," *General Magazine and Historical Chronicle* (February 1741), 120–122.

2. Charles Chauncy, *Enthusiasm Described and Cautioned Against. A Sermon Preach'd at the Old Brick Meeting House in Boston, the Lord's Day after the Commencement, 1742. With a Letter to the Reverend Mr. James Davenport* (Boston: Printed by J. Draper for S. Eliot in Cornhill, 1742), 15.

3. Histories of the "Great Awakening" and its New Light supporters abound. Joseph Tracy popularized the term *Great Awakening* in his genre-pioneering work, *The Great Awakening: A History of the Revival of Religion in the Time of Edwards and Whitefield* (Boston: Tappan and Dennet, 1842). See also J. M. Bumsted, *What Must I Do to Be Saved? The Great Awakening in Colonial America* (Hinsdale, Ill.: Dryden, 1976); Richard Bushman, ed., *The Great Awakening: Documents on the Revival of Religion, 1740–1745* (New York: Atheneum, 1970); Cedric B. Cowing, *The Great Awakening and the American Revolution* (Chicago: Rand McNally, 1971); Edwin Gausted, *The Great Awakening in New England* (New York: Harper and Brothers, 1957); Wesley Gewehr, *The Great Awakening in Virginia, 1740–1790* (Durham, N.C.: Duke University Press, 1930); C. C. Goen, *Revivalism and Separatism in New England, 1740–1800: Strict Congregationalists and Separate Baptists in the Great Awakening* (New Haven: Yale University Press, 1972); Timothy Hall, *Contested Boundaries: Itinerancy and the Reshaping of the Colonial American Religious World* (Durham, N.C.: Duke University Press, 1994); Alan Heimert, *Religion and the American Mind: From the Great Awakening to the Revolution* (Cambridge: Harvard University Press, 1966); Alan Heimert and Perry Miller, eds., *The Great Awakening: Documents Ilustrating the Crisis and its Consequences* (Indianapolis: Indiana University Press, 1967); Rhys Isaac, *The Transformation of Virginia, 1740–1790* (Chapel Hill: University of North Carolina Press, 1982); Frank Lambert, *Inventing the Great Awakening* (Princeton, N.J.: Princeton University Press, 1999); Perry Miller, *Errand into the Wilderness* (Cambridge: Harvard University Press, 1956); Perry Miller, *Jonathan Edwards* (New York: Meridian Books, 1949); Harry Stout, *The New England Soul: Preaching and Religious Culture in Colonial New England* (New York: Oxford University Press, 1986); and Marilyn Westerkamp, *Triumph of the Laity: Scots-Irish Piety and the Great Awakening, 1625–1760* (New York: Oxford University Press, 1988). Allen Guelzo provides a graceful review of Great Awakening historiography in "God's Designs: The Literature of the Colonial Revivals of Religion, 1735–1760," in *New Directions in American Religious History*, ed. Harry Stout and D. G. Hart (New York: Oxford University Press, 1997), 141–172, while Jonathan Butler presents an alternate and critical view in "Enthusiasm Described and Decried: The Great Awakening as Interpretive Fiction," *Journal of American History* 69 (1982–83): 305–325.

4. "Extracts from Several Authors," *The Christian History* 27 (September 3, 1743), 215.

5. Nancy Ruttenburg, *Democratic Personality: Popular Voice and the Trial of American Authorship* (Palo Alto, Calif.: Stanford University Press, 1998), 114.

6. Charles Chauncy, *Seasonable Thoughts on the State of Religion in New*

England (Boston: Rogers and Fowle, for Samuel Eliot in Cornhill, 1743), 226.

7. Erik R. Seeman, "'Justise Must Take Plase': Three African Americans Speak of Religion in Eighteenth-Century New England," *William and Mary Quarterly* 3d ser., 56.2 (April 1999): 395.

8. For the story of Shepherd's Tent, see Richard Warch, "The Shepherd's Tent: Education and Enthusiasm in the Great Awakening," *American Quarterly* 30.2 (summer 1978): 177–198. On Old Light leader Charles Chauncy, see Edward Griffin, *Old Brick: Charles Chauncy of Boston, 1705–1787* (Minneapolis: University of Minnesota Press, 1980); Amy Schrager Lang, "'A Flood of Errors': Chauncy and Edwards in the Great Awakening," in *Jonathan Edwards and the American Experience*, ed. Nathan Hatch and Harry Stout (Oxford: Oxford University Press, 1988), 160–173; and Charles Lippy, *Seasonable Revolutionary: The Mind of Charles Chauncy* (Chicago: Nelson-Hall, 1981).

9. Heimert, *Religion and the American Mind*; Heimert and Miller, *The Great Awakening*.

10. Ruttenburg, *Democratic Personality.*

11. Lambert, *Inventing the Great Awakening*, 128.

12. On the career of George Whitefield, see Harry Stout, *The Divine Dramatist: George Whitefield and the Rise of Modern Evangelicalism* (Grand Rapids, Mich.: Wm. B. Eerdmans Publishing, 1991); Frank Lambert, *Pedlar in Divinity: George Whitefield and the Transatlantic Revivals, 1737–1770* (Princeton, N.J.: Princeton University Press, 1994); and Lambert, *Inventing the Great Awakening*. On Selina Hastings and the Huntingdon Connexion, see Helen C. Knight, *Lady Huntington and Her Friends; or, The Revival of the Work of God in the Days of Wesley, Whitefield, Romaine, Venn, and Others in the Last Century* (New York: New York American Tract Society, 1853); Abel Stevens, *The Women of Methodism; Its Three Foundresses, Susanna Wesley, the Countess of Huntingdon, and Barbara Heck* (New York: Carlton and Porter, 1866); Boyd Stanley Schlenther, *Queen of the Methodists: The Countess of Huntingdon and the Eighteenth-century Crisis of Faith and Society* (Durham, England: Durham Academic Press, 1997); A. C. H. Seymour, *The Life and Times of Selina, Countess of Huntingdon*, 2 vols. (1840; reprint Stoke-on-Trent, England: Tentmaker Publications, 2000).

13. Bushman, *The Great Awakening*, 27.

14. George Whitefield, *Three Letters from the Reverend Mr. G. Whitefield: Letter I. To a Friend in London, concerning Archbishop Tillotson; Letter II. To the Same, on the Same Subject; Letter III. To the Inhabitants of Maryland, Virginia, North and South Carolina, Concerning their Negroes* (Philadelphia: Printed and Sold by B. Franklin, at the New Printing-office near the market, 1740), 15.

15. On David Margate, see Schlenther, *Queen of the Methodists*, 91; Sylvia Frey and Betty Wood, *Come Shouting to Zion: African American Protestantism in the American South and British Caribbean to 1830* (Chapel Hill: University of North Carolina Press, 1998), 112–113; and Winthrop Jordan, *White Over Black: American Attitudes Toward the Negro, 1550–1812* (Chapel Hill: University of North Carolina Press, 1968), 209–210.

16. Olaudah Equiano, *The Interesting Narrative and Other Writings*, ed. Vincent Carretta (1789; reprint, New York: Penguin Books, 1995), 132.

17. Studies of New Light evangelicism, the Huntingdon Connexion, and African-Americans take shape along regional lines. For New England, see William Piersen, *Black Yankees: The Development of an Afro-American Subculture in Eighteenth-Century New England* (Amherst: University of Massachusetts Press, 1988), 65–73; David Lovejoy, *Religious Enthusiasm in the New World: Heresy to Revolution* (Cambridge: Harvard University Press, 1985), 199–203; and Erik Seeman, "'Justise Must Take Plase,'" 393–413. In the southern colonies, see John Boles, ed., *Masters and Slaves in the House of the Lord: Race and Religion in the American South, 1740–1870* (Lexington: University of Kentucky Press, 1988); Jon Butler, *Awash in a Sea of Faith: Christianizing the American People* (Cambridge: Harvard University Press, 1990), 129–163; Janet Duitsman Cornelius, *"When I Can Read My Title Clear": Literacy, Slavery, and Religion in the Antebellum South* (Columbia: University of South Carolina Press, 1991); Frey and Wood, *Come Shouting to Zion*, 80–117; Mechal Sobel, *Trabelin' On: The Slave Journey to an Afro-Baptist Faith* (1979; reprint, Princeton, N.J.: Princeton University Press, 1988), 79–108; and Mechal Sobel, *The World They Made Together: Black and White Values in Eighteenth-Century Virginia* (Princeton, N.J.: Princeton University Press, 1987), 178–203. On Wheatley and the Connexion, see Mukhtar Ali Isani, "The Methodist Connection: New Variants of Some of Phillis Wheatley's Poems," *Early American Literature* 22 (1987): 108–113, and Samuel J. Rogal, "Phillis Wheatley's Methodist Connection," *Black American Literature* 21 (spring-summer 1987): 85–95.

18. Stephen Marini, *Radical Sects of Revolutionary New England* (Cambridge: Harvard University Press, 1982), 173. Many of the works cited in note 1 detail the American history of the revivals and the rise of the New Light evangelical movement. For Jonathan Edwards's contributions to the controversy, see C. C. Goen, ed., *The Great Awakening*, Vol. 4, *The Works of Jonathan Edwards* (New Haven: Yale University Press, 1972).

19. Samson Occom, "A Short Narrative of My Life," in *The Heath Anthology of American Literature*, ed. Paul Lauter et al. (Lexington, Mass.: D. C. Heath, 1994), 942.

20. Bernd Peyer, *The Tutor'd Mind: Indian Missionary-Writers in Antebellum America* (Amherst: University of Massachusetts Press, 1997), 54–110; William Simmons, "Red Yankees: Narragansett Conversion in the Great Awakening," *American Ethnologist* 10.2 (May 1983): 253–271; William Simmons, ed., *Old Light on Separate Ways: The Narragansett Diary of Joseph Fish, 1765–1776* (Hanover, N.H.: University Press of New England, 1982).

21. On the early history of American Methodism, see John H. Wigger, *Taking Heaven by Storm: Methodism and the Rise of Popular Christianity in America* (New York: Oxford University Press, 1998); Dee Andrews, *The Methodists and Revolutionary America, 1760–1800: The Shaping of an Evangelical Culture* (Princeton, N.J.: Princeton University Press, 2000). For Methodism's engagements with slavery and African-Americans, see Harry Richardson, *Dark Salvation: The Story of Methodism as It Developed Among Blacks in America* (New York: Anchor, 1976); Milton Sernett, *Black Religion and American Evangelicism* (Metuchen, N.J.: Scarecrow, 1975); Carol V. R. George, *Segregated Sabbaths, 1760–1840* (New York: Oxford University Press, 1973); and Frey and Wood, *Come*

Shouting to Zion. Finally, the organization of the African Methodist Episcopal church is documented in Richard Allen's autobiography, *The Life Experience and Gospel Labors of the Rt. Rev. Richard Allen* (1833; reprint New York: Abingdon, 1960).

22. Samuel Hopkins's writings include *A Dialogue, Concerning the Slavery of the Africans* (Norwich: Judah P. Spooner, 1776); *A Discourse upon the Slave-Trade, and the Slavery of the Africans* (Providence: J. Carter, 1793); *A Treatise on the Millennium* (Boston: Isaiah Thomas and Ebenezer T. Andrews, 1793). On the New Divinity and its relationship to slavery, see Joseph Conforti, *Samuel Hopkins and the New Divinity: Calvinism, the Congregational Ministry, and Reform in New England between the Great Awakenings* (Grand Rapids, Mich.: Eerdmans, 1981), 125–141, 143–158; John Saillant, "Slavery and Divine Providence in New England Calvinism: The New Divinity and a Black Protest, 1775–1805," *New England Quarterly* 68.4 (1995): 584–608; David Lovejoy, "Samuel Hopkins: Religion, Slavery, and the Revolution," *New England Quarterly* 40 (1967): 227–243. On Lemuel Haynes, see the modern edition of his writings, *Black Preacher to White America: The Collected Writings of Lemuel Haynes, 1774–1833*, ed. Richard Newman (Brooklyn: Carlson, 1990); the standard biography, Timothy Mather Coolley's *Sketches of the Life and Character of the Rev. Lemuel Haynes, A. M.* (1837; reprint, New York: Negro Universities Press, 1969); and John Saillant, *Black Puritan, Black Republican: Faith and Antislavery in the Life of Lemuel Haynes, 1753–1833* (New York: Oxford University Press, 2002).

23. Cotton Mather, *The Negro Christianized* (Boston: Printed by B. Green, 1706), 24–25.

24. Whitefield, *Three Letters*, 15.

25. Jonathan Edwards, *The "Miscellanies,"* vol. 13, *The Works of Jonathan Edwards* (New Haven: Yale University Press, 1994), 13:26, 212–213.

26. Ibid., 13:262, 369.

27. Ibid., 13:379, 449.

28. Jonathan Edwards, *History of the Work of Redemption*, Vol. 9, *The Works of Jonathan Edwards* (New Haven: Yale University Press, 1989), 9: 155.

29. Ibid., 9:178.

30. Ibid., 9:180.

31. On the *History* as analogy, see William J. Scheick, "The Grand Design: Jonathan Edwards' History of the Work of Redemption," *Eighteenth-Century Studies* 8.3 (spring 1975): 300–314.

32. Edwards, *History*, 9:471–472.

33. Ibid., 9:434.

34. Ibid., 9:520.

35. Ibid., 9:520.

36. Scheick, "The Grand Design," 304–305.

37. Jonathan Edwards, *The Great Awakening*, vol. 4, *The Works of Jonathan Edwards* (New Haven: Yale University Press, 1972), 4:159.

38. Ibid., 4:329.

39. Ibid., 4:346.

40. Ibid., 4: 285.

41. Ibid., 4:295.

42. Jonathan Edwards, *Religious Affections*, vol. 2, *The Works of Jonathan Edwards* (New Haven: Yale University Press, 1959), 2:206.

43. Ibid., 2:340.

44. Ibid., 2:340.

45. Ibid., 2:341–342.

46. Ibid., 2:341–343.

47. Ibid., 4:151.

48. See Kenneth P. Minkema, "Jonathan Edwards on Slavery and the Slave Trade," *William and Mary Quarterly* 3d ser. 54.4 (October 1997): 823–824. Minkema identifies besides Titus three more slaves owned by Edwards during his lifetime: Joseph, Lee, and Venus. The receipt for the slave Venus, dated 1731, is reprinted in *A Jonathan Edwards Reader*, ed. John E. Smith, Harry Stout, and Jonathan Minkema (New Haven: Yale University Press, 1995), 296–97.

49. Jonathan Edwards, *Letters and Personal Writings*, Vol. 16, *The Works of Jonathan Edwards* (New Haven: Yale University Press, 1998), 16: 389.

50. The Reverend John Williams is the author of *The Redeemed Captive, Returning to Zion* (Boston: B. Green, 1707); see also John Demos, ed., *The Unredeemed Captive: A Family Story from Early America* (New York: Knopf, 1994). Gerald McDermott reviews Edwards's record on Indian affairs in "Jonathan Edwards and American Indians: The Devil Sucks Their Blood," *New England Quarterly* 72.4 (December 1999): 539–557.

51. Benjamin Braude, "The Sons of Noah and the Construction of Ethnic and Geographical Identities in the Medieval and Early Modern Periods," *William and Mary Quarterly*, 3d ser., 54.1 (January 1997), 127–128, 137–138.

52. Londa Schiebinger, "The Anatomy of Difference: Race and Sex in Eighteenth-Century Science," *Eighteenth-Century Studies* 23.4 (Summer 1990): 387–405. In *The Complexion of Race: Categories of Difference in Eighteenth-Century British Culture* (Philadelphia: University of Pennsylvania Press, 2000), Roxann Wheeler finds no clear "consensus" on the value of race in British philosophical and literary texts of the eighteenth century. In England, the emergence of race as a marker of social status was preceded, determined, and often superseded by older "proto-racial ideologies" such as "Christianity, civility and rank"; not until the "third quarter of the eighteenth century" did skin color emerge as a significant marker of identity in Britain, Wheeler argues (7–9). However, she admits that this state of affairs does not necessarily extend to America. This is evident in the case of Olaudah Equiano, a supremely canny negotiator of race, civility, sympathy, and Englishness, whose *Interesting Narrative* nonetheless reveals, according to Wheeler, that "dark skin color overrides the privileges of free status and British masculinity in certain contexts, especially in the West Indies and America" (236). His literacy, Christianity, humanity, manhood, or Englishness cannot protect Equiano against capture and abasement by race slavery.

53. Emmanuel Chukwudi Eze surveys eighteenth-century philosophical and scientific conceptions of race in *Race and the Enlightenment: A Reader* (Oxford: Blackwell, 1997); see also Peter J. Kitson, ed., *Theories of Race*, vol. 8, *Slav-*

ery, Abolition, and Emancipation: Writings in the British Romantic Period (London: Pickering and Chatto, 1999). On racialization in the new nation, see Carroll Smith-Rosenberg, "Dis-Covering the Subject of the 'Great Constitutional Discussion,' 1786–1789," *The Journal of American History* 79.3 (December 1992): 841–873; Dana Nelson, *National Manhood: Capitalist Citizenship and the Imagined Fraternity of White Men* (Durham, N.C.: Duke University Press, 1998), 29–60; Ronald Takaki, *Iron Cages: Race and Culture in Nineteenth-Century America* (1979; rev. ed. New York: Oxford University Press, 2000), 1–65.

54. On late colonial and early national American Indian relations, see Vine Deloria, Jr., and David E. Wilkins, *Tribes, Treaties, and Constitutional Tribulations* (Austin: University of Texas, 1999), 3–31; Vine Deloria, Jr., *Behind the Trail of Broken Treaties: An Indian Declaration of Independence* (1974; reprint, Austin: University of Texas, 1985), 85–139; and Philip Deloria, *Playing Indian* (New Haven: Yale University Press, 1998), 1–37.

55. Marcus W. Jernegan, "Slavery and Conversion in the American Colonies," *American Historical Review* 21 (1915–16): 504–527; George Frederickson, *The Arrogance of Race: Historical Perspectives on Slavery, Racism, and Social Inequality* (Middletown, Conn.: Wesleyan University Press, 1988), 189–205.

56. William Blackstone, *Commentaries on the Laws of England*, 2 vols. (New York: W. E. Dean, 1844), 1:425.

57. James Oldham, "New Light on Mansfield and Slavery," *Journal of British Studies* 27.1 (January 1988), 45–68; Carretta, *Unchained Voices*, 4–6; David Brion Davis, *The Problem of Slavery in the Age of Revolution, 1770–1823* (Ithaca, N.Y.: Cornell University Press, 1975), 469–522; Teresa Michals, "'That Sole and Despotic Dominion': Slaves, Wives, and Game in Blackstone's Commentaries," *Eighteenth-Century Studies* 27.2 (winter 1993–94): 195–216.

58. Joanne Pope Melish, *Disowning Slavery: Gradual Emancipation and "Race" in New England, 1780–1860* (Ithaca, N.Y.: Cornell University Press, 1998), 86.

59. Patrick Rael, *Black Identity and Black Protest in the Antebellum North* (Chapel Hill: University of North Carolina Press, 2002), 25.

60. Colonial and early national policies affecting African-Americans are reviewed in Melish, *Gradual Emancipation*; Cheryl I. Harris, "Whiteness as Property," *Harvard Law Review* 107 (June 1993): 1707; and in Winthrop Jordan's magisterial *White Over Black: American Attitudes Toward the Negro, 1550–1812* (Chapel Hill: University of North Carolina Press, 1968), 103–110, 315–341, 403–426.

61. On the transition from ethnic African to African-American identities, see Michael Gomez, *Exchanging Our Country Marks: The Transformation of African Identities in the Colonial and Antebellum South* (Chapel Hill: University of North Carolina Press, 1998), 1–16, 154–290; Sterling Stuckey, *Slave Culture: Nationalist Theory and the Foundations of Black America* (New York: Oxford University Press, 1987), 1–97; Piersen, *Black Yankees*, 3–22, 74–113, 143–160.

62. Abdul R. JanMohamed, "Negating the Negation as a Form of Affirmation in Minority Discourse: The Construction of Richard Wright as Subject," in *The Nature and Context of Minority Discourse*, ed. Abdul JanMohamed and David Lloyd (New York: Oxford University Press, 1990), 103.

63. Thomas Jefferson, *Notes on the State of Virginia.*, ed. William Peden (1787; reprint, New York: Norton, 1982), 163.

64. Stuckey, *Slave Culture*, 1–97.

Chapter 2

1. The known papers of Samson Occom are located at Dartmouth College and the Connecticut Historical Society. Dartmouth holds most of Occom's extant letters, diaries, and sermons, which are filed among the papers of Eleazar Wheelock. A sixteen-reel microfilm edition of *The Papers of Eleazar Wheelock* was published by University Microfilm International, in Ann Arbor, Michigan; see especially reel 14. Citations from the Dartmouth Wheelock Papers are indicated "DWP" and noted by document number. Dartmouth Special Collections library also holds a three-volume typescript of Occom's diary (D.C. History E/98/M6/O172), a vertical file of Occom-related materials (VF), as well as a number of relevant rare books. The Samson Occom Papers at the Connecticut Historical Society (Index 79998) comprise 236 items, including sermons, letters, and account books, written by Samson Occom, Mary Occom, Joseph Johnson, and Mohegan tribal leaders, during the years 1727–1808. I have relied upon a CHS-produced microfilm edition of the papers. Citations from the Connecticut Historical Society Samson Occom Papers are indicated "SOP" and noted by document number.

Wheelock comments about his "pain & sorrow of heart" for Occom found in Leon Burr Richardson, *An Indian Preacher in England* (Hanover, N.H.: Dartmouth College Publications, 1933), 356.

2. DWP, 771424.

3. Ibid., 771205.1.

4. Laurie Weinstein, "Samson Occom: Charismatic Eighteenth-Century Mohegan Leader," in *Enduring Traditions: The Native Peoples of New England*, ed. Laurie Weinstein (Westport, Conn.: Bergin and Garvey, 1994), 96.

5. On April 1, 1774, the New London *Gazette* announced that "Mr. Occum's Collection of Poems, will be published on Wednesday next" (3, 3); a front-page notice appeared on April 8. The *Gazette* ran advertisements from April 15 to June 17, 1774; a second printing was advertised during August and September 1776. The hymnal was also advertised in the *Newport Mercury* (May 16–July 25, 1774); the Norwich, Connecticut *Packet* (August 4, 1774); the Connecticut *Courant* (July 5, 1774; July 15–August 26, 1776); and the New York *Packet* (June 20–August 8, 1776).

6. The early history of sectarian American hymnody is reviewed by Stephen Marini in *Radical Sects of Revolutionary New England* (Cambridge: Harvard University Press, 1982), 156–171, and "Rehearsal for Revival: Sacred Singing and the Great Awakening in America," *JAAR Thematic Studies* 50.1 (1983): 71–91. On early African-American hymnody, see William Piersen, *Black Yankees: The Development of an Afro-American Subculture in Eighteenth Century New England* (Amherst: University of Massachusetts Press, 1988), 66–67; Sylvia Frey and Betty Wood, *Come Shouting to Zion: African American Protestantism in the American South and British Caribbean to 1830* (Chapel Hill: University of

North Carolina Press, 1998), 143–145; and Kenneth L. Waters, Sr., "Liturgy, Spirituality, and Polemic in the Hymnody of Richard Allen," *The North Star: A Journal of African-American Religious History* 2.2 (spring 1999): http://northstar. vassar.edu/. See also Richard Allen, *A Collection of Spiritual Songs and Hymns Selected from Various Authors* (Philadelphia: John Ormrod, 1801).

7. Occom was already active in editorial, bookbinding, and bookselling concerns. Advertisements for Phillis Wheatley's *Poems* name Occom as a sales agent; other records show that he transacted with the African-American minister Lemuel Haynes, to whom he sold a copy of John Eliot's Algonkian-language Bible and a seventeenth-century book of sermons. See W. Deloss Love, *Samson Occom and the Christian Indians of New England* (Boston: Pilgrim, 1899), 47; Bernd Peyer, *The Tutor'd Mind: Indian Missionary-Writers in Antebellum America* (Amherst: University of Massachusetts Press, 1997), 330n128; item, Dartmouth Occom VF. Occom recorded one of his interactions with Lemuel Haynes in a May 30, 1787, diary entry: "Got Mr Hainess about 10 he is a Preacher among the People, he is mustee, half white and half Negro an Extraordinary man in understanding & a great Preacher I was there Some Time, took Dinner there, and Some in the after Noon, I went on my way again." See Samson Occom, Diary, 1743–1790, 3 vols. (Typescript. Dartmouth College, Special Collections, Manuscript 4), 3: 292.

8. Bernd Peyer, "Samson Occom: Mohegan Missionary and Writer of the 18th Century," *American Indian Quarterly* 6.3–4 (1982): 208–217; David Murray, *Forked Tongues: Speech, Writing, and Representation in North American Indian Texts* (Bloomington: Indiana University Press, 1991), 49–57; Michael Elliott, "'This Indian Bait': Samson Occom and the Voice of Liminality," *Early American Literature* 29.3 (1994): 233–253; Robert Allen Warrior, *Tribal Secrets: Recovering American Indian Intellectual Traditions* (Minneapolis: University of Minnesota Press, 1995), 3–4; Dana Nelson, "'(I Speak Like a Fool but I Am Constrained)': Samson Occom's Short Narrative and Economies of the Racial Self," in *Early Native American Writing: New Critical Essays*, ed. Helen Jaskoski (New York: Cambridge University Press, 1996), 46–65; Bernd C. Peyer, *The Tutor'd Mind*, 54–116; Jace Weaver, *That the People Might Live: Native American Literatures and Native American Community* (New York: Oxford University Press, 1997),49–53; Eileen Razzari Elrod, "'I Did Not Make Myself So . . .': Samson Occom and American Religious Autobiography," in *Christian Encounters with the Other*, ed. John C. Hawley (New York: New York University Press, 1998), 135–149; Sandra Gustafson, *Eloquence is Power: Oratory and Performance in Early America* (Chapel Hill, N.C.: Omohundro Institute of Early American History and Culture, University of North Carolina Press, 2000), 90–101; Hilary Wyss, *Writing Indians: Literacy, Christianity, and Native Community in Early America* (Amherst: University of Massachusetts Press, 2000), 123–153; and Keely McCarthy, "Conversion, Identity, and the Indian Missionary," *Early American Literature* 36.3 (2001): 353–370. The major biography of Samson Occom is W. DeLoss Love, *Samson Occom and the Christian Indians of New England* (1899; reprint, Syracuse, N.Y.: Syracuse University Press, 2000).

9. See Jace Weaver, ed., *Native Religious Identity: Unforgotten Gods* (Mary-

knoll, N.Y.: Orbis Books, 1998), and James Treat, ed., *Native and Christian: In-digenous Voices on Religious Identity in the United States and Canada* (New York: Routledge, 1996).

10. James Clifford, *The Predicament of Culture: Twentieth-Century Ethnography, Literature, and Art* (Cambridge: Harvard University Press, 1988), 277–346.

11. Samson Occom, "A Short Narrative of My Life," in *The Heath Anthology of American Literature*, ed. Paul Lauter, et al. (Lexington, Mass.: D. C. Heath, 1994), 942.

12. William S. Simmons and Cheryl L. Simmons, *Old Light on Separate Ways: The Narragansett Diary of Joseph Fish, 1765–1776* (Hanover, N.H.: University Press of New England, 1982), xxxi; and William S. Simmons, "Red Yankees: Narragansett Conversion in the Great Awakening," *American Ethnologist* 10.2 (May 1983): 253–271.

13. Peyer, *The Tutor'd Mind*, 60.

14. SOP, 0019.

15. DWP, 766504.4.

16. Ibid., 765900.1.

17. Ibid., 768126.

18. Simmons and Simmons, *Old Light on Separate Ways*, 5.

19. Ezra Stiles discusses Samuel Niles in his *Literary Diary* (New York: C. Scribner's, 1901), 1:244. See also Simmons and Simmons, *Old Light on Separate Ways*, 263, and Simmons, "Red Yankees," 57. On funeral services, see Simmons, "Red Yankees," 263.

20. On Samuel Ashpo, see William Allen, *Memoirs of Samson Occom, The Mohegan Indian Missionary, Including His Own Journal of Many Years, With Specimens of his Sermons, and various Notices Relating to the Indians of his Tribe* (Unpub. mss., 1859; Dartmouth, Vault Mss.), 4. Occom's involvement in the Mason controversy is discussed in DWP 765212.7; DWP 765212.10; Richardson, *An Indian Preacher in England*, 28; and Weinstein, "Samson Occom," 95–96.

21. DWP, 765511.1.

22. Ibid., 767503.3; *Connecticut Courant* May 5, 1766, 3.1.

23. Ibid., 765656.2.

24. Ibid., 765628.1.

25. Richardson, *An Indian Preacher in England*, 83.

26. Samson Occom, Diary, 2:231.

27. DWP, 765656.2.

28. Occom, "A Short Narrative," 947.

29. On Occom's sermons, see Laura Arnold, *Crossing Cultures: Algonquin Indians and the Invention of New England* (Diss., University of California, Los Angeles, 1995), 141–145.

30. SOP, 488.

31. See Paula Gunn Allen, *The Sacred Hoop: Recovering the Feminine in American Indian Traditions* (Boston: Beacon Press, 1986), and Theda Perdue, "Native Women in the Early Republic: Old World Perceptions, New World Realities," in *Native Americans and the Early Republic*, ed. Frederick Hoxie et al. (Charlottesville, Va.: University Press of Virginia, 1999), 85–122.

32. Allen, *Memoirs of Samson Occom*, 153.

33. Jonathan Edwards, *The Great Awakening*, vol. 4, *The Works of Jonathan Edwards* (New Haven: Yale University Press, 1972), 4:118.

34. Ibid., 4:407.

35. Ibid., 4:490.

36. Robert Stevenson, "Protestant Music in America," in *Protestant Church Music: A History*, ed. Friedrich Blume (New York: W. W. Norton, 1974), 644.

37. Paul Larson, "Mahican and Lenape Moravians and Moravian Music," *Unitas Fratrum* 21–22 (1988), 184.

38. James Dow McCallum, ed., *Letters of Eleazar Wheelock's Indians* (Hanover, N.H.: Dartmouth College Publications, 1932), 73–74. See also John Heckwelder, *A Narrative of the Mission of the United Brethren Among the Delaware and Mohegan Indians, from Its Commencement in the Year 1740, to the Close of the Year 1808* (New York: Arno, 1971), 428; and Julius Edward Witinger, *Hymnody of the Early American Indian Missions* (Diss., Catholic University, 1971), 115–118. On Watts and the Housatonic, see Samuel Hopkins, *Historical Memoirs Relating to the Housatonic Indians* (1753; reprint, New York: W. Abbatt, 1911), 128.

39. Michael McNally, *Ojibwe Singers: Hymns, Grief, and a Native Culture in Motion* (New York: Oxford University Press, 2000), 12.

40. Craig Womack, *Red on Red: Native American Literary Separatism* (Minneapolis: University of Minnesota Press, 1999), 16.

41. Louise Burkhart, "The Amanuenses Have Appropriated the Text: Interpreting a Nahuatl Song of Santiago," in *On the Translation of Native American Literatures*, ed. Brian Swann (Washington, D.C.: Smithsonian, 1992), 339–355.

42. Beverly Diamond Cavanagh, "Christian Hymns in Eastern Woodlands Communities: Performance Contexts," in *Musical Repercussions of 1492: Encounters in Text and Performance*, ed. Carol E. Robertson (Washington, D.C.: Smithsonian, 1992), 381–394, and Beverly Diamond Cavanagh, "The Transmission of Algonkian Indian Hymns: Between Orality and Literacy," in *Musical Canada*, ed. John Beckwith and Frederick A. Hall (Toronto: University of Toronto Press, 1988), 3–28.

43. Stevenson, "Protestant Music," 643.

44. Thomas Commuck, *Indian Melodies* (New York: G. Lane and C. B. Tippet, 1845), 63.

45. Harold Blodgett, *Samson Occom*, Dartmouth College Manuscript Series, Number 3 (Hanover, N.H.: Dartmouth, 1935), 46.

46. McCallum, *Letters*, 94.

47. Ibid., 117.

48. Laura Murray, ed., *To Do Good to My Indian Brethren: The Writings of Joseph Johnson, 1751–1776* (Amherst: University of Massachusetts Press, 1998), 60.

49. Murray, *To Do Good to My Indian Brethren*, 67; McCallum, *Letters*, 128.

50. Simmons and Simmons, *Old Light on Separate Ways*, 8, 31.

51. SOP, 0088.

52. Richardson, *An Indian Preacher in England*, 83, 104, 284–287; Love, *Samson Occom*, 178; McCallum, *Letters*, 112; and Robert Stevenson, "American Tribal Musics at Contact," *Inter-American Music Review* 14.1 (spring-summer 1994): 28

53. Murray, *To Do Good to My Indian Brethren*, 109–126, passim.

54. SOP, 0117–0118.

55. DWP, 771205.1.

56. Murray, *To Do Good to My Indian Brethren*, 155.

57. Ibid., 161, emphasis added.

58. Two more evidences of this adoption merit notice here. One is a cryptic letter written by Jacob Fowler to Samson Occom on March 27, 1772, which breaks into quasi-hymnodic verse—"Good News I do Bring, I hear the Christians Sing"—and closes with a quatrain—"I Direct my Love to You / Which is but just Your Due. / And to my Sister Dear / Which I hope will him Fear"— and a postscript corrective to the last line—"I mean, In Gods Time will him Fear" (SOP 244). The second is Joseph Johnson's farewell sermon at Farmington, delivered in February 1773. Johnson used hymnody as a metonym for his relationship with the community: "You See his face no more, nor hear his Voice Sounding amongst you as Usual, Either Exhortin or weeping or making melody to God." See Murray, *To Do Good to My Indian Brethren*, 165.

59. Samson Occom, *A Choice Collection of Hymns and Spiritual Songs; Intended for the Edification of Sincere Christians, of All Denominations* (New London, Conn.: Printed and sold by Timothy Green, a few rods west of the courthouse, 1774), 3.

60. Ibid., 4.

61. According to musicologist Robert Stevenson, Richard Allen adopted two hymns—"What poor despised company" and "Lord when together here we meet"—first published by Occom and followed Occom's lead by implementing extended choral refrains. See Stevenson, "American Tribal Musics," 29.

62. In determining authorship for the contents of Occom's 1774 *Collection*, I have relied on John Julian, ed., *A Dictionary of Hymnology*, 2 vols. (New York: Dover Publications, 1957) and the Hymn Society of America's *Dictionary of American Hymnology: First Line Index*, ed. Leonard Ellinwood, 179 microfilm reels (New York: University Music Editions, 1984).

63. Occom's early biographers Harold Blodgett and W. DeLoss Love once credited him with as many as twenty-four compositions in the *Collection*, citing these hymns' "naiveté" and "earnest simplicity" (Blodgett, *Samson Occom*, 145; Love, *Samson Occom*, 187). Blodgett and Love were, however, incorrect: two of the characteristically "naïve" hymns they attribute to Occom were authored by George Herbert and Charles Wesley. An undated, anonymous typescript in the Dartmouth College Special Collections Samson Occom file (VF) attributes twenty-six hymns to Occom, including twenty-four of the unattributed hymns in the 1774 *Collection*; manuscript sources neither confirm or deny Occom's authorship of these twenty-four hymns.

64. Murray, *To Do Good to My Indian Brethren*, 239.

65. Occom, *A Choice Collection*, 4.

66. Heckwelder, *A Narrative of the Mission of the United Brethren*, 208.

67. Melissa Fawcett, *The Lasting of the Mohegans. Part 1: The Story of the Wolf People* (Uncasville, Conn.: Mohegan Tribe, 1995), 37, and Melissa Fawcett, *Medicine Trail: The Life and Lessons of Gladys Tantaquidgeon* (Tucson: University of Arizona Press, 2000), 4, 135.

68. Occom, *A Choice Collection*, 4.

69. *Divine hymns, or, Spiritual songs: for the use of religious assemblies and private Christians: being a collection by Joshua Smith, Samson Okcum [sic], and others* (Wilkes-Barre, Pa.: Printed by Asher and Charles Miner, 1802). See also *Divine hymns, or, Spiritual songs: for the use of religious assemblies and private Christians: being a collection by Joshua Smith, Samson Ockum [sic] and others. Sixth edition, greatly improved* (Troy, N.Y.: Printed by Moffitt and Lyon, 1803); *Divine hymns, or, Spiritual songs: for the use of religious assemblies and private Christians: being a collection by Joshua Smith, Samson Ockum, and others. Sixth edition, greatly improved* (Albany, N.Y.: Printed by C. R. and G. Webster, and sold at their bookstore, and by Daniel Steele, 1804.)

70. Occom-written manuscript copies of "The Slow Traveller," or "O happy souls how fast you go," and "Come all my young companions, come" survive in the Dartmouth College Rauner Special Collections Library (000194). For full attribution and publication histories, see my article "Six Hymns by Samson Occom," *Early American Literature* 38.1 (2003). See also Robert Shaw, "Samson Occom (1723–1792): His Life and Work as a Hymnist" (M.A. thesis, New Orleans Baptist Theological Seminary, 1986), and John Julian, *A Dictionary of Hymnology* (New York: Dover, 1957), 1:855. The hymn "When shall we three meet again" has sometimes been incorrectly attributed to Occom. Julian, *A Dictionary of Hymnology*, notes that this attribution is based only a "doubtful" bit of Dartmouth folklore (855).

71. Robert Daly, *God's Altar: The World and the Flesh in Puritan Poetry* (Berkeley: University of California Press, 1978), 156.

72. Occom, Diary, 2:162; Blodgett, *Samson Occom*, 181.

73. Ibid., 2:164.

74. Ibid., 2:165; Blodgett, *Samson Occom*, 182–183.

75. Occom, Diary, 2:218; Peyer, *The Tutor'd Mind*, 97.

76. See Gladys Tantaquidgeon, *Folk Medicine of the Delaware and Related Algonkian Indians*. Anthropological Series, number 3 (Harrisburg, Pa.: The Pennsylvania Historical and Museum Commission, 1972), 7–8, 11; M. R. Harrington, *Religion and Ceremonies of the Lenape*, Indian Notes and Monographs series, vol. 19 (New York: Museum of the American Indian, Heye Foundation, 1921), 61–80; John Bierhorst, *Mythology of the Lenape: Guide and Texts* (Tucson: University of Arizona Press, 1987), 61, 65, 73; William Simmons, *Spirit of the New England Tribes: Indian History and Folklore, 1620–1984* (Hanover: University Press of New England, 1986), 247–256.

Chapter 3

1. Sylvia Frey and Betty Wood, *Come Shouting to Zion: African American Protestantism in the American South and British Caribbean to 1830* (Chapel Hill: University of North Carolina Press, 1998), 118.

2. Vincent Carretta suggests that Marrant "may have fabricated" his naval career, because Marrant's name does not appear on muster lists of the ships named in his *Narrative*: the *Scorpion* and the *Princess Amelia*. See *Unchained Voices: An Anthology of Black Authors in the English-Speaking World of the*

Eighteenth-Century (Lexington: University of Kentucky Press, 1996), 130–131, n47. However, "John Morant" does appear on a list of prisoners taken from American privateers during the War of Independence. The list was compiled in 1888 from British War Department Papers and has been published online by the United States Merchant Marine: www.usmm.net/revdead.html. It should be noted that letters and legal records concerning John Marrant often misspell his last name as "Morant."

3. John Marrant, *A Narrative of the Lord's Wonderful Dealings with John Marrant, a Black, (Now Going to Preach the Gospel in Nova-Scotia). Fourth Edition, Enlarged by Mr. Marrant, and Printed (with Permission) for His Sole Benefit, with Notes Explanatory* (London: Printed for the Author, by R. Hawes, No. 40, Dorset-Street, Spitalfields, 1785), 38.

4. Marrant's ordination was also memorialized in Samuel Whitchurch's *The Negro Convert, A Poem; Being the Substance of the Experience of Mr. John Marrant, A Negro, as related by himself, previous to his Ordination* (Bath: Printed and sold by S. Hazard, [1785]). Whitchurch, an author of naval epics, emphasized Marrant's naval career and seafaring trials.

5. John Marrant, *A Journal of the Rev. John Marrant, From August the 18th, 1785, to The 16th of March, 1790. To which are added Two Sermons; One Preached on Ragged Island on Sabbath Day, the 27th Day of October 1787; the Other at Boston in New England, On Thursday, the 24th of June, 1789* (London: Printed for the Author, 1790), 32.

6. The *Journal* of John Marrant has received slight critical notice since its publication in 1790. In *The Negro Author: His Development in America to 1900* (New York: Kennikat, 1964), Vernon Loggins incorrectly and dismissively characterized the *Journal* as "scarcely more than an adaptation of the *Narrative*" (33); see also brief mentions in Angelo Costanzo, *Surprizing Narrative: Olaudah Equiano and the Beginnings of Black Autobiography* (New York: Greenwood Press, 1987): 102–104; and *Black Writers of the Eighteenth Century*, eds. Adam Burr and Susan Potkay (New York: St. Martin's, 1995): 69–70. For more extensive analyses, see John Saillant's "'Wipe Away all Tears from Their Eyes': John Marrant's Theology in the Black Atlantic, 1785–1808," *Journal of Millennial Studies* 1.2 (winter 1999): www.mille.org/publications/journal.html, and my own article, "The *Journal* of John Marrant: Providence and Prophecy in the Eighteenth-Century Black Atlantic," *The North Star: A Journal of African American Religious History* 3.1 (fall 1999): http://northstar.vassar.edu/. The only modern edition of the *Journal* appears in *Face Zion Forward: First Writers of the Black Atlantic, 1785–1798*, ed. Joanna Brooks and John Saillant (Boston: Northeastern University Press, 2002), 93–159.

7. Although he may have modeled his subscription list after that which prefaces Olaudah Equiano's *Interesting Narrative* (1789), Marrant's forty-one-name subscription list is nowhere as large or as luminous as his predecessor's.

8. Sylvia Frey, *Water from the Frock: Black Resistance in a Revolutionary Age* (Princeton, N.J.: Princeton University Press, 1991), 63–64, 113–114, 192–193.

9. On the history of Birchtown, see James W. St. G. Walker, *The Black Loyalists: The Search for a Promised Land in Nova Scotia and Sierra Leone* (New York: Dalhousie University Press, 1976); Ellen Gibson Wilson, *The Loyal Blacks* (New

York: G. P. Putnam's Sons, 1976); Phyllis R. Blakeley and John N. Grant, eds., *Eleven Exiles: Accounts of Loyalists in the American Revolution* (Toronto: Dundurn, 1982); Neil MacKinnon, "The Loyalists: 'A Different People,'" in *Banked Fires: The Ethnics of Nova Scotia*, ed. Douglass Campbell (Ontario: Scribbler's Press, 1978), 69–92; Donald Clairmont and Fred Wien, "Blacks and Whites: The Nova Scotia Race Relations Experience," in *Banked Fires: The Ethnics of Nova Scotia*, ed. Douglass Campbell (Ontario: Scribbler's Press, 1978), 141–182; Anthony Kirk-Greene, "David George: The Nova Scotian Experience," *Sierra Leone Studies* 14 (1960): 96–110; P. E. McKerrow, *A Brief History of the Coloured Baptists of Nova Scotia, 1783–1895* (Halifax: Afro Nova Scotian Enterprises, 1976); A. F. Walls, "The Nova Scotian Settlers and their Religion," *Sierra Leone Bulletin of Religion* 1.1 (June 1959): 19–31; Christopher Fyfe, "The Countess of Huntingdon's Connection in Nineteenth-Century Sierra Leone," *Sierra Leone Bulletin of Religion* 4.2 (December 1962): 53–61; Christopher Fyfe, *A History of Sierra Leone* (New York: Oxford University Press, 1962); Christopher Fyfe, ed., *"Our Children Free and Happy": Letters from Black Settlers in Africa* (Edinburgh: Edinburgh University Press, 1991); Mary Louise Clifford, *From Slavery to Freetown: Black Loyalists after the American Revolution* (Jefferson, N.C.: McFarland, 1999); Graham Russell Hodges, *The Black Loyalists Directory* (New York: Garland, 1996); John Pulis, ed., *Moving On: Black Loyalists in the Afro-Atlantic World* (New York: Garland, 1999); John Saillant, "Hymnody and the Persistence of an African-American Faith in Sierra Leone," *The Hymn* 48 (January 1997): 8–17; John Saillant, "'Wipe away All Tears from Their Eyes': John Marrant's Theology in the Black Atlantic, 1785–1808," *Journal of Millennial Studies* 1 (winter 1999): www.mille.org/publications/journal.html; and Robin W. Winks, *The Blacks in Canada: A History*, 2d ed. (Montreal: McGill-Queens University Press, 1997).

10. George A. Rawlyk, *Ravished by the Spirit: Religious Revivals, Baptists, and Henry Alline* (Kingston: McGill-Queen's University Press, 1984), 10. See also Alline's *New Light Letters and Songs*, ed. George Rawlyk (Nova Scotia: Lancelot Press, 1983), and *The Journal of Henry Alline*, eds. James Beverley and Barry Moody (Nova Scotia: Lancelot Press, 1982).

11. For David George's firsthand account of his career, see "An Account of the Life of Mr. David George, from Sierra Leone in Africa," *Baptist Annual Register* 1 (1793): 473–484; reprinted in Brooks and Saillant, *Face Zion Forward*, 177–190.

12. Walker, *The Black Loyalists*, 68.

13. Blakely and Grant, *Eleven Exiles*, 278; Wilson, *The Loyal Blacks*, 96.

14. Nathan Bangs, ed., *The Life of the Rev. Freeborn Garrettson*, 4th ed. (New York: T. Mason and G. Lane, 1839), 161; Robert Drew Simpson, ed., *American Methodist Pioneer: The Life and Journals of the Rev. Freeborn Garrettson, 1752–1827* (Rutland, Vt.: Academy Books, 1984), 250–251.

15. Boston King also wrote his own account of his life in Nova Scotia and after. See "Memoirs of the Life of Boston King, a black preacher, written by himself during his residence at Kingswood School," *Methodist Magazine* 21 (1798): 105–110; reprinted in Brooks and Saillant, *Face Zion Forward*, 209–231.

16. On David Margate, see Boyd Samuel Schlenther, *Queen of the Method-*

ists: The Countess of Huntingdon and the Eighteenth-Century Crisis of Faith and Society (Durham, England: Durham Academic Press, 1997), 91; Frey and Wood, *Come Shouting to Zion*, 111–112; Winthrop Jordan, *White Over Black: American Attitudes Toward the Negro, 1550–1812* (Chapel Hill: University of North Carolina Press, 1968), 209–210.

17. Bangs, *The Life of the Rev. Freeborn Garrettson*, 152; Simpson, *American Methodist Pioneer*, 246.

18. Bangs, *The Life of the Rev. Freeborn Garrettson*, 161; Simpson, *American Methodist Pioneer*, 251.

19. Marrant, *Journal*, 39.

20. Bangs, *The Life of the Rev. Freeborn Garrettson*, 158; Simpson, *American Methodist Pioneer*, 249.

21. The much reprinted "Extract of a late letter from a gentleman at Constantinople, to his friend in London" recorded in verse "The Prophecy of Ackmet Almack of Cordistan" in the *Boston Evening Post* 10 December 1770: 2, 2; *Massachusetts Spy-Boston* 7–10 December 1770: 3, 2; *Boston Post Boy* 10 December 1770: 1,1–1,2; *New Hampshire Gazette-Portsmouth* 28 December 1770: 1, 2. See also "The Story of Zeyn Alasman, Prince of Balsora," *New Hampshire Gazette-Portsmouth* 19 February 1762: 3, 1. Paul Baepler surveys the Algerian captivity narrative genre in *White Slaves, African Masters: An Anthology of Barbary Captivity Narratives* (Chicago: University of Chicago Press, 1999). See also Robert J. Allison, *The Crescent Obscured: The United States and the Muslim World, 1776–1815* (New York: Oxford University Press, 1995), 35–59.

22. Increase Mather, *The Doctrine of Divine Providence Opened and Applied* (1684; reprint, New York: AMS Press, 1983), 12.

23. R. W. B. Lewis, *The American Adam: Innocence, Tragedy, and Tradition in the Nineteenth Century* (Chicago: University of Chicago Press, 1955), 5.

24. Marrant's *Narrative* went through no less than fifteen editions, many of which were abridged or manipulated by white editors. I use the fourth edition, considered definitive by Marrant scholars. For full bibliographical information, see the preface to the *Narrative* in *Black Writers of the Eighteenth Century*, eds. Adam Burr and Susan Potkay (New York: St. Martin's, 1995). A modern edition of Marrant's *Narrative* appears in Brooks and Saillant, *Face Zion Forward*, 47–76.

25. Review of *A Narrative of the Lord's Wonderful Dealings with John Marrant, a Black*, by John Marrant, *Monthly Review* (November 1785), 399.

26. For critical commentary on Hammon and Marrant, see Benilde Montgomery, "Recapturing John Marrant," in *A Mixed Race: Ethnicity in Early America*, ed. Frank Shuffleton (Oxford: Oxford University Press, 1993), 105–115; Frances Smith Foster, "Briton Hammon's Narrative: Some Insights into Beginnings," *College Language Association Journal* 21 (1977): 179–86; Frances Smith Foster, *Witnessing Slavery: The Development of Antebellum Slave Narratives* (1979; reprint, Madison: University of Wisconsin Press, 1994), 39–43; John Sekora, "Is the Slave Narrative a Species of Autobiography?" in *Studies in Autobiography*, ed. James Olney (Oxford: Oxford University Press, 1988), 99–111; John Sekora, "Red, White, and Black: Indian Captivities, Colonial Printers, and Early African-American Narrative," in *A Mixed Race: Ethnicity in Early America*, ed.

Frank Shuffleton (Oxford: Oxford University Press, 1993), 92–104; Angelo Costanzo, *Surprizing Narrative: Olaudah Equiano and the Beginnings of Black Autobiography* (New York: Greenwood Press, 1987), 91–102; William Andrews, *To Tell a Free Story: The First Century of African-American Autobiography* (Urbana: University of Illinois Press, 1986), 32–60; Henry Louis Gates, Jr., *The Signifying Monkey: A Theory of African-American Literary Criticism* (New York: Oxford University Press, 1988), 138, 142–146; Rafia Zafar, *We Wear the Mask: African-Americans Write American Literature, 1760–1870* (New York: Columbia University Press, 1996), 54–62; Karen Weyler, "Race, Redemption, and Captivity," in *A Narrative of the Lord's Wonderful Dealings with John Marrant, a Black* and *Narrative of the Uncommon Sufferings and Surprizing Deliverance of Briton Hammon, A Negro Man*," in *Genius in Bondage: Literature of the Early Black Atlantic*, ed. Vincent Carretta and Philip Gould (Lexington: University of Kentucky Press, 2001), 39–53; and Philip Gould, "'Remarkable Liberty': Language and Identity in Eighteenth-Century Black Autobiography," in Carretta and Gould, *Genius in Bondage*, 116–129.

27. Lawrence Levine, *Black Culture and Black Consciousness: Afro-American Folk Thought from Slavery to Freedom* (New York: Oxford University Press, 1977), 120.

28. Carol Wilson, *Freedom at Risk: The Kidnapping of Free Blacks in America, 1780–1785* (Lexington: University of Kentucky Press, 1994).

29. Orlando Patterson, *Slavery and Social Death: A Comparative Study* (Cambridge: Harvard, 1982), 51.

30. Briton Hammon, "A Narrative of the Uncommon Sufferings, and Surprizing Deliverance of Briton Hammon, a Negro Man," in Carretta, *Unchained Voices*, 24.

31. Marrant, *Narrative*, 26–27.

32. Ibid., 29.

33. Phillip Richards, "The 'Joseph Story' as Slave Narrative: On Genesis and Exodus as Prototypes for Early Black Anglophone Writing," in *African-Americans and the Bible: Sacred Texts and Social Textures*, ed. Vincent Wimbush (New York: Continuum, 2000), 221–235.

34. On this post-African view of death, see Michael Gomez, *Exchanging our Country Marks: The Transformation of African Identities in the Colonial and Antebellum South* (Chapel Hill: University of North Carolina Press, 1998), 277.

35. Marrant, *Narrative*, 10.

36. Ibid., 11.

37. Ibid., 12.

38. Ibid., 13.

39. Ibid., 13–14.

40. Ibid., 14.

41. Ibid., 16.

42. Ibid., 36–37.

43. Ibid., 31–32.

44. Ibid., 32.

45. Paul Gilroy, *The Black Atlantic: Modernity and Double-Consciousness* (Cambridge: Harvard University Press, 1993), 68.

46. Marrant, *Journal*, 11.

47. On the checkered career of Colonel Stephen Blucke, see Margaret Blucke's letter to John Marrant in the *Journal* (82–84). See also Barry Cahill, "Stephen Blucke: The Peril of Being a 'White Negro' in Loyalist Nova Scotia." *Nova Scotia Historical Review* 11.1 (1991): 129–134.

48. Marrant, *Journal*, 46–47.

49. Ibid., 50.

50. Ibid., 49.

51. Ibid., 16.

52. For an excellent discussion of Haynes, the New Divinity, and race, see chapter 3 of John Saillant, *Black Puritan, Black Republican: Faith and Antislavery in the Life of Lemuel Haynes, 1753–1833* (New York: Oxford University Press, 2002).

53. Saillant, "Hymnody and the Persistence," 12.

54. Marrant, *Journal*, 11.

55. Sterling Stuckey, *Slave Culture: Nationalist Theory and the Foundations of Black America* (New York: Oxford University Press, 1987), 104–106.

56. Marrant, *Journal*, 12.

57. Ibid., 27.

58. Ibid., 88.

59. Ibid., 88.

60. Ibid., 90.

61. Ibid., 102.

62. Ibid., 95–96.

63. Ibid., 95.

64. Ibid., 99.

65. Ibid., 92, 97, 99.

66. Ibid., 102.

67. Ibid., 21.

68. Ibid., 22.

69. Ibid., 22.

70. Ibid., 25.

71. Ibid., 61.

72. Ibid., 50.

73. Ibid., 59.

74. Ibid., 55.

75. Ibid., 64.

76. Ibid., 65.

77. Ibid., 65–66.

78. Ibid., 66.

79. Ibid., 12, 17, 19.

80. Ibid., 12, 18.

81. Ibid., 12, 34.

82. Ibid., 18.

83. Ibid., 44.

84. Melville J. Herskovits applied the theory of retention and reinterpretation to black religion in his landmark *The Myth of the Negro Past* (1941; reprint,

Boston: Beacon Press, 1958), 215–235. This line of thought continues to influence historical studies of black culture. A noteworthy recent example is Mechal Sobel, *The World They Made Together: Black and White Values in Eighteenth-Century Virginia* (Princeton, N.J.: Princeton University Press, 1987).

85. Frey and Wood, *Come Shouting to Zion*, 99.

86. Sterling Stuckey's masterful analysis of the ring shout appears in *Slave Culture*, chap. 1; on water baptism, see Herskovits, *The Myth of the Negro Past*, 233–235, and Gomez, *Exchanging our Country Marks*, 244–290.

87. Gilroy, *The Black Atlantic*, 37.

88. Marrant, *Journal*, 66.

89. In addition to the brother (or brother-in-law) who invited him to Birchtown, Marrant may have had other relations there as well. The *Journal* mentions, incidentally, that a young "boy" sometimes accompanied him in his itinerancy, and it reports allegations (later disproved) that he had married another man's wife. Historical records further document his family life in Nova Scotia. *The Register of Marriages in the Parish of St. George and St. Patrick, in the County of Shelburne, in the Province of Nova Scotia* notes that John Marrant married Elizabeth Herries (or Harries) on August 15, 1788. The *Book of Negroes* lists "Mellia Marrant," "formerly the property of John Marrant near Santee, Carolina," as well as two Marrant children, "Amelia," 6, and "Ben," 4. Some scholars argue that these three individuals were indeed the chattel slaves of John Marrant, while others believe that Melia was rather a sibling or a former spouse. See Carretta, *Unchained Voices*, 129 n9, and Margaret Washington Creel, *"A Peculiar People": Slave Religion and Community Culture Among the Gullahs* (New York: New York University Press, 1988), 376n12. Finally, genealogical records document a number of "John Marrant"s in the Charleston area in the late eighteenth century. John Mayrant (1725/6–1767) was a prominent planter of St. James, Santee Parish, South Carolina; in 1750, he helped found the Charleston Library Society. His son John Mayrant (1762–1836) served in the War of Independence as a lieutenant in the South Carolina navy, then moved from the Santee-Charleston area to Camden District, Claremont County, South Carolina, where 1790 census records show him owning sixty-five slaves. Mellia, Amelia, and Ben Marrant were likely enslaved to this white planter John Mayrant rather than the black evangelist John Marrant.

90. Marrant, *Journal*, 87.

91. Fyfe, *"Our Children Free and Happy,"* 1; Walker, *The Black Loyalists*, 128.

92. Saillant, "Hymnody and the Persistence," 16.

Chapter 4

1. John Marrant, *A Journal of the Rev. John Marrant, From August the 18th, 1785, to The 16th of March, 1790. To which are added Two Sermons; One Preached on Ragged Island on Sabbath Day, the 27th Day of October 1787; the Other at Boston in New England, On Thursday, the 24th of June, 1789* (London: Printed for the Author, 1790), 32.

2. Marrant, *Journal*, 69.

3. Prince Hall's life history, like the history of black Freemasonry, has been

a subject of some debate. William Grimshaw's 1903 *Official History of Freemasonry Among the Colored People of North America* initiated the popular story that Prince Hall was born in Barbados to a white father and free French mulatto mother, that his family immigrated to America, and that Hall later became a Methodist minister. Contemporary scholars of black Freemasonry have observed inconsistencies in Grimshaw's account and for the most part rejected it. A number of men named "Prince Hall" appear in Boston marriage records after 1770 and in the records of the Revolutionary War. One of these men was aboard the *Charming Polly* when it was captured in 1777 and subsequently spent three months with black abolitionist Paul Cuffe under British imprisonment in New York. See Charles H. Wesley, *Prince Hall: Life and Legacy* (Philadelphia: Afro-American Historical and Cultural Museum; Washington, D. C.: United Supreme Council, Prince Hall Affiliation, 1977), 38.

4. See Michael Gomez, *Exchanging our Country Marks: The Transformation of African Identities in the Colonial and Antebellum South* (Chapel Hill: University of North Carolina Press, 1998), 88–103. Sterling Stuckey also connects secret societies to African culture in *Slave Culture: Nationalist Theory and the Foundations of Black America* (New York: Oxford University Press, 1987), 14, 15, 25, 64, 69, 86, 95.

5. Bernard Fay, "Learned Societies in Europe and America in the Eighteenth Century," *The American Historical Review* 37.2 (January 1932): 255–266.

6. Margaret C. Jacob, "Forum: Exits from the Enlightenment," *Eighteenth-Century Studies* 33.2 (1999–2000): 251.

7. White Masons decried Prince Hall Freemasonry as illegitimate well into the twentieth-century. In response, both black and white Masonic scholars published defenses of the order. The first was Martin Delaney's *Origin and Objects of Ancient Freemasonry; Its Introduction into the United States, and Legitimacy Among Colored Men. A Treatise Delivered Before St. Cyprian Lodge, No. 13, June 24th, A.D. 1853-AL 5853* (Pittsburgh: W. S. Haven, 1853). See also William Upton, *Negro Masonry, Being a Critical Examination of Objections to the Legitimacy of the Masonry Existing Among the Negroes of America* (Massachusetts: Prince Hall Grand Lodge, 1902); William Grimshaw, *Official History of Freemasonry Among the Colored People of North America* (New York: n. p., 1903); George Crawford, *Prince Hall and His Followers: Being a Monograph on the Legitimacy of Negro Masonry* (New York: The Crisis, 1914); Harold Van Buren Voorhis, *Negro Masonry in the United States* (New York: Henry Emmerson, 1945); Joseph A. Walkes, Jr., *Black Square and Compass: 200 Years of Prince Hall Freemasonry* (Richmond: Macoy Publishing and Masonic Supply, 1979). Voorhis later rescinded his published work because it drew from Grimshaw's erroneous account of Prince Hall's life and early Freemasonry.

8. Dorothy Porter was the first to republish both the 1792 and the 1797 *Charges* verbatim in her landmark collection *Early Negro Writing 1760–1837* (1970; reprint, Baltimore: Black Classics Press, 1995); the two *Charges* also appear unabridged in *Face Zion Forward: First Writers of the Black Atlantic, 1785–1798*, ed. John Saillant and Joanna Brooks (Northeastern University Press, 2002), 191–197; 199–207. Marrant's 1789 *Sermon* appears in Brooks and Saillant, *Face Zion Forward*, 77–91. Although it is likely that Marrant and Hall collabo-

rated in the composition of the sermon, the title page of the work identifies Marrant as its author.

9. W. E. B. Du Bois describes the black church as "the most characteristic expression of African character" and a "microcosm" of "all that great world from which the Negro is cut off by color-prejudice and social condition" in *The Souls of Black Folk* (1899; reprint, New York: Penguin Books, 1989), 158–159; in *The Philadelphia Negro* (Philadelphia: University of Pennsylvania, 1899), he claims that the church "really represented all that was left of African tribal life, and was the sole expression of the organized efforts of the slaves" (197); and in *The Negro Church* (Atlanta: Atlanta University Press, 1903) he writes, "There can be no reasonable doubt, however, but that the scattered remains of religious systems in Africa today among the Negro tribes are survivals of the religious ideas upon which the Egyptian was based" (2).

10. See St. Clair Drake, *The Redemption of Africa and Black Religion* (Chicago: Third World Press, 1970); Martin Bernal, *Black Athena* (New Brunswick, N.J.: Rutgers University Press, 1987); Mary Lefkowitz, *Not Out of Africa: How Afrocentrism Became an Excuse to Teach Myth as History* (New York: Basic Books, 1996); and Molefi Asante, *The Afrocentric Idea* (Philadelphia: Temple University Press, 1987). Wilson Jeremiah Moses provides an invaluable review of this long debate in his *Afrotopia: The Roots of African American Popular History* (Cambridge: Cambridge University Press, 1998).

11. Sterling Stuckey credits Pan-Africanism to an "almost elemental, instinctual recoil from the constraints of a narrow nationalism" and to the "detribalizing" process of the slave trade in *The Ideological Origins of Black Nationalism* (Boston: Beacon Press, 1972), 11. Wilson Jeremiah Moses claims that Ethiopianism "sprang organically out of certain shared political and religious experiences of English-speaking Africans during the late eighteenth and early nineteenth centuries" in "The Poetics of Ethiopianism," *American Literature* 47.3 (November 1975): 411; see also his *Classical Black Nationalism: From the American Revolution to Marcus Garvey* (New York: New York University Press, 1996) and *The Wings of Ethiopia: Studies in African-American Life and Letters* (Ames: Iowa State University Press, 1990). Finally, in *To Awaken My Afflicted Brethren: David Walker and the Problem of Antebellum Slave Resistance* (University Park: Pennsylvania State University Press, 1997), Peter Hinks concludes that the early black nationalists were "as indebted to . . . ideological assumptions about black character and slavery as they were to the still very limited body of archeological, anthropological, and historical knowledge about early Egypt and Africa" (192).

12. Gomez, *Exchanging Our Country Marks*, 12.

13. Moses, *Classical Black Nationalism*, 6; Drake, *The Redemption of Africa*.

14. Bruce Dain, "Haiti and Egypt in Early Black Racial Discourse in the United States." *Slavery and Abolition* 14.3 (November 1993): 150.

15. Matthew Carey, "A Philosophical Dream," *Columbian Magazine* (October 1786): 21.

16. Thomas Jefferson, *Notes on the State of Virginia*, ed. William Peden (1787; reprint, New York: Norton, 1982), 87, 143.

17. Samuel Hopkins, *The Works of Samuel Hopkins*, 2 vols. (Boston: Doctrinal Tract and Book Society, 1854), 1:144–145.

18. Phillis Wheatley, *The Poems of Phillis Wheatley*, ed. Julian D. Mason, Jr. (Chapel Hill: University of North Carolina Press, 1989), 211.

19. *Boston Independent Ledger* 30 December 1782, 3,1.

20. Wesley, *Prince Hall*, 210.

21. Ibid., 66–68.

22. Harry E. Davis, "Documents Relating to Negro Masonry in America," *Journal of Negro History* 21.4 (October 1936): 414.

23. Steven C. Bullock, *Revolutionary Brotherhood: Freemasonry and the Transformation of the American Social Order, 1730–1840* (Williamsburg, Virginia: Institute of Early American History and Culture, 1996), 14.

24. Margaret Jacob, *Living the Enlightenment: Freemasonry and Politics in Eighteenth-Century Europe* (Oxford: Oxford University Press, 1991), 154.

25. Bullock, *Revolutionary Brotherhood*, 89.

26. Wellins Calcott, *A Candid Disquisition of the Principles and Practices of the Most Antient and Honourable Society of Free and Accepted Masons; Together with some Strictures on the Origin, Nature, and Design of that Institution* (Boston: Reprinted and sold by Brother William M'Alpine, in Marlborough-Street, Boston, 1772), 80.

27. Grand Lodge of Pennsylvania, *Ahiman Rezon Abridged and Digested: As a Help to all that are, or would be, Free and Accepted Masons* (Philadelphia: Hall and Sellers, 1783), x.

28. Grand Lodge of Pennsylvania, *Ahiman Rezon*, 5.

29. "The African Lodge, An Oration delivered before the Grand Master, Wardens, and Brethren of the most Ancient and venerable Lodge of African Masons," *Columbian Magazine* 2.8 (1788): 467.

30. "The African Lodge," 467.

31. John Marrant, *A Sermon Preached on the 24th Day of June 1789, Being the Festival of Saint John the Baptists, at the Request of the Right Worshipful the Grand Master Prince Hall, and the Rest of the Brethren of the African Lodge of the Honorable Society of Free and Accepted Masons in Boston* (Boston: Printed and sold by T. and J. Fleet at the Bible and Heart, Cornhill, 1789), 4; emphasis added.

32. Marrant, *Sermon*, 5.

33. Potkay and Burr, *Black Writers of the Eighteenth Century*, 74.

34. Wesley, *Prince Hall*, 214. Although the title of this work apparently resembles the dispensationalist history of Jonathan Edwards, it may also refer to the English dispensationalist author John Edwards (1637–1716), *Polpoikilos sophia, a compleat history or survey of all the dispensations and methods of religion, from the beginning of the world to the consummation of all things, as represented in the Old and New Testament* (London: Printed for Daniel Brown, Jonathan Brown, Andrew Bell, John Wyatt, and E. Harris, 1699).

35. On chiasmus, repetition, and reversal, see Henry Louis Gates, Jr., *The Signifying Monkey: A Theory of African-American Literary Criticism* (New York: Oxford University Press, 1988), xxiv–xxv, 153–154.

36. Marrant, *Sermon*, 5–6.

37. Ibid., 6–7.

38. Ibid., *Sermon*, 8.

39. Ibid., *Sermon*, 8–9.

40. Ibid., *Sermon*, 9.

41. Ibid., *Sermon*, 9.

42. Genesis 4:15 records that God "set a mark" upon Cain, but it does not specify the nature of this mark. Consequently, the attribution of blackness to Cain has no clear biblical basis. Benjamin Braude investigates the uneven historical development of Cain, Ham, and Canaan-related theories of blackness in "The Sons of Noah and the Construction of Ethnic and Geographical Identities in the Medieval and Early Modern Periods," *William and Mary Quarterly*, 3d ser., 54.1 (January 1997): 103–142.

43. Marrant, *Sermon*, 10.

44. Ibid., 12–13; emphasis added.

45. Ibid., 11.

46. Sidney Kaplan, *The Black Presence in the Era of the American Revolution, 1770–1800* (Washington, D.C.: Smithsonian Institution, 1973), 183; see also Carol Wilson, *Freedom at Risk: The Kidnapping of Free Blacks in America, 1780–1785* (Lexington: University of Kentucky Press, 1994).

47. Davis, "Documents," 429.

48. Joanne Pope Melish, *Disowning Slavery: Gradual Emancipation and "Race" in New England, 1780–1860* (Ithaca, N.Y.: Cornell University Press, 1998), 102 n40.

49. Davis, "Documents," 430.

50. Marrant, *Sermon*, 13.

51. Ibid., 13.

52. Ibid., 13–14.

53. Ibid., 15.

54. Ibid., 15.

55. Ibid., 16–17.

56. Ibid., 18.

57. Ibid., 20.

58. Ibid., 20.

59. Ibid., 20.

60. Ibid., 24.

61. Ibid., 24.

62. James H. Cone, "The Story Context of Black Theology," *Theology Today* 32 (July 1975): 148.

63. Recontextualization of biblical writings within the present historical needs of black peoples has long been a central feature of black theologies. In the 1960s and 1970s, black theologians—most eminently, James Cone and James H. Evans, Jr.,—documented, systematized, and theorized this practice within the framework of liberation theology. See also Cain Felder, *Troubling Biblical Waters: Race, Class, and Family* (Maryknoll, N.Y.: Orbis, 1989); Cain Felder, "The Bible, Re-Contextualization, and the Black Religious Experience," in *African American Religious Studies: An Interdisciplinary Anthology*, ed. Gayraud Wilmore (Durham, N.C.: Duke University Press, 1989), 155–171;

Charles Copher, "Three Thousand Years of Biblical Interpretation with Reference to Black Peoples," in Wilmore, *African American Religious Studies*, 105–128; Vincent Wimbush, "Biblical Historical Study as Liberation: Toward an Afro-Christian Hermeneutic," in Wilmore, *African American Religious Studies*, 140–154; and Vincent Wimbush, ed., *African-Americans and the Bible: Sacred Texts and Social Textures* (New York: Continuum, 2000).

64. Cone, "The Story Context," 150.

65. Prince Hall, *A Charge Delivered to the Brethren of the African Lodge on the 25th of June, 1792* (Boston: Printed and sold by T. and J. Fleet at the Bible and Heart, Cornhill, 1792), 1.

66. Hall, *A Charge* [1792], 1.

67. Michael Kennedy, "The Foundation of the Jacobin Clubs and the Development of the Jacobin Club Network, 1789–1791," *The Journal of Modern History* 51.4 (December 1979): 701–733.

68. David Shields, "Anglo-American Clubs: Their Wit, Their Heterodoxy, Their Sedition." *William and Mary Quarterly* 51.2 (April 1994): 295.

69. Withrop Jordan, *White Over Black: American Attitudes Toward the Negro, 1550–1812* (Chapel Hill: University of North Carolina Press, 1968), 130.

70. Davis, "Documents," 431.

71. Ibid. 424–425.

72. Hall, *A Charge* [1792], 12.

73. Ibid., 1–2.

74. Ibid., 4.

75. At least one African-American was indicted for participation in Shay's Rebellion: Moses Sash of Worthington, Massachusetts, described in court records as a "labourer" and as a "captain" of Shay's troops, was indicted on two counts associated with the Rebellion. See Kaplan, *Black Presence*, 224–225.

76. Hall, *A Charge* [1792], 9–10.

77. Ibid., 11–12.

78. Ibid., 12.

79. Ibid., 10; emphasis in the original.

80. Ibid., 10.

81. Although charges of "other-worldly" or "compensatory" belief are as old as the black church itself, criticisms of black Christianity intensified in the twentieth century along two ideological vectors: Marxist fundamentalism, which held religion to be "opium," and mainline Protestantism, which held black Christianity to be a dysfunctional permutation of tradition. In 1938, Dr. Benjamin Mays, then a professor of religion at Howard University, published *The Negro's God as Reflected in His Literature* (Boston: Chapman and Grimes), which scrutinized this stereotypical view of black religion in relation to African-American literature, 1760 to 1930. The black theology movement of the 1960s and 1970s further established the systematicity and coherence of black Christian belief and practice.

82. Hall, *A Charge* [1792], 13.

83. Davis, "Documents," 425.

84. Prince Hall, *A Charge Delivered to the African Lodge, June 24, 1797, at Meno-*

tomy (Boston: Printed by Benjamin Edes, for and sold at Prince Hall's Shop, opposite the Quaker Meeting House, Quaker Lane, 1797), 3.

85. Julia Stern, *The Plight of Feeling: Sympathy and Dissent in the Early American Novel* (Chicago: University of Chicago Press, 1997), 19.

86. Hall, *Charge* [1797], 18. Paul Baepler surveys this genre in *White Slaves, African Masters: An Anthology of Barbary Captivity Narratives* (Chicago: University of Chicago Press, 1999).

87. Davis, "Documents," 429.

88. Hall, *Charge* [1797], 10.

89. Ibid., 11–12.

90. Ibid., 5.

91. Melish, *Disowning Slavery*, 140–150.

92. Hall, *Charge* [1797], 7, 9.

93. Bullock, *Revolutionary Brotherhood*, 161.

94. Hall, *Charge* [1797], 12.

95. Ibid., 12–13.

96. Ibid., 13.

97. Ibid., 18, emphasis added.

98. Ibid., 18.

99. Frantz Fanon, *The Wretched of the Earth* (New York: Grove, 1963), 210.

100. Stuart Hall, "Cultural Identity and Diaspora," in *Colonial Discourse and Post-colonial Theory: A Reader*, ed. Patrick Williams and Laura Chrisman (New York: Columbia University Press, 1994), 393.

101. Hall, "Cultural Identity and Diaspora," 394.

102. Women were routinely denied admission to most Masonic Lodge meetings. They did, however, participate in the public activities of the lodge and in the more intimate work of sewing their male relatives' Masonic regalia. A Masonic women's auxiliary, the Eastern Star, was established in the nineteenth century.

103. Homi Bhabha, *The Location of Culture* (London: Routledge, 1994), 231.

104. Maurice Wallace has argued the connection between Masonic ritual and processes of masculine self-construction among African-Americans in "'Are We Men?': Prince Hall, Martin Delaney, and the Masculine Ideal in Black Freemasonry, 1775–1865," *American Literary History* 9.3 (fall 1997): 396–424. William Muraskin's *Middle-class Blacks in a White Society: Prince Hall Freemasonry in America* (Berkeley: University of California Press, 1975) advances a view of black Freemasonry as a mode of class differentiation and a mark of bourgeois distinction for African-Americans.

105. David Walker, "Appeal to the Colored Citizens of the World," in *Walker's Appeal and Garnet's Address to the Slaves of the United States of America* (Nashville, Tenn.: James C. Winston, 1994), 52.

106. Henry Highland Garnet, "Address to the Slaves of the United States of America," in *Walker's Appeal and Garnet's Address*, vi.

107. W. P. Palmer and H. W. Flournoy, eds., *Calendar of Virginia State Papers and other Manuscripts Preserved in the Capitol at Richmond*, 11 vols. (Richmond: Commonwealth of Virginia, 1875–1893), 9:150–152.

108. Herbert Aptheker, *American Negro Slave Revolts* (New York: International Publishers, 1969), 50.

109. Richard A. Rutyna and Peter C. Stewart, *The History of Freemasonry in Virginia* (Lanham, Md.: University Press of America, 1998), 300–301.

110. Jacqueline Tobin and Raymond Dobard, *Hidden in Plain View: The Secret Story of Quilts and the Underground Railroad* (New York: Doubleday, 1999).

111. On the ideological implications of Enlightenment-era classification, see Jordan, *White Over Black*, 482–511, and Cornel West, *Prophesy Deliverance: An Afro-American Revolutionary Christianity* (Philadelphia: Westminster, 1982), 50–65.

Chapter 5

1. Richard Allen, *The Life Experience and Gospel Labors of the Rt. Rev. Richard Allen* (1833; reprint, New York: Abingdon, 1960), 24.

2. W. E. B. Du Bois, *The Philadelphia Negro* (Philadelphia: University of Pennsylvania, 1899), 19.

3. Allen, *The Life Experience*, 25.

4. Julie Winch, *Philadelphia's Black Elite: Activism, Accommodation, and the Struggle for Autonomy, 1787–1848* (Philadelphia: Temple University Press, 1988), 17; Gary B. Nash, *Forging Freedom: The Formation of Philadelphia's Black Community* (Cambridge: Harvard University Press, 1988), 63.

5. Benjamin Rush, *Letters of Benjamin Rush*. Vol. 2, *1793–1813*, ed. L. H. Butterfield (Princeton, N.J.: Published for the American Philosophical Society by Princeton University Press, 1951), 655.

6. Susan Klepp, "Appendix I: 'How Many Precious Souls are Fled'?: The Magnitude of the 1793 Yellow Fever Epidemics," in *A Melancholy Scene of Devastation: The Public Response to the 1793 Philadelphia Yellow Fever Epidemic*, ed. J. Worth Estes and Billy G. Smith (Canton, Mass.: Science History Publishers, 1997), 167.

7. Rush, *Letters*, 684.

8. Phillip Lapsansky, "'Abigail, a Negress': The Role and the Legacy of African Americans in the Yellow Fever Epidemic," in Estes and Smith, *A Melancholy Scene of Devastation*, 67; Klepp, "Appendix I: How Many," 168.

9. P. Lapsansky, "'Abigail, A Negress,'" 61.

10. Debbie Lee, "Yellow Fever and the Slave Trade: Coleridge's *The Rime of the Ancient Mariner*," *English Literary History* 65.3 (1998): 680.

11. On the metaphorical suggestiveness of yellow fever, see Robert Levine, *Conspiracy and Romance: Studies in Brockden Brown, Cooper, Hawthorne and Melville* (New York: Cambridge University Press, 1989), 15–57; Robert A. Ferguson, "Yellow Fever and Charles Brockden Brown: Context of the Emerging Novelist," *Early American Literature* 14 (1979–1980): 293–305; Shirley Samuels, "Infidelity and Contagion: The Rhetoric of Revolution," *Early American Literature* 22.2 (Fall 1987): 183–191; Mark A. Smith, "Andrew Brown's 'Earnest Endeavor': The Federal Gazette's Role in Philadelphia's Yellow Fever Epidemic of 1793," *Pennsylvania Magazine of History and Biography* 1204 (1996): 321–342;

Philip Gould, "Race, Commerce, and the Literature of Yellow Fever in Early National Philadelphia," *Early American Literature* 35.2 (2000): 157–186.

12. William Currie, *A description of the malignant, infectious fever prevailing at present in Philadelphia; with an account of the means to prevent infection, and the remedies and method of treatment, which have been found most successful* (Philadelphia: Printed by T. Dobson, no. 41, South Second-Street, 1793), 12.

13. Ibid., 12–13.

14. David de Isaac Cohen Nassy, *Observations on the cause, nature, and treatment of the epidemic disorder, prevalent in Philadelphia* (Philadelphia: Printed by Parker and Co. for M. Carey, Nov. 26, 1793), 21.

15. Benjamin Rush, *An enquiry into the origin of the late epidemic fever in Philadelphia: in a letter to Dr. John Redman, president of the College of Physicians, from Doctor Benjamin Rush* (Philadelphia: From the press of Mathew Carey, December 11, 1793), 14.

16. John Lining, *A description of the American yellow fever, which prevailed at Charleston, in South Carolina, in the year 1748* (Philadelphia: Printed for Thomas Dobson, at the stone-house, no 41, South Second Street, 1799), 7.

17. Winthrop Jordan, *White Over Black: American Attitudes Toward the Negro, 1550–1812* (Chapel Hill: University of North Carolina Press, 1968), 529.

18. Cotton Mather, *Selected Letters of Cotton Mather*, comp. Kenneth Silverman (Baton Rouge: Louisiana State University Press, 1971), 214.

19. Cotton Mather, *Account of the Method and Success of Inoculating the Smallpox in Boston in New England (1722)*, in *Smallpox in Colonial America* (New York: Arno, 1977), 24.

20. William Douglass in *A Dissertation Concerning Inoculation of the Small-Pox* (1730), in *Smallpox in Colonial America* (New York: Arno, 1977), 7.

21. James Kilpatrick, *An Essay on Inoculation, Occassioned by the Small-Pox being brought into South Carolina in the Year 1738 (1743)*, in *Small-Pox in Colonial America* (New York: Arno, 1977), 14.

22. Kilpatrick, *An Essay on Inoculation*, 48; Jordan, *White Over Black*, 260 n92.

23. Samuel Stanhope Smith, *An Essay on the Causes of the Variety of Complexion in the Human Species*, in *Slavery, Abolition, and Emancipation: Writings in the British Romantic Period*, 8 vols., ed. Peter J. Kitson (London: Pickering and Chatto, 1999), 8: 83–84.

24. Ibid., 84.

25. Ibid., 89–90.

26. William Currie, *A Treatise on the Synochus Iteroides* (Philadelphia: Printed by Thomas Dobson, 1794), 14.

27. Benjamin Rush, *An account of the bilious remitting yellow fever, as it appeared in the city of Philadelphia, in the year 1793* (Philadelphia, Printed by Thomas Dobson, at the Stone-house, no. 41, South Second-street, 1794), 97.

28. Rush, *An account of the bilious remitting yellow fever*, 94–95.

29. Jordan, *White Over Black*, 529.

30. Rush, *Letters*, 786. On Rush and black leprosy, see Ronald Takaki, *Iron Cages: Race and Culture in 19th-Century America* (1979; reprint, New York: Oxford University Press, 2000), 30–34, and Dana Nelson, *National Manhood: Capi-*

talist Citizenship and the Imagined Fraternity of White Men (Durham, N.C.: Duke University Press, 1998), 57–60.

31. P. Lapsansky, "'Abigail, A Negress,'" 64.

32. Mark A. Smith, "Andrew Brown's 'Earnest Endeavor': The Federal Gazette's Role in Philadelphia's Yellow Fever Epidemic of 1793," *Pennsylvania Magazine of History and Biography* 1204 (1996): 327.

33. Rush, *Letters*, 669.

34. *Minutes of the proceedings of the committee, appointed on the 14th September, 1793, by the citizens of Philadelphia, the Northern Liberties and the District of Southwark, to attend to and alleviate the sufferings of the afflicted with the malignant fever, prevalent, in the city and its vicinity, with an appendix* (Philadelphia: Printed by R. Aitken and Son, and sold by J. Crukshank, W. Young, T. Dobson and the other booksellers, 1794), 188.

35. Matthew Carey, *Autobiography* (New York: Research Classics, 1942), 25–26.

36. Mathew Carey, *A short account of the malignant fever, lately prevalent in Philadelphia: with a statement of the proceedings that took place on the subject in different parts of the United States, third edition, improved* (Philadelphia: Printed by the author, November 30, 1793), 33, 35.

37. Carey, *A short account*, third edition, 79.

38. Ibid., 78.

39. Ibid., 78–79.

40. Mathew Carey, *A short account of the malignant fever, lately prevalent in Philadelphia*, fourth edition (Philadelphia: Printed by the author, January 16, 1794), 63.

41. Carey, *A short account*, third edition, 99.

42. Ibid., 105.

43. Ibid., 97.

44. Ibid., 101.

45. Mathew Carey, "A Philosophical Dream," *Columbian Magazine* (October 1786): 21.

46. Currie, *A description*, 27.

47. J. H. Powell, *Bring Out your Dead; The Great Plague of Yellow Fever in Philadelphia in 1793* (Philadelphia: University of Pennsylvania Press, 1993), 288.

48. Carey, *A short account*, third edition, 79.

49. Richard Allen and Absalom Jones, *A narrative of the proceedings of the black people, during the late awful calamity in Philadelphia, in the year 1793: and a refutation of some censures, thrown upon them in some late publications* (Philadelphia: Printed for the authors, by William W. Woodward, at Franklin's Head, no. 41, Chesnut-Street, 1794), 3, 10.

50. Ibid., 7–8.

51. Ibid., 8.

52. Ibid., 10.

53. Ibid., 13.

54. Ibid., 12–13.

55. Ibid., 3.

56. Ibid., 3.

57. Ibid., 11.

58. Ibid., 12.

59. Ibid., 12.

60. Ibid., 15.

61. Ibid., 15.

62. Ibid., 15.

63. Ibid., 17.

64. Nash, *Forging Freedom*, 123.

65. Allen and Jones, *A narrative of the proceedings*, 16.

66. Jacquelyn Miller, "An 'Uncommon Tranquility of Mind': Emotional Self-Control and the Construction of a Middle-class Identity in Eighteenth-Century Philadelphia," *Journal of Social History* 301 (1996): 129–148.

67. Allen and Jones, *A narrative of the proceedings*, 14.

68. Ibid., 16.

69. Ibid., 16–17.

70. Ibid., 19.

71. Ibid., 15.

72. Ibid., 20.

73. Ibid., 17–18.

74. Ibid., 25.

75. Michele Wallace, *Invisibility Blues: From Pop to Theory* (London: Verso, 1990), 2.

76. Abdul JanMohamed and David Lloyd, "Toward a Theory of Minority Discourse: What Is to Be Done?" in *The Nature and Context of Minority Discourse*, ed. Abdul JanMohamed and David Lloyd (New York: Oxford University Press, 1990), 10.

77. In England, Olaudah Equiano availed himself of copyright protection for his *Interesting Narrative* in March 1789. See Vincent Carretta's "Introduction" to Equiano, *Interesting Narrative and Other Writings* (New York: Penguin, 1995), xv, and his article "'Property of Author': Olaudah Equiano's Place in the History of the Book," in *Genius in Bondage: Literature of the Early Black Atlantic*, ed. Vincent Carretta and Philip Gould (Lexington: University of Kentucky Press, 2001), 130–150.

78. In 1794, Darton and Harvey, publishers of American anti-slavery and Quaker writings, published a slightly shorter twenty-four-page version of the *Narrative* in London.

79. Carey, *A short account*, third edition, 56–57.

80. Mathew Carey, *Address of M. Carey to the Public* (Philadelphia: Printed by Mathew Carey, 1794), 8.

81. Carey, *Address*, 7–8.

82. Rosemary Coombe, *The Cultural Life of Intellectual Properties: Authorship, Appropriation, and the Law* (Durham, N.C.: Duke University Press, 1998); Mark Rose, *Authors and Owners: The Invention of Copyright* (Cambridge: Harvard University Press, 1993).

83. Prince Hall, *A Charge Delivered to the African Lodge, June 24, 1797, at Menotomy* (Boston: Printed by Benjamin Edes, for and sold at Prince Hall's Shop, opposite the Quaker Meeting House, Quaker Lane, 1797), 10.

84. Joanne Pope Melish, *Disowning Slavery: Gradual Emancipation and "Race" in New England, 1780–1860* (Ithaca, N.Y.: Cornell University Press, 1998), 1.

85. Emma Jones Lapsansky, "'Since They Got Those Separate Churches': Afro-Americans and Racism in Jacksonian Philadelphia," *American Quarterly* 32.1 (spring 1980): 54–78.

86. *Articles of Association of the African Methodist Episcopal Church, of the City of Philadelphia, in the Commonwealth of Pennsylvania* (1799; reprint, Philadelphia: Rhistoric Publications, 1969), 4, 6, 9.

87. Charles Brockden Brown, *Arthur Mervyn: or, Memoirs of the year 1793*, in *Charles Brockden Brown: Three Gothic Novels* (New York: The Library Company of America, 1998), 231.

88. Brown, *Arthur Mervyn*, 566.

89. Joan Dayan, "Amorous Bondage: Poe, Ladies, and Slaves," *American Literature* 66.2 (June 1994): 239–273.

90. Brown, *Arthur Mervyn*, 363–364.

91. Michael Warner, *Letters of the Republic* (Cambridge: Harvard University Press, 1990), 166–167.

Conclusion

1. Pauline Brunette Danforth, "Native City Arts: Singing Is like Praying Twice," *The Circle* 18.8 (August 31, 1997): 10; Kathryn D. Green, *The Hymnody of the Seneca Native Americans of Western New York* (DMA, Music: University of Cincinnati, 1996); Terence O'Grady, "The Singing Societies of the Oneida," *American Music* 9.1 (spring 1991): 67–91; Lynn Whidden, "Cree Hymnody as Traditional Song," *Hymn* 4 (July 1989): 21–25; Michael McNally, *Ojibwe Singers: Hymns, Grief, and a Native Culture in Motion* (New York: Oxford University Press, 2000); Luke Eric Lassiter, Clyde Ellis, and Ralph Kotay, *The Jesus Road: Kiowas, Christianity, and Indian Hymns* (Lincoln: University of Nebraska Press, 2002).

2. Coria Holland, "Prince Hall Masons Head to U.K. for Recognition after 200 Years," *Bay State Banner* 31.38 (June 13, 1996): 1; "Prince Hall Masons Important Contributors To Black History," *Atlanta Inquirer* 37.31 (February 28, 1998): 2.

Bibliography

A Dream dreamed by one in the year 1757, concerning Philadelphia, and repeated again, in the same manner, about eleven years after, by the same person. Germantown, Pa.: Printed by Peter Leibert, 1793.

"The African Lodge, An Oration delivered before the Grand Master, Wardens, and Brethren of the most Ancient and venerable Lodge of African Masons." *Columbian Magazine* 2.8 (1788): 467–469.

Allen, Paula Gunn. *The Sacred Hoop: Recovering the Feminine in American Indian Traditions.* Boston: Beacon Press, 1986.

Allen, Richard. *A Collection of Spiritual Songs and Hymns Selected from Various Authors.* Philadelphia: John Ormrod, 1801.

———. *The Life Experience and Gospel Labors of the Rt. Rev. Richard Allen.* 1833. Reprint, New York: Abingdon, 1960.

———, and Absalom Jones. *A narrative of the proceedings of the black people, during the late awful calamity in Philadelphia, in the year 1793: and a refutation of some censures, thrown upon them in some late publications.* Philadelphia: Printed for the authors, by William W. Woodward, at Franklin's Head, no. 41, Chesnut-Street, 1794.

Allen, William. *Memoirs of Samson Occom, The Mohegan Indian Missionary, Including His Own Journal of Many Years, With Specimens of his Sermons, and various Notices Relating to the Indians of his Tribe.* Unpub. mss., 1859. Rauner Special Collections Library, Dartmouth College, Hanover, N.H.

Allison, Robert J. *The Crescent Obscured: The United States and the Muslim World, 1776–1815.* New York: Oxford University Press, 1995.

Anderson, Benedict. *Imagined Communities: Reflections on the Origin and Spread of Nationalism.* 1983. Reprint, London: Verso, 1991.

Andrews, Dee. *The Methodists and Revolutionary America, 1760–1800: The Shaping of an Evangelical Culture.* Princeton, N.J.: Princeton University Press, 2000.

Andrews, William. *To Tell a Free Story: The First Century of African-American Autobiography.* Urbana: University of Illinois Press, 1986.

Apess, William. *On Our Own Ground: The Complete Writings of William Apess, a*

Pequot. Ed. Barry O'Connell. Amherst: University of Massachusetts Press, 1992.

Aptheker, Herbert. *American Negro Slave Revolts*. New York: International Publishers, 1969.

Arnold, Laura. "Crossing Cultures: Algonquin Indians and the Invention of New England." Ph.D. diss., University of California, Los Angeles, 1995.

Articles of Association of the African Methodist Episcopal Church, of the City of Philadelphia, in the Commonwealth of Pennsylvania. 1799. Reprint, Philadelphia: Rhistoric Publications, 1969.

Asante, Molefi. *The Afrocentric Idea*. Philadelphia: Temple University Press, 1987.

Axtell, James. *The Invasion Within: The Contest of Cultures in Colonial North America*. New York: Oxford University Press, 1985.

Baepler, Paul, ed. *White Slaves, African Masters: An Anthology of Barbary Captivity Narratives*. Chicago: University of Chicago Press, 1999.

Baker, Houston. *The Journey Back: Issues in Black Literature and Criticism*. Chicago: University of Chicago Press, 1980.

Bangs, Nathan, ed. *The Life of the Rev. Freeborn Garrettson*. 4th ed. New York: T. Mason and G. Lane, 1839.

Bassard, Katherine Clay. *Spiritual Interrogations: Culture, Gender, and Community in Early African American Women's Writing*. Princeton, N.J.: Princeton University Press, 1999.

Beauchamp, William, ed. *Moravian Journals Relating to Central New York, 1745–1766*. New York: AMS, 1976.

Benjamin, Walter. *Illuminations*. New York: Harcourt, Brace and World, 1968.

Bernal, Martin. *Black Athena*. New Brunswick, N.J.: Rutgers University Press, 1987.

Beverley, James, and Barry Moody, eds. *The Journal of Henry Alline*. Nova Scotia: Lancelot Press, 1982.

Bhabha, Homi. *The Location of Culture*. London: Routledge, 1994.

Bierhorst, John. *Mythology of the Lenape: Guide and Texts*. Tucson: University of Arizona Press, 1987.

Blakeley, Phyllis R., and John N. Grant, eds. *Eleven Exiles: Accounts of Loyalists in the American Revolution*. Toronto: Dundurn, 1982.

Blodgett, Harold. *Samson Occom*. Dartmouth College Manuscript Series, no. 3. Hanover, N.H.: Dartmouth College Publications, 1935.

Boles, John, ed. *Masters and Slaves in the House of the Lord: Race and Religion in the American South, 1740–1870*. Lexington: University of Kentucky Press, 1988.

Boylston, Zabdiel. *An Historical Account of the Small-Pox Inoculated in New England, Upon all Sorts of Persons, Whites, Blacks, and of All Ages and Constitutions*. 1726. Reprint, *Small-Pox in Colonial America*. New York: Arno, 1977.

Bradford, William. *Of Plymouth Plantation, 1620–1647*. New York: McGraw-Hill, 1981.

Brooke, John L. "A Deacon's Orthodoxy: Religion, Class, and the Moral Economy of Shay's Rebellion." In *In Debt to Shays: The Bicentennial of an*

Agrarian Rebellion, ed. Robert Gross, 205–238. Charlottesville: University Press of Virginia, 1993.

Brooks, Joanna. "The *Journal* of John Marrant: Providence and Prophecy in the Eighteenth-Century Black Atlantic." *The North Star: A Journal of African American Religious History* 3.1 (fall 1999): http://northstar.vassar.edu/.

———. Prince Hall, Freemasonry, and Genealogy." *African-American Review* 34.2 (summer 2000): 197–216.

———. "Six Hymns by Samson Occom." *Early American Literature* 38.1 (2003).

———, and John Saillant, eds. *Face Zion Forward: First Writers of the Black Atlantic, 1785–1798*. Boston: Northeastern University Press, 2002.

Brown, Charles Brockden. *Arthur Mervyn: or, Memoirs of the year 1793*. 1799. Reprint, *Charles Brockden Brown: Three Gothic Novels*. New York: The Library Company of America, 1998.

———. *Ormond: Or, The Secret Witness*. 1799. Ed. Mary Chapman. Reprint, New York: Broadview, 1999.

Bruce, Jr., Dickson D. *The Origins of African American Literature, 1680–1865*. Charlottesville: University Press of Virginia, 2001.

Bumsted, J. M. *What Must I Do to Be Saved? The Great Awakening in Colonial America*. Hinsdale, Ill.: Dryden, 1976.

Bullock, Steven C. *Revolutionary Brotherhood: Freemasonry and the Transformation of the American Social Order, 1730–1840*. Williamsburg, Va.: Institute of Early American History and Culture, 1996.

Burkhart, Louise M. "The Amanuenses Have Appropriated the Text: Interpreting a Nahuatl Song of Santiago." In *On the Translation of Native American Literatures*, ed. Brian Swann, 339–355. Washington, D.C.: Smithsonian, 1992.

Burr, Sandra and Adam Potkay, eds. *Black Writers of the Eighteenth Century*. New York: St. Martin's, 1995.

Bushman, Richard, ed. *The Great Awakening: Documents on the Revival of Religion, 1740–1745*. New York: Atheneum, 1970.

Butler, Jonathan. *Awash in a Sea of Faith: Christianizing the American People*. Cambridge: Harvard University Press, 1990.

———. "Enthusiasm Described and Decried: The Great Awakening as Interpretive Fiction." *Journal of American History* 69 (1982–83): 305–325.

Cahill, Barry. "Stephen Blucke: The Peril of Being a 'White Negro' in Loyalist Nova Scotia." *Nova Scotia Historical Review* 11.1 (1991): 129–134.

Calcott, Wellins. *A Candid Disquisition of the Principles and Practices of the Most Antient and Honourable Society of Free and Accepted Masons; Together with some Strictures on the Origin, Nature, and Design of that Institution*. Boston: Reprinted and sold by Brother William M'Alpine, in Marlborough-Street, Boston, 1772.

Carey, Mathew. *Address of M. Carey to the public*. Philadelphia: Printed by Mathew Carey, 1794.

———. *Autobiography*. New York: Research Classics, 1942.

———. *A desultory account of the yellow fever, prevalent in Philadelphia, and of the present state of the city*. Philadelphia: Printed by Mathew Carey, 1793.

———. *Observations on Dr. Rush's Enquiry into the origin of the late epidemic fever in Philadelphia*. Philadelphia: From the press of the author, December 14, 1793.

———. "A Philosophical Dream." *Columbian Magazine* (October 1786): 21.

———. *A short account of the malignant fever, lately prevalent in Philadelphia*. 4th ed. Philadelphia: Printed by the author, January 16, 1794.

———. *A short account of the malignant fever, lately prevalent in Philadelphia: with a statement of the proceedings that took place on the subject in different parts of the United States*. Philadelphia: Printed by the author, November 14, 1793.

———. *A short account of the malignant fever, lately prevalent in Philadelphia: with a statement of the proceedings that took place on the subject in different parts of the United States*. 2d ed. Philadelphia: Printed by the author, November 23, 1793.

———. *A short account of the malignant fever, lately prevalent in Philadelphia: with a statement of the proceedings that took place on the subject in different parts of the United States*. 3d ed. Philadelphia: Printed by the author, November 30, 1793.

Carlisle, Rodney. *The Roots of Black Nationalism*. New York: National University Publications, 1975.

Carretta, Vincent, ed. *Unchained Voices: An Anthology of Black Authors in the English-Speaking World of the 18th Century*. Lexington: University of Kentucky Press, 1996.

———, and Philip Gould, eds. *Genius in Bondage: Literature of the Early Black Atlantic*. Lexington: University of Kentucky Press, 2001.

Cavanagh, Beverley Diamond. "Christian Hymns in Eastern Woodlands Communities: Performance Contexts." In *Musical Repercussions of 1492: Encounters in Text and Performance*, ed. Carol E. Robertson, 381–394. Washington, D.C.: Smithsonian, 1992.

———. "The Transmission of Algonkian Indian Hymns: Between Orality and Literacy." In *Musical Canada*, ed. John Beckwith and Frederick A. Hall, 3–28. Toronto: University of Toronto Press, 1988.

Chauncy, Charles. *Enthusiasm Described and Cautioned Against. A Sermon Preach'd at the Old Brick Meeting House in Boston, the Lord's Day after the Commencement, 1742. With a Letter to the Reverend Mr. James Davenport*. Boston: Printed by J. Draper for S. Eliot in Cornhill, 1742.

———. *Seasonable Thoughts on the State of Religion in New England*. Boston: Rogers and Fowle, for Samuel Eliot in Cornhill, 1743.

Clairmont, Donald, and Fred Wien. "Blacks and Whites: The Nova Scotia Race Relations Experience." In *Banked Fires: The Ethnics of Nova Scotia*, ed. Douglass Campbell. 141–182. Ontario: Scribbler's, 1978.

Clifford, James. *The Predicament of Culture*. Cambridge: Harvard University Press, 1988.

Commuck, Thomas. *Indian Melodies*. New York: G. Lane and C. B. Tippet, 1845.

Cone, James H. "The Story Context of Black Theology." *Theology Today* 32 (July 1975): 144–150.

Conforti, Joseph. *Jonathan Edwards, Religious Tradition, and American Culture*. Chapel Hill: University of North Carolina Press, 1995.

———. *Samuel Hopkins and the New Divinity: Calvinism, the Congregational Ministry, and Reform in New England between the Great Awakenings.* Grand Rapids, Mich.: Eerdmans, 1981.

Cooley, Timothy Mather. *Sketches of the Life and Character of the Rev. Lemuel Haynes, A.M.* 1837. Reprint, New York: Negro Universities Press, 1969.

Coombe, Rosemary. *The Cultural Life of Intellectual Properties: Authorship, Appropriation, and the Law.* Durham, N.C.: Duke University Press, 1998.

Copher, Charles. "Three Thousand Years of Biblical Interpretation with Reference to Black Peoples." In *African American Religious Studies: An Interdisciplinary Anthology,* ed. Gayraud Wilmore, 105–128. Durham, N.C.: Duke University Press, 1989.

Cornelius, Janet Duitsman. *"When I Can Read My Title Clear": Literacy, Slavery, and Religion in the Antebellum South.* Columbia: University of South Carolina Press, 1991.

Costanzo, Angelo. *Surprizing Narrative: Olaudah Equiano and the Beginnings of Black Autobiography.* New York: Greenwood, 1987.

Cowing, Cedric B. *The Great Awakening and the American Revolution.* Chicago: Rand McNally, 1971.

Crawford, George. *Prince Hall and His Followers: Being a Monograph on the Legitimacy of Negro Masonry.* New York: The Crisis, 1914.

Creel, Margaret Washington. *"A Peculiar People": Slave Religion and Community Culture Among the Gullahs.* New York: New York University Press, 1988.

Currie, William. *A description of the malignant, infectious fever prevailing at present in Philadelphia; with an account of the means to prevent infection, and the remedies and method of treatment, which have been found most successful.* Philadelphia: Printed by T. Dobson, no. 41, South Second-Street, 1793.

———. *A Treatise on the Synochus Iteroides.* Philadelphia: Printed by Thomas Dobson, 1794.

Dain, Bruce. "Haiti and Egypt in Early Black Racial Discourse in the United States." *Slavery and Abolition* 14.3 (November 1993): 139–161.

Daly, Robert. *God's Altar: The World and the Flesh in Puritan Poetry.* Berkeley: University of California Press, 1978.

Danforth, Pauline Brunette. "Native City Arts: Singing is like Praying Twice." *The Circle* 18.8 (August 31, 1997): 10.

Davis, Harry E. "Documents Relating to Negro Masonry in America." *Journal of Negro History* 21.4 (October 1936): 411–432.

Dayan, Joan. "Amorous Bondage: Poe, Ladies, and Slaves." *American Literature* 66.2 (June 1994): 239–273.

Delaney, Martin. *Origin and Objects of Ancient Freemasonry; Its Introduction into the United States, and Legitimacy Among Colored Men. A Treatise Delivered Before St. Cyprian Lodge, No. 13, June 24th, A.D. 1853-AL 5853.* Pittsburgh, Pa.: W. S. Haven, 1853.

Deloria, Philip. *Playing Indian.* New Haven: Yale University Press, 1998.

Deloria, Jr., Vine. *Behind the Trail of Broken Treaties: An Indian Declaration of Independence.* 1974. Reprint, Austin: University of Texas, 1985.

———, and David E. Wilkins. *Tribes, Treaties, and Constitutional Tribulations.* Austin: University of Texas, 1999.

Derrida, Jacques and Gianni Vattimo, eds. *Religion*. Palo Alto: Stanford University Press, 1998.

Deveze, Jean. *An enquiry into, and observations upon the causes and effects of the epidemic disease, which raged in Philadelphia from the month of August till towards the middle of December, 1793*. Philadelphia: Printed by Parent, 1794.

Douglass, William. *A Dissertation Concerning Inoculation of the Small-Pox*. 1730. Reprint, *Small Pox in Colonial America*. New York: Arno, 1977.

Drake, St. Clair. *The Redemption of Africa and Black Religion*. Chicago: Third World, 1970.

Du Bois, W. E. B. *The Negro Church*. Atlanta: Atlanta University Press, 1903.

———. *The Philadelphia Negro*. Philadelphia: University of Pennsylvania, 1899.

———. *The Souls of Black Folk*. 1899. Reprint, New York: Penguin Books, 1989.

Edwards, Jonathan. *The Great Awakening*. Ed. C. C. Goen. *The Works of Jonathan Edwards*, vol. 4. New Haven: Yale University Press, 1972.

———. *History of the Work of Redemption*. Ed. John F. Wilson. *The Works of Jonathan Edwards*, vol. 9. New Haven: Yale University Press, 1989.

———. *A Jonathan Edwards Reader*, eds. John E. Smith, Harry Stout, and Jonathan Minkema. New Haven: Yale University Press, 1995.

———. *Letters and Personal Writings*. Ed. George S. Claghorn. *The Works of Jonathan Edwards*, vol. 16. New Haven: Yale University Press, 1998.

———. *The "Miscellanies."* Ed. Thomas A. Schafer. *The Works of Jonathan Edwards*, vol. 13. New Haven: Yale University Press, 1994.

———. *Religious Affections*. Ed. John Smith. *The Works of Jonathan Edwards*, vol. 2. New Haven: Yale University Press, 1959.

Equiano, Olaudah. *The Interesting Narrative and Other Writings*. Ed. Vincent Carretta. New York: Penguin Books, 1995.

Estes, J. Worth, and Billy G. Smith, eds. *A Melancholy Scene of Devastation: The Public Response to the 1793 Philadelphia Yellow Fever Epidemic*. Canton, Mass.: Science History Publishers, 1997.

"Extracts from Several Authors." *The Christian History* 27 (September 3, 1743): 215–216.

Eze, Emmanuel Chukwudi, ed. *Race and the Enlightenment: A Reader*. Oxford: Blackwell, 1997.

Fanon, Frantz. *The Wretched of the Earth*. New York: Grove, 1963.

Fawcett, Melissa. *The Lasting of the Mohegans. Part 1: The Story of the Wolf People*. Uncasville, Conn.: Mohegan Tribe, 1995.

———. *Medicine Trail: The Life and Lessons of Gladys Tantaquidgeon*. Tucson: University of Arizona Press, 2000.

Fay, Bernard. "Learned Societies in Europe and America in the Eighteenth Century." *The American Historical Review* 37.2 (January 1932): 255–266.

Felder, Cain. "The Bible, Re-Contextualization, and the Black Religious Experience." In *African American Religious Studies: An Interdisciplinary Anthology*, ed. Gayraud Wilmore, 155–171. Durham, N.C.: Duke University Press, 1989.

———. *Troubling Biblical Waters: Race, Class, and Family*. Maryknoll, N.Y.: Orbis, 1989.

Ferguson, Robert A. "Yellow Fever and Charles Brockden Brown: Context of the Emerging Novelist." *Early American Literature* 14 (1979–1980): 293–305.

Foster, Frances Smith. "Briton Hammon's Narrative: Some Insights into Beginnings." *College Language Association Journal* 21 (1977): 179–86.

———. *Witnessing Slavery: The Development of Antebellum Slave Narratives.*
Westport, Conn.: Greenwood, 1979.

Frederickson, George. *The Arrogance of Race: Historical Perspectives on Slavery,
Racism, and Social Inequality.* Middletown, Conn.: Wesleyan University
Press, 1988.

Frey, Sylvia. *Water from the Frock: Black Resistance in a Revolutionary Age.* Princeton, N.J.: Princeton University Press, 1991.

———, and Betty Wood. *Come Shouting to Zion: African American Protestantism
in the American South and British Caribbean to 1830.* Chapel Hill: University of
North Carolina Press, 1998.

Fyfe, Christopher. "The Countess of Huntingdon's Connection in Nineteenth-Century Sierra Leone." *Sierra Leone Bulletin of Religion* 4.2 (December 1962): 53–61.

———, ed. *"Our Children Free and Happy": Letters from Black Settlers in Africa.*
Edinburgh: Edinburgh University Press, 1991.

Garnet, Henry Highland. "Address to the Slaves of the United States of
America." In *Walker's Appeal and Garnet's Address to the Slaves of the United
States of America.* Nashville, Tenn.: James C. Winston, 1994.

Gates, Henry Louis, Jr. *Figures in Black: Words, Signs, and the "Racial" Self.* New
York: Oxford University Press, 1985.

———. *The Signifying Monkey: A Theory of African-American Literary Criticism.*
New York: Oxford University Press, 1988.

Gausted, Edwin. *The Great Awakening in New England.* New York: Harper and
Brothers, 1957.

George, Carol V. R. *Segregated Sabbaths, 1760–1840.* New York: Oxford University Press, 1973.

George, David. "An Account of the Life of Mr. David George, from Sierra
Leone in Africa." *Baptist Annual Register* 1 (1793): 473–484.

Gewehr, Wesley. *The Great Awakening in Virginia, 1740–1790.* Durham, N.C.:
Duke University Press, 1930.

Gilroy, Paul. *The Black Atlantic: Modernity and Double-Consciousness.* Cambridge: Harvard University Press, 1993.

Glaude, Eddie, Jr. *Exodus! Religion, Race, and Nation in Early Nineteenth-Century
Black America.* Chicago: University of Chicago Press, 2000.

Goen, C. C. *Revivalism and Separatism in New England, 1740–1800: Strict Congregationalists and Separatist Baptists in the Great Awakening.* New Haven: Yale
University Press, 1972.

Gomez, Michael. *Exchanging Our Country Marks: The Transformation of African
Identities in the Colonial and Antebellum South.* Chapel Hill: University of
North Carolina Press, 1998.

Gould, Philip. "Race, Commerce, and the Literature of Yellow Fever in
Early National Philadelphia." *Early American Literature* 35.2 (2000): 157–
186.

———. "'Remarkable Liberty': Language and Identity in Eighteenth-Century
Black Autobiography." In *Genius in Bondage: Literature of the Early Black At-*

lantic, ed. Vincent Carretta and Philip Gould, 116–129. Lexington: University of Kentucky Press, 2001.

Grand Lodge of Pennsylvania. *Ahiman Rezon Abridged and Digested: As a Help to all that are, or would be, Free and Accepted Masons*. Philadelphia: Hall and Sellers, 1783.

Green, Kathryn D. "The Hymnody of the Seneca Native Americans of Western New York." DMA diss., University of Cincinnati, 1996.

Griffin, Edward. *Old Brick: Charles Chauncy of Boston, 1705–1787*. Minneapolis: University of Minnesota Press, 1980.

Grimshaw, William. *Official History of Freemasonry Among the Colored People of North America*. New York: n.p., 1903.

Guelzo, Allen. "God's Designs: The Literature of the Colonial Revivals of Religion, 1735–1760." In *New Directions in American Religious History*, ed. Harry Stout and D. G. Hart, 141–172. New York: Oxford University Press, 1997.

Guha, Ranajit, and Gayatri Spivak, eds. *Selected Subaltern Studies*. Oxford: Oxford University Press, 1988.

Gustafson, Sandra. *Eloquence is Power: Oratory and Performance in Early America*. Chapel Hill: Omohundro Institute of Early American History and Culture, University of North Carolina Press, 2000.

Hall, Prince. *A Charge Delivered to the African Lodge, June 24, 1797, at Menotomy*. Boston: Printed by Benjamin Edes, for and sold at Prince Hall's Shop, opposite the Quaker Meeting House, Quaker Lane, 1797.

———. *A Charge Delivered to the Brethren of the African Lodge on the 25th of June, 1792*. Boston: Printed and sold by T. and J. Fleet at the Bible and Heart, Cornhill, 1792.

Hall, Stuart. "Cultural Identity and Diaspora." In *Colonial Discourse and Postcolonial Theory: A Reader*, ed. Patrick Williams and Laura Chrisman, 392–403. New York: Columbia University Press, 1994.

Hall, Timothy. *Contested Boundaries: Itinerancy and the Reshaping of the Colonial American Religious World*. Durham, N.C.: Duke University Press, 1994.

Hammon, Briton. "A Narrative of the Uncommon Sufferings, and Surprizing Deliverance of Briton Hammon, a Negro Man." 1760. In *Unchained Voices*, ed. Vincent Carretta, 20–25. Lexington: University of Kentucky Press, 1996.

Harrington, M. R. *Religion and Ceremonies of the Lenape*. Indian Notes and Monographs series, vol. 19. New York: Museum of the American Indian, Heye Foundation, 1921.

Harris, Cheryl I. "Whiteness as Property." *Harvard Law Review* 107 (June 1993): 1707.

Hatch, Nathan. *The Democratization of American Christianity*. New Haven: Yale University Press, 1989.

Haynes, Lemuel. *Black Preacher to White America: The Collected Writings of Lemuel Haynes, 1774–1833*. Ed. Richard Newman. Brooklyn: Carlson, 1990.

Heckwelder, John. *History, Manners, and Customs of the Indian Nations who Once Inhabited Pennsylvania and the Neighbouring States*. Philadelphia: Historical Society of Pennsylvania, 1881.

———. *A Narrative of the Mission of the United Brethren Among the Delaware and*

Mohegan Indians, from Its Commencement in the Year 1740, to the Close of the Year 1808. New York: Arno, 1971.

Heimert, Alan. *Religion and the American Mind: From the Great Awakening to the Revolution.* Cambridge: Harvard University Press, 1966.

———, and Perry Miller. *The Great Awakening: Documents Illustrating the Crisis and its Consequences.* Indianapolis: Indiana University Press, 1967.

Herskovits, Melville. *The Myth of the Negro Past.* 1941. Reprint, Boston: Beacon, 1958.

Hinks, Peter. *To Awaken My Afflicted Brethren: David Walker and the Problem of Antebellum Slave Resistance.* University Park: Pennsylvania State University Press, 1997.

Holland, Coria. "Prince Hall Masons Head to U.K. for Recognition after 200 years." *Bay State Banner* 31.38 (June 13, 1996): 1.

Holland, Sharon Patricia. *Raising the Dead: Readings of Death and (Black) Subjectivity.* Durham, N.C.: Duke University Press, 2000.

Hopkins, Samuel. *A dialogue, concerning the slavery of the Africans; shewing it to be the duty and interest of the American colonies to emancipate all their African slaves: with an address to the owners of such slaves.* Norwich: Printed and sold by Judah P. Spooner, 1776.

———. *A discourse upon the slave-trade, and the slavery of the Africans. Delivered in the Baptist meeting-house at Providence, before the Providence Society for Abolishing the Slave-Trade, &c. At their annual meeting, on May 17, 1793.* Providence: J. Carter, 1793.

———. *Historical Memoirs Relating to the Housatonic Indians.* 1753. Reprint, New York: W. Abbatt, 1911.

———. *A treatise on the millennium, showing from Scripture prophecy, that it is yet to come; when it will come; in what it will consist; and the events which are first to take place, introductory to it.* Boston: Isaiah Thomas and Ebenezer T. Andrews, 1793.

———. *The Works of Samuel Hopkins.* 2 vols. Boston: Doctrinal Tract and Book Society, 1854.

Hudson, Nicholas. "From 'Nation' to "Race': The Origin of Racial Classification in Eighteenth-Century Thought." *Eighteenth Century Studies* 29.3 (1996): 247–264.

Hymn Society of America. *Dictionary of American Hymnology: First Line Index.* Ed. Leonard Ellinwood. 179 microfilm reels. New York: University Music Editions, 1984.

Imlay, Gilbert. *Topographical Description of the Western Territory of North America.* 3d. ed. London: J. Debrett, 1797.

Isaac, Rhys. "Evangelical Revolt: The Nature of the Baptists' Challenge to the Traditional Order in Virginia, 1765–1775." *William and Mary Quarterly* 31 (1974): 345–368.

———. *The Transformation of Virginia, 1740–1790.* Chapel Hill: University of North Carolina Press, 1982.

Isani, Mukhtar Ali. "The Methodist Connection: New Variants of Some of Phillis Wheatley's Poems." *Early American Literature* 22 (1987): 108–113.

Jacob, Margaret C. "Forum: Exits from the Enlightenment," *Eighteenth-Century Studies* 33.2 (1999–2000): 251–279.

———. *Living the Enlightenment: Freemasonry and Politics in Eighteenth-Century Europe.* Oxford: Oxford University Press, 1991.

JanMohamed, Abdul R. "Negating the Negation as a Form of Affirmation in Minority Discourse: The Construction of Richard Wright as Subject." In *The Nature and Context of Minority Discourse*, ed. Abdul JanMohamed and David Lloyd, 102–123. New York: Oxford University Press, 1990.

———, and David Lloyd. "Toward a Theory of Minority Discourse: What Is to Be Done?" In *The Nature and Context of Minority Discourse*, ed. Abdul Jan-Mohamed and David Lloyd, 1–16. New York: Oxford University Press, 1990.

Jefferson, Thomas. *Notes on the State of Virginia.* Ed. William Peden. 1787. Reprint, New York: Norton, 1982.

Jernegan, Marcus W. "Slavery and Conversion in the American Colonies." *American Historical Review* 21 (1915–16): 504–527.

Jordan, Winthrop. *White Over Black: American Attitudes Toward the Negro, 1550–1812.* Chapel Hill: University of North Carolina Press, 1968.

Julian, John, ed. *A Dictionary of Hymnology.* 2 vols. New York: Dover Publications, 1957.

Kaplan, Sidney. *The Black Presence in the Era of the American Revolution, 1770–1800.* Washington, D.C.: Smithsonian Institution, 1973.

———. "Veteran Officers and Politics in Massachusetts, 1783–1787." *William and Mary Quarterly* 9.1 (January 1952): 29–57.

Kennedy, Michael. "The Foundation of the Jacobin Clubs and the Development of the Jacobin Club Network, 1789–1791." *The Journal of Modern History* 51.4 (December 1979): 701–733.

Kilpatrick, James. *An Essay on Inoculation, Occassioned by the Small-Pox being brought into South Carolina in the Year 1738.* 1743. Reprint, *Small-Pox in Colonial America.* New York: Arno, 1977.

King, Boston. "Memoirs of the Life of Boston King, a Black Preacher, Written by Himself during his Residence at Kingswood School." *Methodist Magazine* 21 (1798): 105–110.

Kirk-Greene, Anthony. "David George: The Nova Scotian Experience." *Sierra Leone Studies* 14 (1960): 96–110.

Kitson, Peter J., ed. *Theories of Race, Slavery, Abolition, and Emancipation: Writings in the British Romantic Period*, vol. 8. London: Pickering and Chatto, 1999.

Klepp, Susan. "Appendix I: 'How Many Precious Souls are Fled'?: The Magnitude of the 1793 Yellow Fever Epidemics." In *A Melancholy Scene of Devastation: The Public Response to the 1793 Philadelphia Yellow Fever Epidemic*, ed. J. Worth Estes and Billy G. Smith, 163–182. Canton, Mass.: Science History Publishers, 1997.

Knight, Helen C. *Lady Huntington and her Friends; or, The Revival of the Work of God in the Days of Wesley, Whitefield, Romaine, Venn, and Others in the Last Century.* New York: New York American Tract Society, 1853.

Krupat, Arnold. *The Turn to the Native: Studies in Criticism and Culture.* Lincoln: University of Nebraska Press, 1996.

———. *The Voice in the Margin: Native American Literature and the Canon.* Berkeley: University of California Press, 1988.

Lambert, Frank. *Inventing the Great Awakening.* Princeton, N. J.: Princeton University Press, 1999.

———. *Pedlar in Divinity: George Whitefield and the Transatlantic Revivals, 1737–1770.* Princeton, N.J.: Princeton University Press, 1994.

Lang, Amy Schrager. "'A Flood of Errors': Chauncy and Edwards in the Great Awakening." In *Jonathan Edwards and the American Experience,* ed. Nathan Hatch and Harry Stout, 160–173. Oxford: Oxford University Press, 1988.

Lapsansky, Emma Jones. "'Since They Got Those Separate Churches': Afro-Americans and Racism in Jacksonian Philadelphia." *American Quarterly* 32.1 (spring 1980): 54–78.

Lapsansky, Phillip. "'Abigail, a Negress: The Role and the Legacy of African Americans in the Yellow Fever Epidemic." In *A Melancholy Scene of Devastation: The Public Response to the 1793 Philadelphia Yellow Fever Epidemic,* ed. J. Worth Estes and Billy G. Smith, 61–78. Canton, Mass.: Science History Publishers, 1997.

Larson, Paul. "Mahican and Lenape Moravians and Moravian Music." *Unitas Fratrum* 21–22 (1988): 173–187.

Lee, Debbie. "Yellow Fever and the Slave Trade: Coleridge's *The Rime of the Ancient Mariner.*" *English Literary History* 65.3 (1998): 675–700.

Lefkowitz, Mary. *Not Out of Africa: How Afrocentrism Became an Excuse to Teach Myth as History.* New York: Basic Books, 1996.

Levine, Lawrence W. *Black Culture and Black Consciousness: Afro-American Folk Thought from Slavery to Freedom.* Oxford: Oxford University Press, 1977.

Levine, Robert. *Conspiracy and Romance: Studies in Brockden Brown, Cooper, Hawthorne and Melville.* New York: Cambridge University Press, 1989.

Lewis, R. W. B. *The American Adam: Innocence, Tragedy, and Tradition in the Nineteenth Century.* Chicago: University of Chicago Press, 1955.

Lining, John. *A description of the American yellow fever, which prevailed at Charleston, in South Carolina, in the year 1748.* Philadelphia: Printed for Thomas Dobson, at the stone-house, no 41, South Second Street, 1799.

Lippy, Charles. *Seasonable Revolutionary: The Mind of Charles Chauncy.* Chicago: Nelson-Hall, 1981.

Loggins, Vernon. *The Negro Author: His Development in America to 1900.* New York: Kennikat, 1964.

Long, Edward. "'Negroes' from *History of Jamaica.*" In *Theories of Race, Slavery, Abolition, and Emancipation: Writings in the British Romantic Period,* vol. 8, ed. Peter J. Kitson, 1–22. London: Pickering and Chatto, 1999.

Love, W. Deloss. *Samson Occom and the Christian Indians of New England.* Boston: Pilgrim, 1899.

Lovejoy, David. *Religious Enthusiasm in the New World: Heresy to Revolution.* Cambridge: Harvard University Press, 1985.

———. "Samuel Hopkins: Religion, Slavery, and the Revolution." *New England Quarterly* 40 (1967): 227–243.

McBride, Dwight. *Impossible Witnesses: Truth, Abolitionism, and Slave Testimony.* New York: New York University Press, 2001.

McCallum, James Dow, ed. *Letters of Eleazar Wheelock's Indians.* Hanover, N.H.: Dartmouth College Publications, 1932.

McDermott, Gerald. "Jonathan Edwards and American Indians: The Devil Sucks Their Blood." *New England Quarterly* 72.4 (December 1999): 539–557.

McKerrow, P. E. *A Brief History of the Coloured Baptists of Nova Scotia, 1783–1895.* Halifax: Afro Nova Scotian Enterprises, 1976.

MacKinnon, Neil. "The Loyalists: 'A Different People.'" In *Banked Fires: The Ethnics of Nova Scotia,* ed. Douglass Campbell, 69–92. Ontario: Scribbler's, 1978.

McNally, Michael. *Ojibwe Singers: Hymns, Grief, and a Native Culture in Motion.* New York: Oxford University Press, 2000.

Marini, Stephen. *Radical Sects of Revolutionary New England.* Cambridge: Harvard University Press, 1982.

———. "Rehearsal for Revival: Sacred Singing and the Great Awakening in America." *JAAR Thematic Studies* 50.1 (1983): 71–91.

Marrant, John. *A Journal of the Rev. John Marrant, From August the 18th, 1785, to The 16th of March, 1790. To which are added Two Sermons; One Preached on Ragged Island on Sabbath Day, the 27th Day of October 1787; the Other at Boston in New England, On Thursday, the 24th of June, 1789.* London: Printed for the Author, 1790.

———. *A Narrative of the Lord's Wonderful Dealings with John Marrant, a Black, (Now Going to Preach the Gospel in Nova-Scotia) Born in New York, in North-America. Enlarged by Mr. Marrant, and Printed (with Permission) for his Sole Benefit, With Notes Explanatory.* London: R. Hawes of No. 40, Dorset Street, Spitalfields, 1785.

———. *A Sermon Preached on the 24th Day of June 1789, Being the Festival of Saint John the Baptists, at the Request of the Right Worshipful the Grand Master Prince Hall, and the Rest of the Brethren of the African Lodge of the Honorable Society of Free and Accepted Masons in Boston.* Boston: Printed and sold by T. and J. Fleet at the Bible and Heart, Cornhill, 1789.

Marx, Anthony. *Making Race and Nation: A Comparison of South Africa, the United States and Brazil.* Cambridge: Cambridge University Press, 1998.

Mather, Cotton. *An Account of the Method and Success of Inoculating the Small-Pox, In Boston in New England.* 1722. Reprint, *Smallpox in Colonial America.* New York: Arno, 1977.

———. *Magnalia Christi Americana.* Ed. Kenneth B. Murdock. Cambridge, Mass.: Belknap Press, 1977.

———. *Selected Letters of Cotton Mather.* Comp. Kenneth Silverman. Baton Rouge: Louisiana State University Press, 1971.

Mather, Increase. *The Doctrine of Divine Providence Opened and Applied.* 1684. Reprint, New York: AMS Press, 1983.

Mays, Benjamin. *The Negro's God as Reflected in His Literature.* Boston: Chapman and Grimes, 1938.

Melish, Joanne Pope. *Disowning Slavery: Gradual Emancipation and "Race" in New England, 1780–1860.* Ithaca, N.Y.: Cornell University Press, 1998.

Miller, Jacquelyn. "An 'Uncommon Tranquility of Mind': Emotional Self-

Control and the Construction of a Middle-class Identity in Eighteenth-Century Philadelphia," *Journal of Social History* 301 (1996): 129–148.

Miller, Perry. *Errand into the Wilderness.* Cambridge: Harvard University Press, 1956.

———. *Jonathan Edwards.* New York: Meridian Books, 1959.

Minkema, Kenneth P. "Jonathan Edwards on Slavery and the Slave Trade," *William and Mary Quarterly* 3d ser. 54.4 (October 1997): 823–824.

Minutes of the proceedings of the committee, appointed on the 14th September, 1793, by the citizens of Philadelphia, the Northern Liberties and the District of Southwark, to attend to and alleviate the sufferings of the afflicted with the malignant fever, prevalent, in the city and its vicinity,: with an appendix. Philadelphia: Printed by R. Aitken and Son, and sold by J. Crukshank, W. Young, T. Dobson and the other booksellers, 1794.

Montgomery, Benilde. "Recapturing John Marrant." In *A Mixed Race: Ethnicity in Early America,* ed. Frank Shuffleton, 105–115. Oxford: Oxford University Press, 1993.

Moore-Gilbert, Bart. *Postcolonial Theory: Contexts, Practices, Politics.* London: Verso, 1997.

Moses, Wilson Jeremiah. *Afrotopia: The Roots of African American Popular History.* Cambridge: Cambridge University Press, 1998.

———. "The Poetics of Ethiopianism." *American Literature* 47.3 (November 1975): 411–426.

———. *The Wings of Ethiopia: Studies in African-American Life and Letters.* Ames: Iowa State University Press, 1990.

———, ed. *Classical Black Nationalism: From the American Revolution to Marcus Garvey.* New York: New York University Press, 1996.

Muraskin, William. *Middle-Class Blacks in a White Society: Prince Hall Freemasonry in America.* Berkeley: University of California Press, 1975.

Murray, David. *Forked Tongues: Speech, Writing, and Representation in North American Indian Texts.* Bloomington: Indiana University Press, 1991.

Murray, Laura, ed. *To Do Good to My Indian Brethren: The Writings of Joseph Johnson, 1751–1776.* Amherst: University of Massachusetts Press, 1998.

Nash, Gary B. *Forging Freedom: The Formation of Philadelphia's Black Community.* Cambridge: Harvard University Press, 1988.

———. "New Light on Richard Allen: The Early Years of Freedom." *William and Mary Quarterly* 462 (1989): 332–340.

———. *The Urban Crucible: Social Change, Political Consciousness, and the Origins of the American Revolution.* Cambridge: Harvard University Press, 1979.

Nassy, David de Isaac Cohen. *Observations on the cause, nature, and treatment of the epidemic disorder, prevalent in Philadelphia.* Philadelphia: Printed by Parker and Co. for M. Carey, Nov. 26, 1793.

Nelson, Dana. *National Manhood: Capitalist Citizenship and the Imagined Fraternity of White Men.* Durham, N.C.: Duke University Press, 1998.

Niles, Nathaniel. *Samson Occom, The Mohegan Indian Teacher, Preacher and Poet, with a Short Sketch of His Life.* Rauner Special Collections Library, Dartmouth College, Hanover, N.H.

Nisbet, Richard. *The Capacity of Negroes for Religious and Moral Improvement Considered*. London: J. Phillips, 1789.

Occom, Samson. *A Choice collection of hymns and spiritual songs; intended for the edification of sincere Christians, of all denominations*. New London, Conn.: Printed and sold by Timothy Green, a few rods west of the court-house, 1774.

————. Diary, 1743–1790. 3 vols. Typescript. Rauner Special Collections Library, Darmouth College, Hanover, N.H.

————. *A sermon, preached at the execution of Moses Paul, an Indian, who was executed at New-Haven, on the 2d of September 1772, for the murder of Mr. Moses Cook, late of Waterbury, on the 7th of December 1771*. New London, Conn.: T. Green, 1772.

————. "A Short Narrative of my Life." 1768. Reprint, *The Heath Anthology of American Literature*, vol. 1, 2d ed., ed. Paul Lauter et al., 942–947. Lexington, Mass.: D. C. Heath, 1994.

O'Grady, Terence J. "The Singing Societies of the Oneida." *American Music* 9.1 (spring 1991): 67–91.

Omi, Michael, and Howard Winant. *Racial Formation in the United States: From the 1960s to the 1990s*. 2d ed. New York: Routledge, 1994.

Palmer, W. P., and H. W. Flournoy, eds. *Calendar of Virginia State Papers and other Manuscripts Preserved in the Capitol at Richmond*, vol. 9. Richmond: Commonwealth of Virginia, 1875–1893.

Patterson, Orlando. *Slavery and Social Death: A Comparative Study*. Cambridge: Harvard, 1982.

Perdue, Theda. "Native Women in the Early Republic: Old World Perceptions, New World Realities." In *Native Americans and the Early Republic*, ed. Frederick Hoxie et al., 85–122. Charlottesville: University Press of Virginia, 1999.

Peyer, Bernd. *The Tutor'd Mind: Indian Missionary-Writers in Antebellum America*. Amherst: University of Massachusetts Press, 1997.

Piersen, William D. *Black Yankees: The Development of an Afro-American Subculture in Eighteenth-Century New England*. Amherst: University of Massachusetts Press, 1988.

Porter, Dorothy, ed. *Early Negro Writing 1760–1837*. 1971. Reprint, Baltimore: Black Classics, 1995.

Powell, J. H. *Bring Out Your Dead: The Great Plague of Yellow Fever in Philadelphia in 1793*. Philadelphia: University of Pennsylvania Press, 1993.

"Prince Hall Masons Important Contributors To Black History." *Atlanta Inquirer* 37.31 (February 28, 1998): 2.

Rael, Patrick. *Black Identity and Black Protest in the Antebellum North*. Chapel Hill: University of North Carolina Press, 2002.

Rawlyk, George A. *Ravished by the Spirit: Religious Revivals, Baptists, and Henry Alline*. Kingston, Canada: McGill-Queen's University Press, 1984.

————, ed. *New Light Letters and Songs*. Nova Scotia: Lancelot Press, 1983.

Reed, Harry. *Platform for Change: The Foundations of the Northern Free Black Community, 1775–1865*. East Lansing: Michigan State University Press, 1994.

Review of *A Narrative of the Lord's Wonderful Dealings with John Marrant, a Black*, by John Marrant. *Monthly Review* (November 1785): 399.

Richards, Phillip. "The 'Joseph Story' as Slave Narrative: On Genesis and Exodus as Prototypes for Early Black Anglophone Writing." In *African-Americans and the Bible: Sacred Texts and Social Textures*, ed. Vincent Wimbush, 221–235. New York: Continuum, 2000.

Richardson, Harry. *Dark Salvation: The Story of Methodism as It Developed Among Blacks in America*. New York: Anchor, 1976.

Richardson, Leon Burr. *An Indian Preacher in England*. Hanover, N.H.: Dartmouth College Publications, 1933.

Roach, Joseph. *Cities of the Dead: Circum-Atlantic Performance*. New York: Columbia University Press, 1996.

Rogal, Samuel J. "Phillis Wheatley's Methodist Connection." *Black American Literature* 21 (spring-summer 1987): 85–95.

Rose, Mark. *Authors and Owners: The Invention of Copyright*. Cambridge: Harvard University Press, 1993.

Rush, Benjamin. *An account of the bilious remitting yellow fever, as it appeared in the city of Philadelphia, in the year 1793*. Philadelphia, Printed by Thomas Dobson, at the Stone-house, no. 41, South Second-street, 1794.

———. *An enquiry into the origin of the late epidemic fever in Philadelphia: in a letter to Dr. John Redman, president of the College of Physicians, from Doctor Benjamin Rush*. Philadelphia: From the press of Mathew Carey, December 11, 1793.

———. *Letters of Benjamin Rush*. Vol. 2. *1793–1813*. Ed. L. H. Butterfield. Princeton, N.J.: Published for the American Philosophical Society by Princeton University Press, 1951.

Ruttenburg, Nancy. *Democratic Personality: Popular Voice and the Trial of American Authorship*. Palo Alto, Calif.: Stanford University Press, 1998.

Rutyna, Richard A., and Peter C. Stewart. *The History of Freemasonry in Virginia*. Lanham, Md.: University Press of America, 1998.

Saillant, John. "Hymnody and the Persistence of an African-American Faith in Sierra Leone." *Hymn* 48.1 (January 1997): 8–17.

———. "Slavery and Divine Providence in New England Calvinism: The New Divinity and a Black Protest, 1775–1805." *New England Quarterly* 68.4 (1995): 584–608.

———. "'Wipe away All Tears from Their Eyes': John Marrant's Theology in the Black Atlantic, 1785–1808." *Journal of Millennial Studies* 1.2 (winter 1999): www.mille.org/journal.html.

Samuels, Shirley. "Infidelity and Contagion: The Rhetoric of Revolution." *Early American Literature* 22.2 (fall 1987): 183–191.

Sandiford, Keith. *Measuring the Moment: Strategies of Protest in Eighteenth-Century Afro-English Writing*. London: Associated University Presses, 1988.

Sargeant, John. "To the Rev. Mr. Isaac Hollis." *Christian History* 19 (July 9, 1743): 151–152.

Scheick, William J. "The Grand Design: Jonathan Edwards' History of the Work of Redemption," *Eighteenth-Century Studies* 8.3 (spring 1975): 300–314.

Schlenther, Boyd Samuel. *Queen of the Methodists: The Countess of Huntingdon* and the Eighteenth-century Crisis of Faith and Society. Durham, England: Durham Academic Press, 1997.

Seeman, Erik R. "'Justise Must Take Plase': Three African Americans Speak of Religion in Eighteenth-Century New England." *William and Mary Quarterly* 3d ser., 56.2 (April 1999): 393–413.

Sekora, John. "Is the Slave Narrative a Species of Autobiography?" In *Studies in Autobiography*, ed. James Olney, 99–111. New York: Oxford University Press, 1988.

———. "Red, White, and Black: Indian Captivities, Colonial Printers, and Early African-American Narrative." In *A Mixed Race: Ethnicity in Early America*, ed. Frank Shuffleton, 92–104. Oxford: Oxford University Press, 1993.

Sernett, Milton. *Black Religion and American Evangelicism*. Metuchen, N.J.: Scarecrow, 1975.

Seymour, A. C. H. *The Life and Times of Selina, Countess of Huntingdon*, 2 vols. 1840. Reprint, Stoke-on-Trent, England: Tentmaker Publications, 2000.

Shaw, Robert. "Samson Occom (1723–1792): His Life and Work as a Hymnist." M.A. thesis, New Orleans Baptist Theological Seminary, 1986.

Shields, David. "Anglo-American Clubs: Their Wit, Their Heterodoxy, Their Sedition." *William and Mary Quarterly* 3d ser., 51.2 (April 1994): 293–304.

Simmons, William S. *Old Light on Separate Ways: The Narragansett Diary of Joseph Fish, 1765–1776*. Hanover, N.H.: University Press of New England, 1982.

———. "Red Yankees: Narragansett Conversion in the Great Awakening." *American Ethnologist* 10.2 (May 1983): 253–271.

———. *Spirit of the New England Tribes: Indian History and Folklore, 1620–1984*. Hanover, N.H.: University Press of New England, 1986.

Simpson, Robert Drew, ed. *American Methodist Pioneer: The Life and Journals of the Rev. Freeborn Garrettson, 1752–1827*. Rutland, Vt.: Academy Books, 1984.

Smith, Mark A. "Andrew Brown's 'Earnest Endeavor': The Federal Gazette's Role in Philadelphia's Yellow Fever Epidemic of 1793." *Pennsylvania Magazine of History and Biography* 1204 (1996): 321–342.

Smith, Samuel Stanhope. *An Essay on the Causes of the Variety of Complexion in the Human Species*. 1787. Reprint, *Theories of Race, Slavery, Abolition, and Emancipation: Writings in the British Romantic Period*, vol. 8., ed., Peter J. Kitson, 67–96. London: Pickering and Chatto, 1999.

Smith-Rosenberg, Carroll. "Dis-Covering the Subject of the 'Great Constitutional Discussion,' 1786–1789." *The Journal of American History* 79.3 (December 1992): 841–873.

Sobel, Mechal. *Trabelin' On: The Journey to an Afro-Baptist Faith*. Princeton, N.J.: Princeton University Press, 1979.

———. *The World They Made Together: Black and White Values in Eighteenth-Century Virginia*. Princeton, N.J.: Princeton University Press, 1987.

Stern, Julia. *The Plight of Feeling: Sympathy and Dissent in the Early American Novel*. Chicago: University of Chicago Press, 1997.

Stevens, Abel. *The Women of Methodism; its Three Foundresses, Susanna Wesley,* the Countess of Huntingdon, and Barbara Heck. New York: Carlton and Porter, 1866.

Stevenson, Robert. "American Tribal Musics at Contact." *Inter-American Music Review* 14.1 (spring-summer 1994): 1–56.

———. "The First Native American (American Indian) Published Composer." *Inter-American Music Review* 4.2 (spring-summer 1982): 79–84.

———. "Protestant Music in America." In *Protestant Church Music: A History*, ed. Friedrich Blume, 639–690. New York: W. W. Norton, 1974.

Stiles, Ezra. *Literary Diary*. 2 vols. New York: C. Scribner's, 1901.

Stout, Harry. *The Divine Dramatist: George Whitefield and the Rise of Modern Evangelicalism*. Grand Rapids, Mich.: Wm. B. Eerdmans, 1991.

———. *The New England Soul: Preaching and Religious Culture in Colonial New England*. New York: Oxford University Press, 1986.

Stuckey, Sterling. *The Ideological Origins of Black Nationalism*. Boston: Beacon Press, 1972.

Takaki, Ronald. *Iron Cages: Race and Culture in Nineteenth-Century America*. 1979. Reprint, New York: Oxford University Press, 2000.

Tantaquidgeon, Gladys. *Folk Medicine of the Delaware and Related Algonkian Indians*. Anthropological Series, no. 3. Harrisburg: The Pennsylvania Historical and Museum Commission, 1972.

Thornton, Russell. *American Indian Holocaust and Survival: A Population History since 1492*. Norman: University of Oklahoma Press, 1987.

Tracy, Joseph. *The Great Awakening: A History of the Revival of Religion in the Time of Edwards and Whitefield*. Boston: Tappan and Dennet, 1842.

Treat, James, ed. *Native and Christian: Indigenous Voices on Religious Identity in the United States and Canada*. New York: Routledge, 1996.

"A True and Genuine Account of a Wonderful Wandering Spirit." *General Magazine and Historical Chronicle* (February 1741): 120–122.

Upton, William. *Negro Masonry, Being a Critical Examination of Objections to the Legitimacy of the Masonry Existing Among the Negroes of America*. Boston, Mass.: Prince Hall Grand Lodge, 1902.

Visnawathan, Gauri. *Outside the Fold: Conversion, Modernity, and Belief*. Princeton, N.J.: Princeton University Press, 1998.

Voorhis, Harold Van Buren. *Negro Masonry in the United States*. New York: Henry Emmerson, 1945.

Walker, David. "Appeal to the Colored Citizens of the World." In *Walker's Appeal and Garnet's Address to the Slaves of the United States of America*. Nashville, Tenn.: James C. Winston, 1994.

Walker, James W. St. G. *The Black Loyalists: The Search for a Promised Land in Nova Scotia and Sierra Leone*. New York: Dalhousie University Press, 1976.

Walkes, Joseph A., Jr. *Black Square and Compass: 200 Years of Prince Hall Freemasonry*. Richmond, Va.: Macoy Publishing and Masonic Supply, 1979.

Wallace, Maurice. "'Are We Men?': Prince Hall, Martin Delaney, and the Masculine Ideal in Black Freemasonry, 1775–1865." *American Literary History* 9.3 (fall 1997): 396–424.

Wallace, Michele. *Invisibility Blues: From Pop to Theory*. London: Verso, 1990.

Walls, A. F. "The Nova Scotian Settlers and their Religion." *Sierra Leone Bulletin of Religion* 1.1 (June 1959): 19–31.

Warch, Richard. "The Shepherd's Tent: Education and Enthusiasm in the Great Awakening," *American Quarterly* 30.2 (summer 1978): 177–198.

Warner, Michael. *Letters of the Republic.* Cambridge: Harvard University Press, 1990.

Waters, Kenneth L., Sr., "Liturgy, Spirituality, and Polemic in the Hymnody of Richard Allen." *The North Star: A Journal of African-American Religious History* 2.2 (spring 1999): http://northstar.vassar.edu.

Weaver, Jace. *Other Words: American Indian, Law, and Culture.* Norman: University Oklahoma Press, 2001.

———. "From I-Hermeneutics to We-Hermeneutics: Native Americans and the Post-Colonial." In *Native American Religious Identity: Unforgotten Gods,* ed. Jace Weaver, 1–25. Maryknoll, N.Y.: Orbis Books, 1998.

———. *That the People Might Live: Native American Literatures and Native American Community.* New York: Oxford University Press, 1997.

Weinstein, Laurie. "Samson Occom: Charismatic Eighteenth-Century Mohegan Leader." In *Enduring Traditions: The Native Peoples of New England,* ed. Laurie Weinstein, 91–102. Westport, Conn.: Bergin and Garvey, 1994.

Wesley, Charles H. *Prince Hall: Life and Legacy.* Philadelphia: Afro-American Historical and Cultural Museum; and Washington, D.C.: United Supreme Council, Prince Hall Affiliation, 1977.

West, Cornel. *Prophesy Deliverance! An Afro-American Revolutionary Christianity.* Philadelphia: Westminster, 1982.

Westerkamp, Marilyn. *Triumph of the Laity: Scots-Irish Piety and the Great Awakening, 1625–1760.* New York: Oxford University Press, 1988.

Weyler, Karen. "Race, Redemption, and Captivity in *A Narrative of the Lord's Wonderful Dealings with John Marrant, a Black* and *Narrative of the Uncommon Sufferings and Surprizing Deliverance of Briton Hammon, A Negro Man.*" In *Genius in Bondage: Literature of the Early Black Atlantic,* ed. Vincent Carretta and Philip Gould, 39–53. Lexington: University of Kentucky Press, 2001.

Wheatley, Phillis. *The Poems of Phillis Wheatley.* Ed. Julian D. Mason, Jr. Chapel Hill: University of North Carolina Press, 1989.

Wheeler, Roxann. *The Complexion of Race: Categories of Difference in Eighteenth-Century British Culture.* Philadelphia: University of Pennsylvania Press, 2000.

Whidden, Lynn. "Cree Hymnody as Traditional Song." *Hymn* 4 (July 1989): 21–25.

Whitchurch, Samuel. *The Negro Convert, A Poem; Being the Substance of the Experience of Mr. John Marrant, A Negro, As related by himself, previous to his Ordination, at the Countess of Huntingsdon's Chapel in Bath, on Sunday, the 15th of May, 1785.* Bath: Printed and sold by S. Hazard, [1785].

Whitefield, George. *Three Letters from the Reverend Mr. G. Whitefield: Letter I. To a Friend in London, concerning Archbishop Tillotson; Letter II. To the Same, on the Same Subject; Letter III. To the Inhabitants of Maryland, Virginia, North and South Carolina, Concerning their Negroes.* Philadelphia: Printed and Sold by B. Franklin, at the New Printing-office near the market, 1740.

Wigger, John. "Taking Heaven by Storm: Enthusiasm and Early American

Methodism, 1770–1820." *Journal of the Early Republic* 14 (summer 1994): 167–194.

————. *Taking Heaven by Storm: Methodism and the Rise of Popular Christianity in America*. New York: Oxford University Press, 1998.

Wilson, Carol. *Freedom at Risk: The Kidnapping of Free Blacks in America, 1780–1785*. Lexington: University of Kentucky Press, 1994.

Wilson, Ellen Gibson. *The Loyal Blacks*. New York: G. P. Putnam's Sons, 1976.

Wimbush, Vincent. "Biblical Historical Study as Liberation: Toward an Afro-Christian Hermeneutic." In *African American Religious Studies: An Interdisciplinary Anthology*, ed. Gayraud Wilmore, 140–154. Durham, N.C.: Duke University Press, 1989.

————, ed. *African-Americans and the Bible: Sacred Texts and Social Textures*. New York: Continuum, 2000.

Winch, Julie. *Philadelphia's Black Elite: Activism, Accommodation, and the Struggle for Autonomy, 1787–1848*. Philadelphia: Temple University Press, 1988.

Witinger, Julius Edward. "Hymnody of the Early American Indian Missions." Ph.D. diss., Catholic University, 1971.

Womack, Craig S. *Red on Red: Native American Literary Separatism*. Minneapolis: University of Minnesota Press, 1999.

Wyss, Hilary E. *Writing Indians: Literacy, Christianity, and Native Community in Early America*. Amherst: University of Massachusetts Press, 2000.

Young, Robert Alexander. "The Ethiopian Manifesto." In *Pamphlets of Protest: An Anthology of Early African American Protest Literature, 1790–1860*, ed. Richard Newman, Patrick Rael, and Phillip Lapsansky, 85–89. New York: Routledge, 2000.

Young, Robert J. C. *Colonial Desire: Hybridity in Theory, Culture, and Race*. New York: Routledge, 1995.

Zafar, Rafia. *We Wear the Mask: African-Americans Write American Literature, 1760–1870*. New York: Columbia University Press, 1996.

Index

Printed in the United States
85782LV00004B/55/A